D1599375

OXFORD
UNIVERSITY PRESS

Oxford University Press, Inc., publishes works that further
Oxford University's objective of excellence
in research, scholarship, and education.

Oxford   New York
Auckland   Cape Town   Dar es Salaam   Hong Kong   Karachi
Kuala Lumpur   Madrid   Melbourne   Mexico City   Nairobi
New Delhi   Shanghai   Taipei   Toronto

With offices in
Argentina   Austria   Brazil   Chile   Czech Republic   France   Greece
Guatemala   Hungary   Italy   Japan   Poland   Portugal   Singapore
South Korea   Switzerland   Thailand   Turkey   Ukraine   Vietnam

Copyright © 2011 by Oxford University Press, Inc.

Published by Oxford University Press, Inc.
198 Madison Avenue, New York, New York 10016

www.oup.com

Oxford is a registered trademark of Oxford University Press.

Stevenson, Leslie Forster.
Inspirations from Kant : essays / by Leslie Stevenson.
p. cm.
Includes bibliographical references (p.).
ISBN 978-0-19-977822-5
1. Philosophy.   2. Kant, Immanuel, 1724–1804.   I. Title.
B2798.S84   2011
193—dc22   2010035614

1 3 5 7 9 8 6 4 2

Printed in the United States of America
on acid-free paper

Inspirations
from Kant
Essays

Leslie Stevenson

OXFORD
UNIVERSITY PRESS

Inspirations from Kant

CONTENTS

PREFACE

My title is brief, and I hope attractive—except perhaps to those for whom Kant is the very last writer they would look to for inspiration! It is uninformative in two respects, however. First, I concentrate mostly on Kant's theoretical philosophy, and indeed on the *Critique of Pure Reason*, though toward the end I discuss questions of freedom and *Glaube* (belief or faith) that touch on Kantian practical philosophy. I have recently found some inspiration from Kant on religion and aesthetics (Stevenson 2001, 2003, 2006), but those articles are not reprinted in this collection. In revising the essays on theoretical philosophy included here (some published in journals since 2000, others new) I have found more connections between them than I first thought of, so I have taken the opportunity to point these out.

The other way my title might be misleading is that in almost all these essays I deploy ideas from contemporary analytical philosophy in my reading of Kant, so the traffic is two-way, bringing inspirations *to* him and deriving them from him. (Essay 4 is the nearest to pure Kant-exegesis, and essay 8 the most distant.) I thus hope to rescue Kant from what I have heard described as "the Kant church," whose adherents tend to revere his writings like sacred scripture and treat his doctrines as dogmas that may be open to interpretation but not to question. Those scholarly controversies about how to interpret Kant are usually conducted by lifetime specialists, which is understandable given the magnitude of the task of reading his voluminous texts and coming to grips with their notorious difficulties, plus all those lecture notes that keep coming out, and of course the ever-burgeoning secondary literature. In these days of fearsome academic specialization, that means having hardly any time left to keep abreast of other developments in philosophy. There is thus a danger that the Kantians conduct their debates about representations and intuitions, concepts and categories, synthesis and apperception, affection and spontaneity, appearances and things in themselves, phenomena and noumena while assuming it is clear what those formidable technical terms mean. Conversely, most of those working in epistemology, metaphysics, and the philosophies of language, mind, or science (or indeed moral philosophy) have little patience for the nitty-gritty of the seemingly eternal debates about how to interpret Kant and make sense of his paradoxical doctrines, especially "transcendental idealism."

I freely confess that I have not read every word Kant ever wrote, let alone all those that his students noted down from his lectures. And of course no one can pretend to an all-round competence in the enormous range and depth of analytical philosophy. All I can offer is some forty years' experience in trying to discern what is valuable in Kant's philosophy (mostly but not completely on the theoretical side) with the aid of relevant contemporary ideas, especially from the philosophy of mind.

Perhaps in this book I can make some amends for my juvenile effort in *The Metaphysics of Experience* (1982a), in which youthful over-confidence led me to sketch a bicentenary modernization of the *Critique of Pure Reason* in a hundred pages, with some rather uncritical reliance on the later Wittgenstein. Perhaps I did a bit better in my essay "Wittgenstein's Transcendental Deduction and Kant's Private Language Argument" (1982b); and essay 1 here is my latest attempt in that direction. If that early book was a premature ejaculation, perhaps this is a late splurge! The opportunity of early retirement in 2000 gave me the time and energy to return to Kant in what I hope is greater depth. I am reassured that Graham Bird has also found deep affinities between Kant and Wittgenstein in his impressive commentary (2006), in which he relates Kant to many other central themes in twentieth-century analytical philosophy. I am grateful to Graham for his encouraging comments on drafts of some of these essays.

My quotations from the *Critique of Pure Reason* are from the translation by Guyer and Wood in the Cambridge Edition of the works of Immanuel Kant, with the usual A and B page numberings to the first and second editions. Other references to Kant give the volume and page numbers of the Berlin Academy edition of his works. Permissions to reprint my papers are detailed at the beginning of the notes to the relevant essay.

St. Andrews
August 2010

Inspirations from Kant

ESSAY 1

༄

Objects of Representation

Kant's Copernican Revolution Reinterpreted

K ant's Copernican revolution and the transcendental idealism that he
claimed to follow from it continue to attract some philosophers,
but to repel rather more. In the preface to the second edition of the *Critique
of Pure Reason* he famously wrote:

> Up to now it has been assumed that all our cognition must conform to the objects…let
> us once try whether we do not get farther with the problems of metaphysics by assuming
> that the objects must conform to our cognition.
>
> (Bxvi)

It is an understatement to say that there is continuing disagreement about
the meaning and acceptability of this proposed revolution in philosophical
method. I propose to use some concepts from twentieth-century analytical
philosophy of language to see what sense we can now make of it.

I

Sebastian Gardner offered some helpful illumination in his *Guidebook* to
the first *Critique*, his main idea being that the basic propositions of Kant's
philosophy should be understood as expressing "necessities of representation" (Gardner 1999: Ch.1, Ch.8). Gardner introduces Kant's transcendental
method as arising from what he rather melodramatically calls "the problem
of reality":[1]

Now in order for reality or any part of it to become known to us, some sort of condition must obtain whereby it becomes an *object* for us.... But the question is: what makes reality into an object for us? Its being an object for us is not established by its simple existence.

(Gardner 1999: 34)

This is a generalization of the problem Kant raised in his well-known letter to Marcus Herz of February 21, 1772, early in the "silent decade" when he was gestating the *Critique of Pure Reason*. He there posed the question: "What is the ground of the relation of that in us which we call 'representation' to the object?" And about the "intellectual" representations (which he later called the categories, or pure concepts of the understanding), Kant asked: "Whence comes the agreement they are supposed to have with objects?" These are arcane questions indeed, using very abstract notions of "representation" and of "object,"[2] and I fear that many interpreters of Kant have not sufficiently explored their ambiguities. If we invest close attention into how to formulate these questions about objects of representation more precisely, we may receive rich dividends.

Gardner (1999: 34) poses the mind-boggling question: "What makes reality into an object for us?" But thinking of reality as a whole is not something that many people go in for, unless they are cosmologists, metaphysicians, or perhaps transcendental meditators! We might well wonder, on the sort of grounds Kant himself adduces in his discussion of the antinomies, whether there can be any such thing as referring to "reality" as a complete totality (see essays 4 and 5), but it is uncontroversial that we think and talk about particular *parts* of reality. However, there is a fundamental ambiguity between a *relational* conception of representation as relating the subject to particulars existing independently of his or her mental states and a *nonrelational* conception of the mere mental reference to "intentional objects," which may or may not exist outside the mind of the subject. Descartes, applying his method of doubt in his first Meditation, quickly reached a stage where he thought he could doubt the existence of the whole material world, but he never doubted that he had in his mind various "ideas," i.e., representations of things. A fundamental question about representation can be formulated as follows: "What are the necessary conditions for us to represent in the internal, nonrelational sense?" (Or more succinctly: "What makes intentionality possible?")

Yet even this is still ambiguous in several ways. First, we must take account of the fundamental difference between two kinds of representation, namely, singular reference and propositional thought.[3] In language, there is a corresponding distinction between singular terms and sentences (primarily indicative sentences). The former involve the identification of particular objects or items, or at least the attempt to identify them, whereas the latter involve propositions, which represent possible states of affairs. Second, there is a distinction between successful and unsuccessful representations—but there are different kinds of success. The question "What are the conditions for us to represent particular parts of reality?" can be taken as inquiring about conditions for truth, for knowledge, or for mere representation. On the first interpretation one would expect by way of answer a philosophical account of the notion of truth, perhaps in terms of correspondence or coherence, or a minimalist account. But talk of the truth of propositions obviously presupposes that they have representational *contents*, which can be understood without being known or believed to be true. On the second interpretation the question would be about the conditions for knowledge, or perhaps for justification or warrant. Whatever is necessary for representation is of course necessary for knowledge or belief, but the converse does not hold: we can formulate, understand and discuss many propositions for which we have little or no evidence.[4]

All questions about the success of our representations thus presuppose that they have determinate contents, so the most fundamental question of all is *what constitutes representational content*: i.e., what makes it the case that some of our mental states refer to, or are "about" (in the nonrelational sense), particular objects or particular states of affairs? How do our thoughts have "objective reality" in the (now counterintuitive) sense given to that phrase by Descartes, following the medievals?[5] As Gardner puts it, what demands philosophical explanation is "the possibility of there being objects for us, things that we can have experience of and thoughts about" (1999: 37). In short, how can we think of or refer to anything in particular? It is surely this deepest level of philosophical inquiry that Kant was breaking through to in posing his questions about representation.[6]

The basic notion of success for propositional representations is truth, but it comes at the risk of the corresponding kind of failure, namely falsity, and people can of course believe or assert false propositions. Despite Plato's puzzles in the *Sophist*, there is no difficulty in expressing the content of a false belief, for that is precisely what we do in a "that-clause," i.e., the word "that" followed by a sentence. To be sure, there are much-discussed philosophical problems about exactly which sentences are appropriate for making reports of people's beliefs in various contexts. But the notion of different people believing (and asserting, denying, disagreeing, or expressing agnosticism about) the *same thing* is one that we cannot do without, given that we are rational beings who can communicate knowledge or beliefs to each other and raise questions about the truth of what has been asserted or believed by others, or by ourselves at some previous time. We are thus committed to there being "objects" (in yet another sense of that ambiguous word) of belief, assertion, denial, and mere "propounding"—and they are traditionally called "propositions."[7]

A different dimension of success and failure applies to reference. Sometimes we attempt to make a singular reference, but fail to do so. Linguistically expressed examples include "the King of France in 1905," "Father Christmas," and "the rational square root of 2." There are also perceptual illusions or hallucinations, as when Macbeth, in his murderous state of mind, thought he saw a dagger before him, or when someone takes a pattern of shadows to be a man lurking in the bushes, or when a schizophrenic thinks he hears voices speaking to him. As we dangerously put it, people sometimes think or talk of, and "see" or "hear," things that aren't really there (as in the "Irish" use of the phrase "seeing things"). But in such cases we want to be able to understand what the mistake consists in, so we try to express what it is that the subject was thinking of, while remaining agnostic about its actual existence. In one sense we want to identify the "object" of their thought, while leaving it open for ourselves to deny in another sense that there is any such object.

I therefore suggest that we need to distinguish four questions within what Gardner calls "the problem of reality":

1. What makes some mental or linguistic items into propositional representations?—i.e., what constitutes *propositional content*?
2. What makes some propositional representations successful, i.e., true?— i.e., what constitutes *truth*?
3. What makes some mental or linguistic items would-be referential representations?—i.e., what constitutes *referential content*?
4. What makes some would-be referential representations successful, while others fail?—i.e., what constitutes *singular reference*?

Although distinguishable, these questions form a package, in that fully answering any one of them will involve answering the others. Reference is not a separable mental act or speech act; it is only a preparation for saying or thinking something about what is referred to (and thereby propounding a proposition).[8] There are of course general and existential propositions that do not themselves involve singular reference; but to understand them one must be able to understand their instantiations. Questions 1 and 3 therefore seem to be more fundamental, asking how any sort of representation is possible in the first place. Yet any adequate answer must presuppose that we can make distinctions between successful and unsuccessful representations, for the very notion of representation involves the possibility of *mis*representation.[9] Talk of the "objects" of representation is thus ambiguous between two levels—what in one sense is represented, whether or not the attempt is successful (the content or sense), and what is represented in the sense of being successfully referred to. The upshot of this discussion is that we can distinguish four kinds of "object of representation":

(Ia) Propositions (the contents of assertions and beliefs)
(Ib) Facts or "states of affairs" (corresponding to true propositions)
(IIa) The contents of putative acts of singular reference ("intentional objects")
(IIb) Actual objects of successful singular reference

In IIa I have used Brentano's phrase "intentional object," but only in brackets, because it suggests that intentional objects are one kind of objectthat there are, a species of a larger genus of "objects." Thus an overgrowth of Meinongian ontological jungle notoriously threatens this neck of the philosophical woods. Brentano described intentional objects as "inexistent," presumably trying to avoid such ontological inflation. Some philosophers influenced by the phenomenological tradition have said mysteriously that an intentional object may or may not be identical with an actual object; but others deny that the concept of identity can apply in any such case, since intentional objects are categorically different from actual objects.[10] However, I am using "intentional object" only as a synonym for what precedes it in IIa, namely, the *contents* rather than the referents of mental or linguistic acts of putative singular reference. Such contents are at the level of Frege's sense (*Sinn*) as opposed to reference (*Bedeutung*).

According to an influential line of thought stemming from Evans and McDowell, in a situation of reference failure there is no *singular* content of the act of putative reference, and hence no singular thought or proposition.[11] So in the case of someone suffering a perceptual illusion that she is being watched by a man in the bushes, she may think or say "That fellow is looking at me," and we may be tempted to say that she thereby affirms a singular thought, but if we do not ourselves believe there is anybody there, we cannot say *which* man she is referring to. Even if she says "That ugly little guy is looking at me," we still cannot identify any real individual (aesthetically or vertically challenged, or otherwise) to whom she is referring. There is no particular object in sense IIb that she is talking about, and thus no *singular* proposition in sense Ia that she is affirming or entertaining. I accept this analysis: I just insist that there must nevertheless be *some* identifiable content, albeit not *singular*, of the subject's mental state at the time, for she at least believes the *existential* proposition that there is a man, perhaps of a certain general description, in the relevant bushes. In that minimal sense her thought has *content*, and that is all I mean by using the phrase "intentional object" here. If that usage is still deemed misleading, I do not insist on it.

The most familiar cases of IIb and Ib are of course material objects, and states of affairs involving them. These are spatiotemporally located in the physical world (although sometimes only vaguely, e.g., clouds, mountains, tribal lands, political revolutions, and fashions of dress or speech). But IIb and Ib can *also* include abstract objects and facts about them, e.g., numbers, shapes and sets in mathematics, and words, phrases, and sentences conceived of as *types*. Many material objects and states of affairs exist independently of their being represented by anyone, or even of the existence of all human beings (though obviously this does not hold of humanly constructed or social objects such as buildings, works of art, universities, or pension funds). Philosophers of mathematics who have a realist conception of mathematical objects will want to say something similar about *them*. Indeed there are meaningful, contentful, putatively referring phrases in mathematics that can be proved *not* to refer, precisely by reasoning from their content (e.g., "the greatest prime number," "the rational square root of 2"). So success in representing objects of types Ib and IIb is never guaranteed—it depends on matters that are independent of the mind of the subject, and in some sense independent of all mental states of anyone.

The status of Ia and IIa requires careful elucidation. These are *not* representations in the sense of represent*ings*, i.e., mental acts or events such as judgings or recognitions, or longer-lasting mental states of believing. Rather they are the *contents* of such mental acts or states, contents that can be shared by different people, and by one person at different times. In that sense they are independent of any one mind. But they are *internal* objects of representings, as opposed to the mind-independent external "objects" in Ib and IIb. In recent philosophy a distinction has been made between "narrow" and "broad" conceptions of content.[12] Only the former conform to my requirements here, for the latter involve the existence of objects or natural kinds external to the mind of the subject. At the level of narrow content, i.e., internal objects of representation, there is no question of success or failure in representation, no gap between thought and reality—there is merely thought. So in my usage of the term "proposition" in Ia, there can be no such thing as a genuinely singular narrowly construed proposition.[13]

Of course if someone has not *acquired* a certain concept, they will be unable to understand a proposition or referring phrase involving it, even if they pronounce or write the relevant words: in *that* sense they can fail to represent a content of type Ia or IIa. But if someone *does* have the concept and uses it on a certain occasion, there can be no slippage between that deployment and the existence of the relevant content. To talk of concepts is already to invoke publicly shareable standards for concept-possession and concept-application. So there is a sense in which the existence of a concept—a content or "intentional object"—with its relevant norms for correct application, though independent of any one mind, does depend on the existence of human practices. These are typically the practices of minds in the plural, but we can allow the possibility of one-person practices by a Robinson Crusoe on a desert island or indeed in any situation where someone develops a new conceptual practice that she has not yet communicated to anyone else, provided that there is no logical bar to others joining in the practice and thus acquiring the concept. Practices in this Wittgensteinian sense are essentially normative – they involve standards of correctness for concept-application. And we cannot talk of the holding of norms unless there are people (at least one person, anyway) who apply them.[14] The contents or internal objects of representation Ia or IIa are in *that* sense mind-dependent.

But what constitutes these mind-dependent contents? As Gardner notes (1999: 34–37), the mere *existence* of things or states of affairs cannot explain anyone's representation of them. From the bare fact that a certain object exists, it does not follow that any mind has any thoughts about it. And from the existence (the holding true, or obtaining) of a certain state of affairs, it does not follow that anyone understands the relevant proposition, let alone knows it to be true. Obviously, we cannot give any particular examples of unidentified objects or states of affairs, for to do so would be a fortiori to identify them. But, pace Berkeley, we can quite consistently assert that there are many things and states of affairs that have not been, and may never be, individually referred to or represented by anyone—e.g., in the depths of the oceans, on other planetary system, in the deep past, or after the millionth digit in the decimal expansion of pi. And of course we believe that many of the objects and states of affairs that we *do* represent would still exist even if we had never done so.

For our representations to be possible, then, there must, as Gardner puts it, be "some sort of fundamental connecting relation between reality and ourselves" (1999: 34). But what *sort* of relation is needed? In his letter to Herz, Kant seemed to think that for our empirical representations, a causal relation in either direction was enough, and that his question about the possibility of representation was puzzling only for the categories, the pure or "intellectual" concepts, of the understanding. But by the time he wrote the *Critique*, he realized that mere causation does not suffice for *any* sort of representation, as Gardner explains (1999: 30). Even a causal relation that systematically preserves information is not enough. The variable weather of past seasons causes patterns in the growth rings inside tree trunks, so trees are said to contain information about past climate and might incautiously be said to "represent" it, though of course trees do not have thoughts or beliefs about the past climate; they do not *represent* it in the sense we are concerned with. Even with rational beings like us who do represent in the full sense, there may be information about our pasts encoded in causal traces in our bodies (for example, our diet can leave trace minerals in our bones), but that does not entail that we thereby represent our eating habits or the presence of isotopes in our teeth. And even if some physical or mental traumas cause present states of consciousness in the form of tweaks of pain or twinges of objectless anxiety, those mental events do not thereby become representations of their past causes, for no conscious memory of them need remain.

A causal information link in the other direction, from subject to object, is equally insufficient for representation. Someone may leave behind faint smells that a tracker dog can detect, or traces of DNA that can be identified with modern equipment, but that does not imply that the person has any representations of those things. Even when the causation runs from a person's *mind* to the world, e.g., when someone's pains or moods cause anxiety in other people, that need not involve representations of those effects (a child may feel pain, and have the concept of pain, without yet having acquired the concept of anxiety). Of course, in our *actions* we intentionally bring about changes in the world, and in that case the subject *does* have representations of the state of affairs she intends to bring about. But to point to that familiar kind of intentional causation does nothing to *explain* how representation is possible; it just presupposes that we do indeed represent what we intend to do.

II

If causal relations are not enough, what does Kant have to say about the possibility of representation? Let us look in more detail at his programmatic introduction of his Copernican revolution in the B Preface:

> Up to now it has been assumed that all our cognition must conform to the objects; but all attempts to find out something about them *a priori* through concepts that would extend our cognition have, on this presupposition, come to nothing. Hence let us once try whether we do not get farther with the problems of metaphysics by assuming that the objects must conform to our cognition, which would agree better with the requested possibility of an *a priori* cognition of them, which is to establish something about objects before they are given to us.
>
> (Bxvi)

The neat rhetorical contrast between "our cognition conforming to objects" and "objects conforming to our cognition" is one of those memorable turns of phrase in Kant's otherwise turgid prose that tend to dominate our philosophical imagination, so that if we are not careful we can find ourselves repeating his words without asking ourselves what they really mean. But readers of a realist disposition tend to turn away in repugnance from the very idea that objects must conform to our knowledge. How, they say, can the whole universe stoop to accommodate itself to the limited capacities of our human minds? Surely most of it preexisted the evolution of human beings, anyway. But now our distinction between four uses of the term "object" can be applied to relieve some of this perplexity. When Kant suggests that it has been wrongly assumed so far that our cognition must conform to objects, he is surely thinking about *representation* rather than truth or knowledge. For a proposition to be known, it must be true: what is predicated of whatever is referred to must "conform" to the actual properties and relations of the relevant things. And for a putative singular reference to be successful, there must be an appropriate relation to an appropriate object. In *that* sense, Kant can and should accept that our knowledge must conform to objects of the kinds Ib and IIb. He elsewhere affirms the correspondence account of truth (A58/B83, A820/B848), and that is surely part of what he means by his "empirical realism."[15]

What then can Kant mean by his mysterious suggestion that "objects must conform to our cognition"? Not, surely, that objects of types Ib and IIb are *created* by our representing activities, or even that they are *affected* by them. Yet that notorious phrase invites some such idealist misunderstanding, to which a long history of Kant interpretation bears witness, whether the idealism is endorsed or repudiated. I fear Gardner is in danger of contributing to it when he writes that "in a recondite philosophical sense, the subject *constitutes* its objects," "these subject-constituted objects compose the only kind of reality to which we have access," and "our mode of cognition determines the constitution of its objects" (1999: 41, 275).[16] This sounds idealist, unless the "recondite sense" is very carefully explained. In my understanding of Kant (and of Gardner's account of him) it is the *contents*, the senses or "intentional objects," of our representations Ia and IIa that depend on (and are even created by) our representing activities, for there cannot be any such contents unless there are minds with representational practices. There is a tolerably clear sense, then, in which *intentional objects*, the narrowly construed contents of our representations, are mind-dependent and can be said to "conform to our cognition."

Let us now examine how Kant tries to follow up on his statement of his Copernican hypothesis. He applies it first to "intuitions" (i.e., perceptual representations of particular objects):

> If intuition has to conform to the constitution of the objects, then I do not see how
> we can know anything of them *a priori*; but if the object (as an object of the senses)

conforms to the constitution of our faculty of intuition, then I can very well represent this possibility to myself.

(Bxvii)[17]

And the next sentence (one of Kant's monstrously lengthy ones) begins:

Yet because I cannot stop with these intuitions, if they are to become cognitions, but must refer them as representations to something as their object and determine this object through them.

(Bxvii)

He has in mind here his distinction between intuitions and concepts, sensibility and understanding, and the corresponding textual division between the Transcendental Aesthetic and the Transcendental Logic. In the Aesthetic he proposes to examine "our faculty of intuition" *before* dealing with concepts and conceptual cognition, which involve our "faculty of understanding." However, in view of his subsequent statement that intuitions without concepts are blind and that only through the union of sensibility and understanding can cognition arise (A51/B75–76), we may wonder how far it is possible to discuss human perception without bringing in conceptualization (see essay 3). Interpreters have come to agree that Kant's notion of "intuition" (*Anschauung*) is ambiguous between nonconceptualized and conceptualized representations. There is unconceptualized perception in animals and prelinguistic infants, but it is also manifest in human adults, for instance in playing ball games, in our sensitivity to facial expressions and tones of voice, and in our appreciation of music and abstract art. Whether it counts as *representation* depends on how we decide to use the word "representation" as a technical term, but there seems to be no harm in extending the word to nonconceptual cases (as Kant himself does),[18] providing we recognize the differences between them and conceptual representations. Of course, we cannot *say* anything about objects of nonconceptual representation without using concepts ourselves: but that is not to attribute those concepts to the relevant subjects. We know that a lamb can see, hear, and smell things, and we can tell when it recognizes (or misrecognizes) a sheep as its mother, without thereby our having to credit it with the concept of sheep or of motherhood. There is a wide Aristotelian sense of the terms "experience" and "mentality" in which experiences, mental states, and representations can be ascribed to any creature capable of unconceptualized perception, desires, emotional arousal, and perception-guided behavior.

Kant, however, has a narrower notion of experience (*Erfahrung*) that is peculiar to human beings. This involves the subject applying *concepts* to represent objects and states of affairs, to make perceptual *judgments* and to act on them, and to evaluate the reasons or justification for judgments and actions—and all this can be expressed by the subject in language. Our most distinctively human representations are thus conceptual as well as perceptual (see essay 2). But as we have noted, not all our representations are conceptual, we have many perceptions that remain unconceptualized. And not all humans have any conceptual representations: infants lack them, and those affected by brain damage or degeneration may lose them. We can thus say that it is a synthetic yet in some sense a priori truth that human representation—i.e., our *typical, mature* form of representation—is conceptual.

The above discussion is not confined to *presently perceptual* representations, i.e., those that involve the subject's own current perceptions. Any general theory of representation must also apply to our knowledge of the world in geography, history, and the sciences, most of which is acquired from testimony, by believing (and in favorable cases coming to know) what other people (past and present) inform us about (see essay 4). The undeniable core of empiricism is that all knowledge of contingent facts about the material world must be *perception-based*, in the sense that it ultimately depends for its justification on perception by somebody or other. But this does not rule out the conception of a "God's-eye point of view" not itself located in space or time, yet enjoying representations of the physical world that are not perception-based. Theologians have sometimes pictured God's omniscience in such a way, and it is not incoherent, at least at first sight. Kant himself maintained the logical possibility of a non-perception-based representation of reality, which he called "intellectual intuition" (B71–72, B145, B308). This would not involve any causal affection by its objects, and it would be free of the subjective features and limitations that characterize our perceptions from their particular spatiotemporal points of view. Kant was tempted to say that it could represent things "as they are in themselves," independently of the perceptual conditions that apply to our human representation, but he admits that we, whose intuition is "sensible," cannot know what it is like to possess this alleged intellectual intuition. Some philosophers may want to rule it out as impossible or inconceivable; but it is not obvious what the limits of possibility or conceivability are here. Short of a knockdown proof, perhaps we can agree with Kant in saying that it is a synthetic a priori truth that all *human* representations of the spatiotemporal world are perception-based.

What sense can we make, then, of Kant's somewhat shocking suggestion that objects "conform to the constitution of our faculty of *intuition*"? Let us distinguish the following *conceptualized perceptual* subspecies of our previously listed kinds of "object":

(Ia-cp) Propositions about perceivable states of affairs

(Ib-cp) Physical facts (or "states of affairs") that are actual or potential objects of conceptualized perception

(IIa-cp) The *contents* of conceptualized perceptual states (the intentional objects of such perception or putative perception)

(IIb-cp) Material objects or events, the actual or potential objects of conceptualized perception

There is no question of objects of types Ib-cp and IIb-cp "conforming to the constitution of our faculty of intuition," or to the perceptual sensitivity of any particular creature or species. But as we have seen, talk of objects of types Ia-cp and IIa-cp only makes sense as a way of talking about the perceptual sensitivities and recognitional capacities of rational beings like ourselves. The *contents* or intentional objects of our perceptual states must of course depend on, or "conform to," the ways in which we can perceive. We know that the intentional objects of *human* perception have certain properties: for example, everything we can see is colored within certain wavelengths of light, and the sounds humans can hear lie within certain frequencies, whereas bats can hear more, and dogs can smell much more than we can. This, however, is a posteriori knowledge, resting on the physical differences between the sense organs of various species. But when Kant asserts in the Transcendental Aesthetic that space and time are features of "the constitution of our faculty of intuition," he is claiming that the spatio-temporal form of our intuition is a deeper-lying truth about us, involving a stronger kind of necessity than the biological facts about human sense organs. It is surely a necessary truth that all finite rational beings have conceptualized perceptual representations, from their positions in space and time, of things and states of affairs in the physical world.

Let us now examine the next part of Kant's long sentence that I interrupted above:

> I can assume either that the concepts through which I bring about this determination also conform to objects, and then I am once again in the same difficulty about how I could know anything about them a *priori*.
>
> (Bxvii)

As I have acknowledged, there is unconceptualized perception in humans, but our empirical *knowledge* involves the application of concepts to our perceptions. The logical form of singular perceptual judgments is "This F is G," in which the concept F is used with a demonstrative word (and sometime a gesture) to make identifying reference to a presently perceived object (of type IIb-cp), and the concept G expresses a property that the subject presently perceives as holding of that object. We can also say that the subject currently perceives the corresponding fact or state of affairs (of type Ib-cp), namely, that the indicated F falls under the concept G.

Kant's claim in the second part of the quoted sentence is that the notion of "concepts conforming to objects" cannot explain how a priori knowledge is possible. But what could it *mean* to say that concepts "conform" to objects of type IIb-cp? Concepts can *apply* to things, of course. And *natural kind* concepts can be said to aspire to "conform to objects" in a deeper sense, aiming to "carve nature at the joints," i.e., to make the classifications that will prove to be most explanatory in the scientific sense. Kant touches on this topic much later on in the *Critique* in the Appendix to the Dialectic where he discusses the philosophy of science (A642/B670ff.), and also in the Method section when he discusses the possibility of definitions (A727/B755). Finding out *which* natural kind concepts apply in the world—i.e., discovering natural kinds—is an empirical (a posteriori) matter. So there is one sense, consistent with the rejection of "transcendental realism," in which the existence of objects falling into certain natural kinds or species *can* explain why humans have acquired concepts of those natural kinds. Interaction with certain kinds of objects, e.g., the repeated perception of iron, oak trees, or elephants, and indeed the practical use of them,[19] explains how human communities came to form concepts of those kinds of things. But that is empirical historical explanation of the development of specific concepts by certain peoples; whereas we were seeking an explanation at the *philosophical* level of how *any* conceptual representations at all are possible.

Let us proceed to the positive horn of Kant's dilemma:

> or else I assume that the objects, or what is the same thing, the *experience* in which alone they can be cognized (as given objects) conforms to those concepts, in which case I immediately see an easier way out of the difficulty, since experience itself is a kind of cognition requiring the understanding, whose rule I have to presuppose in myself before any object is given to me, hence a priori, which rule is expressed in concepts *a priori*, to which all objects of experience must therefore necessarily conform, and with which they must agree.
>
> (Bxvii)

This passage is, no doubt, one of those that make many readers give up hope of illumination from Kant! Indeed it is puzzling how he can identify objects with *experience* of those same objects. But if we deploy once more our distinction between intentional and actual objects, we can offer a plausible reinterpretation. For Kant, "experience" (*Erfahrung*) means *conceptualized* perceptual experience, expressible in perceptual judgments involving the faculty of understanding (*Verstand*) as well as sensibility (*Sinnlichkeit*). In terms of the distinctions I have been insisting on in this paper, we can take his point to be that the narrowly construed contents or *intentional* objects of experience, Ia-cp and IIa-cp, must "conform" to the a priori concepts, i.e., the categories or "pure concepts of the understanding," that express the necessary conditions to which all of our conceptualized perceptual experience must conform. Thus we have here in the B Preface a sneak preview of the kind of transcendental argument that Kant offers at length in the Transcendental Deduction and the Analogies of Experience. Strictly speaking, we cannot literally *identify* the actual objects with the intentional objects, nor the latter with conceptualized perceptual experiences, but the intentional objects can be said to be the *content* of such experiences.

III

In the rest of this essay, let me explore how this preview fits with the passages in the Transcendental Deduction where Kant explicitly discusses "objects of representation." In the A version he poses the question: "What does one mean, then, if one speaks of an object corresponding to and therefore also distinct from the cognition?" (A104). I suggest that in trying to answer this question, we must be careful about the use of the first-person plural.[20] One person A can distinguish between the objects he believes to exist, and an overlapping but nonidentical set of objects that (he takes it) another person B recognizes—some of which A may *not* believe to exist, and will therefore describe as mere intentional objects of B's thought. A can similarly distinguish between the set of objects he *now* recognizes, and those that he believed in at some stage in the past (e.g., A may say that he used not to believe in God, but now he does). Given two *groups* of people the Cs and the Ds, each with a shared set of beliefs, the Cs can distinguish between their own set of intentional objects of thought and those of the Ds (e.g., we believe in mental illness, but they believe in demon possession), and the Cs may also distinguish their *present* set of objects from those they recognized in the past (e.g., we used to accept the theory of phlogiston, but now we know about oxidization). But of course no individual or group can make a distinction between *their own current* set of intentional objects and the objects they currently believe to exist. I suggest this is why Kant answered his own question as follows:

> It is easy to see that this object must be thought of only as something in general = X, since outside of our cognition we have nothing that we could set over against this cognition as corresponding to it.

(A104)

But that is a dangerously ambiguous statement. Read in one way, a skeptical or idealist abyss threatens to open up, for we are tempted to picture our thought as inevitably and frustratingly cut off from direct contact with the world, so that any knowledge of mind-independent reality may seem impossible. Yet surely this is a philosophical illusion. It is undeniable that if one is to refer to and describe objects one must use some *way* of doing so: there can be no such thing as thinking about a particular item without relying on some humanly usable procedure for identifying exactly which item one "means," i.e., intends to refer to. There can be no reference without sense, if "sense" is understood (with Frege) as a *way* of singling out the item referred to. (And there is almost always more than one conceivable way of singling out the same thing.) So it seems that the notion of an object distinct from all our ways of referring and knowing can only be of some unspecified "thing in itself," like the unknown quantity x in an algebraic equation. The very talk of *an* object presupposes that one particular object, entity, substance, event, process, or state of affairs is already somehow identified determinately and discriminated from all others. But identification (singling out, discrimination) is something that *we have to do* in order to represent any particular aspect of reality, and say or think anything about it. The notion of reality "as it is itself," prior to and independent of all our representing activities, can only be expressed by all-encompassing, indiscriminate, unparticularizing words like "Reality," "the World (as it is in itself)," "Nature," "Being," or "the One" (with a hint of mysticism!) (see essays 4 and 5).[21]

But is there really any such dramatic threat to our sense of objectivity, our assumption that our thoughts (some of them, at least!) refer to mind-independent reality? Although one person cannot distinguish between her present set of intentional objects and the objects she presently believes to exist, she can conceive of *changes* in her beliefs, and the same applies to human communities. We have to allow the possibility that our set of intentional objects and accepted propositions will expand, and occasionally contract, as we gain more knowledge of the world. There are many ways in which present beliefs can be tested by further experience, involving further perceptions by oneself, the testimony of other people, or induction and scientific inference generally. Kant's next sentence is relevant to this:

> We find, however, that our thought of the relation of all cognition to its object carries something of necessity with it, since namely the latter is regarded as that which is opposed to our cognitions being determined at pleasure or arbitrarily rather than being determined *a priori*, since insofar as they are to relate to an object our cognitions must also necessarily agree with each other in relation to it, i.e. they must have that unity that constitutes the concept of an object.

(A104–5)

Our thought of the relation of our present beliefs and theories to their objects thus carries with it an element of necessity, in the sense that there are necessary connections between our present beliefs and many possible perceptions, both our own and other people's. Our beliefs about what there is in the world, including our perceptual judgments, cannot be totally haphazard or arbitrary, having no connection with one another: if various beliefs are to be about particular objects within the world, they must be consistent with each other, not merely logically consistent, but consistent with the general causal laws we believe to hold. Perceptual-based judgments about an object must be interpreted as having a causal relationship with that object, i.e., perceptual confrontations with it must have caused the perceptual experiences on which those judgments were based.

It thus emerges that representation is essentially holistic. Referring to a particular object, or having a singular thought, is not a simple property that a given mental state either possesses or lacks quite independently of what holds true of everything else in the mind of the subject. A given mental state represents an object only in virtue of its conceptual role, which depends on a complex pattern of actual or possible relationships to other representational mental states in that subject (and in other people too, according to Wittgenstein's argument against the possibility of a "private language"). As Kant goes on:

> It is clear, however, that since we have only to do with the manifold of our representations, and that X which corresponds to them (the object), because it should be something distinct from all of our representations, is nothing for us, the unity that the object makes necessary can be nothing other than the formal unity of the consciousness in our synthesis of the manifold of our representations. Hence we say that we cognize the object if we have effected synthetic unity in the manifold of intuition.
>
> (A105)

The same theme is expressed in slightly different terms in the B Transcendental Deduction (where the theory of synthesis is still present, though not given such prominence) when Kant says that "an object, however, is that in the concept of which the manifold of a given intuition is united" (B137).

Toward the end of the A version, Kant sums up, in terms that he himself admits are paradoxical, the idealist-sounding conclusion to which he thinks his argument has led:

> Thus we ourselves bring into the appearances that order and regularity in them that we call nature, and moreover we would not be able to find it there if we, or the nature of our mind, had not originally put it there.
>
> (A125)

...Thus as exaggerated and contradictory as it may sound to say that the understanding is itself the source of the laws of nature, and thus of the formal unity of nature, such an assertion is nevertheless correct and appropriate to the object, namely experience.

(A127)

At the end of the B version, Kant offers an account that is perhaps rather less "exaggerated and contradictory" of how the categories can prescribe laws a priori to appearances:

It is by no means stranger that the laws of appearances in nature must agree with the understanding and its *a priori* form, i.e. its faculty of combining the manifold in general, than that the appearances themselves must agree with the form of sensible intuition *a priori*. For laws exist just as little in the appearances, but rather exist only relative to the subject in which the appearances inhere, insofar as it has understanding, as appearances do not exist in themselves, but only relative to the same being, insofar as it has senses.

(B164)

Here is my suggested interpretation of this less than pellucid passage, in the light of the distinctions deployed in this essay. Just as all the objects of *un*conceptualized perception ("appearances" in one sense of the word)[22] must conform to the conditions for the subject to have perceptions, so all the objects of conceptualized perception ("appearances" in the conceptualized sense, i.e., Ib-cp and IIb-cp) must conform to the conditions for the subject to have concepts of perceivable objects, properties, and states of affairs.

Nearly two centuries after Kant, the Polish philosopher Leszek Kolakowski reiterated the "exaggerated and contradictory" interpretation of transcendental idealism:

The picture of reality sketched by everyday perception and by scientific thinking is a kind of human creation (not imitation) since both the linguistic and the scientific division of the world into particular objects arise from man's practical needs. In this sense the world's products must be considered artificial. In this world the sun and the stars exist because man is able to make them *his* objects, differentiated in material and conceived as "corporeal individuals."

(Kolakowski 1968: 47–48)

But the whole trend of this essay suggests that we should not rest content with such dangerously overstated formulations. David Wiggins in his lifelong study of identity and individuation[23] has wisely insisted that we need to walk a philosophical tightrope between the errors of idealism on one side and a nonconceptualist realism on the other. We must reject any "sense" in which horses, leaves, sun, and stars could be supposed to be our products, while acknowledging that we have to use *our* concepts in singling out those very things among many others that could be singled out by other concepts:

> Conceptualism properly conceived must not entail that before we grasped [the relevant] concepts, their extensions did not exist autonomously.... Its most distinctive contention is that, even though horses, leaves, sun and stars are not inventions or artifacts, still, if such things...were to be singled out in experience at all so as to become objects of thought, then some scheme had to be fashioned or formed, in the back and forth process between recurrent traits in nature and would-be cognitive conceptions of these traits, that made it possible for them to be picked out.
>
> (Wiggins 2001: 149–50)

Nicholas Rescher defended a similar position that he labels "conceptual idealism" in his book of that name (Rescher 1973).[24] He puts rather more emphasis on the laws and hence on the unfulfilled possibilities that are inherent in our conception of the world, whereas Wiggins concentrates on the matter of individuation; but I think the difference between Wiggins's "conceptualist realism" and Rescher's "conceptualistic idealism" is only a matter of terminology and emphasis. The fact that Wiggins calls his position a form of realism, whereas Rescher labels his a form of idealism, shows just how narrow is the tightrope that any interpretation of Kant has to walk between transcendental and empirical idealism, and transcendental and empirical realism. I hope to have provided some balancing aids to that perilous walk.

ESSAY 2

⚭

Synthetic Unities of Experience

I am going to explore various kinds of unity in our experience. My title comes from Kant, and like him I mean it quite literally: the idea is that these forms of unity are produced by mental processes of synthesis. I also derive inspiration from Merleau-Ponty, Wilfrid Sellars, Andrew Brook, and others.[1] Kant was, I submit, asking questions about the relation between preconceptual and conceptual levels of mental functioning that are still of fundamental importance in epistemology, philosophy of mind, and cognitive science.[2] I hope to formulate more precisely some of the principles of unity that he suggested, and some more that he did not.

It is not always easy to decide which claims about our mental functioning are philosophical, and which are scientific. Kant was famously resolute about distinguishing the a priori from the a posteriori, and he showed some awareness of the need to apply this to his own theorizing about human faculties when he distinguished between what he called the "objective" and "subjective" deductions of the categories (Axvi–xvii).[3] Some recent philosophers of mind, however, have rejected any attempt to distinguish the a priori from the empirical in anything more than degree, and thus they see philosophy as merging seamlessly with cognitive science. So when I formulate a number of theses about unity in human experience, the question arises whether I am presenting them as analytic truths about the very concept of experience or as empirical facts about our actual experience. Or are they even empirical falsities, in view of certain kinds of disassociation or disunity manifested in cases of brain damage or mental malfunctioning, or in very unusual experimental conditions? The status I have in mind for my theses does not quite fit into any of these categories: I propose that they are (1) typical of the conceptualized experience of normal human adults in our usual environments; and (2) normative, in that we think of them as essential for proper mental functioning (for example, one expects people to be able to say what they are doing, and to remember a good deal of what they have done that day). Various kinds of exception may be found in infants, in clinical cases, or in abnormal experimental situations (for example, surprising dissociations can be found in split-brain cases, and large-scale memory loss happens in brain damage and dementia). If there are such synthetic unities involved in typical human experience, it will surely help our philosophical and psychological theorizing to have a deeper understanding of them.[4]

I. THE INDIVIDUATION OF EXPERIENCES

The first point is that experience implies the existence of a *subject*, i.e., a persisting being endowed with certain mental capacities. Lichtenberg questioned this when he alleged that the Cartesian *cogito* shows only that there is thinking, not that there is a thinker. But it can be replied on Descartes's behalf that it is a logical truth that every attribute requires a substance of some sort to inhere in, and that mental states and processes involve the existence of mental capacities, which presuppose persisting mental subjects. The experiences of A (whether animal or human) are distinct events from the experiences of B, even if they happen at the very same moment and are exactly similar in content, e.g., if A and B hear the same bang or smell the same pong. With mutual communication, two people can know that they are enjoying experiences with the same content, but we still distinguish A's experiences from B's by the identities of the two subjects.

The suggestion of experience without an identifiable subject also arose in Hume's famous section "On Personal Identity" (Hume [1739] 2007: I.iv.vi), in which he presented his problem as that of how to tie "perceptions" into appropriate bundles to make up selves, as if perceptions could be identified in a way that does not already individuate them by their subjects. Kant's much-quoted premise in the B Transcendental Deduction that it must be possible for the "I think" to accompany all one's representations (B131) can be seen as a rejection of this, though he agreed with Hume that the self is not an identifiable particular *within* experience. Kant's point is that all distinctively human experience involves the self-ascribability of experiences.

A second feature of the logical grammar of experiences is their *temporality*. Experiences are had, undergone, or enjoyed at certain moments in time. We sometimes hear talk of timeless experiences, glimpses of eternity, or even of tenseless divine experience. Some such locutions may only be metaphors for meaning-charged experiences that are perfectly clockable by physical standards ("Our timeless moment of mutual rapture took place as the sun set over the mountains, at 19:37, Eastern Standard Time"). Other such talk may involve controversial metaphysical or theological doctrines, into which I do not propose to enter here. I merely point out that our ordinary notion of animal or human experiences is of mental states or events occurring at identifiable times. But as we shall see below, there are important and subtle issues about integration or synthesis over time, and about the representation of time in experience. Kant says that time is the form of inner sense (A22–23/B37), and by that he meant more than that our experiences are in time; he meant that we *represent* our experiences as occurring at particular times within a public time frame (he says, at B275, "I am conscious of my existence as determined in time"). Animal experiences are in time, but only human beings are *aware* of themselves as being in time. We can thus be aware of our own mortality, that our time span of existence is limited, which is a fact of great existential importance.

Experiences thus fall into the ontological category of events or states in a mentally endowed subject. There is a wide Aristotelian sense of the terms "experience" or "mentality" in which experiences can be ascribed to all creatures capable of sensation, unconceptualized perception, and perception-guided activity. But we can distinguish a narrower, more distinctively Kantian use of "experience" (his term was *Erfahrung*) that is peculiar to human beings. This involves the subject being able to apply concepts to represent states of affairs, to make perceptual judgments about the world, and to evaluate the justification for such judgments. The subject of this conceptualized experience is a rational being who can ask herself: Does the concept F apply to what I now perceive? According to this Kantian conception of experience, then, human beings are unlike other animals in that (1) we apply norms of rational correctness in making judgments and practical decisions, i.e., we can ask about the justification for a belief, and for an action; and (2) we have a concept of ourselves as subjects of conscious experience, i.e., each of us can think of his or her experiences as "mine." Distinctively human experience is both *conceptual*, involving theoretical and practical reason, and *personal* in the sense of being potentially self-conscious.

II. THE PRECONCEPTUAL MENTAL PROCESSES UNDERLYING EXPERIENCE

Kant argued that *Erfahrung*, human conceptualized experience, is the result of preconceptual, subpersonal mental processing. If we are to think of perceived states of affairs and make judgments and decisions about them, there must be psychological processes (which Kant variously called "synthesis," "working up," or "combination") by which the manifold and disparate elements of raw sensory input (the immediate effects of the world on the sense organs) are somehow integrated, organized, or processed into conscious, conceptualized representations of objects and states of affairs. He said as much on the first page of the main text of the *Critique*:

> There is no doubt whatever that all our cognition begins with experience; for how else should the cognitive faculty be awakened into exercise if not through objects that stimulate our senses and in part themselves produce representations, in part bring the activity of our understanding into motion to compare these, to connect or separate them, and thus to work up the raw material of sensible impressions into a cognition of objects that is called experience?
>
> (B1)

Unlike the classic empiricist accounts of perceptual experience as the mere passive reception of Lockean/Berkeleian "ideas" or Humean "impressions," Kant's claim is that conceptualized experience does not come into being until a lot of mental processing has been done. Objects and events affect our sense organs in physical ways, thereby producing "sensible impressions" or "sensations" as the immediate effects on our mental capacities. But these sensible impressions (or sensations) are mere "raw material." They do not involve singular reference, predication, or propositional content; they do not themselves "represent" anything. There must therefore be a process, obviously very rapid, but nevertheless a temporal process, by which the raw material gets worked up into the "finished product" of conceptualized perceptual experiences which do represent objects and states of affairs in the world.

"Experience," "consciousness," and "representation" are multiply ambiguous words that constantly cause confusion in philosophy. Kant's use of them is not without his own peculiar problems, but his most basic claim is that our perceptual experience involves the cooperation of two mental faculties: the "receptivity" of "sensibility," in which we are causally affected by the physical world through our sense organs,[5] and the "spontaneity" of "understanding," by which we apply concepts and make judgments about what we perceive. The famous slogan "Thoughts without content are empty, intuitions without concepts are blind" (A51/B75) is a neat encapsulation of this (and for many people the only bit of Kant that they remember). But there is more to Kant than this. He distinguishes conceptualized experience from the subpersonal processes that make it possible, and he takes it that the latter are largely or usually unconscious, but that the processing, though unconscious, is mental, involving powers of our mind (*Gemut*). Mysteriously, he sometimes attributes synthesis to a third mental faculty called the "imagination," which is supposed to mediate between sensibility and understanding, and at A78/B103 he describes the imagination as "a blind but indispensable function of the soul, without which we should have no knowledge whatsoever, but of which we are scarcely ever conscious,"[6] and in the A version of the Transcendental Deduction he offers his most complicated theorizing about the operations of the imagination in various levels of synthesis.

To get clear about his terminology, we need to take account of the passage in which he gives his most detailed elucidation of his mental terms:[7]

> The genus is representation (*Vorstellung*) in general. Under it stands the representation with consciousness (*Bewusstsein*). A perception that refers to the subject as a modification of its state is a sensation (*Empfindung*); an objective perception is a cognition (*Erkenntnis*). The latter is either an intuition (*Anschauung*) or a concept (*Begriff*). The former is immediately related to the object and is singular; the latter is mediate, by means of a mark, which can be common to several things.
>
> (A320/B376–77, inserting Kant's German terms instead
> of the Latin words he offered)

Kant here allows that some representations (mental states) are unconscious, and he includes raw unsynthesized sense impressions as "representations," even though they do not themselves represent anything. He distinguishes "cognitions" as "objective," by which I take it he means that they have conceptual content about objects and states of affairs distinct from the subject, from sensations (such as pain, heat, blurred vision, and ringing in the ears) that are mere "modifications of the subject's state," available to consciousness but representing nothing extra-mental.[8] Note that Kant here classes intuitions under "objective" representations: so in this passage at least, we are given to understand intuitions as conceptualized, though when he wrote much earlier of intuitions without concepts being "blind" he must have been thinking of unconceptualized intuitions. We can think of conceptualized intuitions as demonstrative ways of thinking of particular objects under concepts, expressible linguistically in the form "this (presently perceived) F."[9] As Patricia Kitcher has noted (1990: 66), the implication that some representations do not represent is only a verbal paradox, not a self-contradiction, like modern physics saying that atoms are divisible. If we wish to avoid all appearance of paradox, we could translate *Vorstellung* as "cognitive state," meaning thereby any state of the subject that contributes to knowledge, and therefore falls within the subject matter of cognitive science.

There may appear to be a conflict with Kant's dictum that it must be possible for the "I think" to accompany all my representations (B131). An easy resolution would be to say that all mental states, all representations, are *potentially* conscious, although not all are actually so. But his statement that we are scarcely ever conscious of the working of our imagination suggests a stronger thesis, that the subpersonal processes of synthesis (or most of them) are not normally available to introspection. We need to read the full sentence of which the much-quoted saying is only the first part:

> It must be possible for the "I think" to accompany all my representations, for otherwise something would be represented in me which could not be thought at all, and that is equivalent to saying that the representation would be impossible, or at least would be nothing to me.
>
> (B131–32)

I suggest we should interpret this as a necessary truth about *conceptual,* "objective" representations, that mental states at *that* level must be potentially self-ascribable. Animals obviously feel sensations and they perceive things, and their perceptions of their environment must be made possible by sensory and cortical processing. But that processing is not as complex as ours, for it does not allow for linguistic representation or conscious self-ascription. It is open for contemporary philosophy and cognitive science to elucidate a sense (or senses) in which there are cognitive states in us that may be said to have *nonconceptual* content, representing states of the world in some nonpropositional way. Thus Kant's wide use of *Vorstellung* could become defensible for a reason that he only dimly foresaw. That is a matter for much ongoing research in philosophy and cognitive science.

There remains a crucial ambiguity that Sellars alerted us to,[10] between

1. Kant's "representations" as mental events or acts (represent*ings*)
2. the content thereby represented—the intentional objects of conceptualized represent*ings* (see essay 1)
3. the external objects that are represent*ed* (in many if not all cases)

It is the conceptualized *representings* (with their contents) that are synthesized, not the mind-independent objects. When I see something and recognize it as a house, my visual representation of it (my intuition) has the conceptual content "house," and that conceptualized perceptual state is a result of information-processing in my mind (or brain). I certainly do not synthesize the house—it was constructed by the builders. Yet there is a temptation to confusion on this point, encouraged by Kant's notorious proneness to suggest that we can know only our own representations, for example:

Everything intuited in space or in time, hence all objects of an experience possible for us, are nothing but appearances, i.e. mere representations, which, as they are represented, as extended beings or series of alterations, have outside our thoughts no existence grounded in itself.

(A490–91/B518–19)

Hence the recurring questions as to how his position differs at bottom from phenomenalism or Berkeleian idealism. But I suggest that such pressure can be reduced by picking up on his use of the word "as," and interpreting him as saying that we can only know things *as* we represent them (see essay 1).[11]

In his talk of synthesis, Kant anticipated cognitive science. The mental processes of synthesis in us are causally necessary for experience, but they are not themselves experienced. We are not introspectively aware of them (not usually, anyway): phenomenologically, we are just aware of things and events in the world. Even if we *try* to introspect, there seems no reason why we should be able to become aware of any or much of our own processes of synthesis. However, philosophers can argue about them in their a priori way, cognitive scientists can postulate theories about them, and experimental psychologists can test those theories by empirical evidence.

III. THE INDIVIDUATION OF CONCEPTUALIZED EXPERIENCES IN TIME

I will now pursue further questions about how to individuate and classify conceptualized experiences, beginning with temporal distinctions. Obviously, there are differences between practically instantaneous experiences (e.g., recognizing a friend, and giving her a peck on the cheek) and longer-lasting ones (e.g., hearing a lecture, being a student or a parent). Sometimes we use the word "experience" as a mass term rather than a count noun, e.g., when we recommend someone to get more experience of life and love before getting married. Experiences in the plural form temporal parts of longer-lasting tracts of experience: for example, Jane's experience of her first term at university is the sum total of the many experiences she undergoes or enjoys in those frantic weeks; and her experience of a lecture or party is itself made up of a succession of experiences of briefer episodes. But how far can we take such subdivision? Is one's experience of hearing a sentence, for example, made up of experiences of hearing its individual words pronounced in order? I suggest there are limits to such microtemporal subdivision.

We say that one subject has two different experiences of the same type if they occur at distinct times, e.g., hearing two playings of the same recording. But beyond this point (noted in section I), interesting unclarities arise.

What if the subject hears two bangs in quick succession? Is that one experience (an experience of succession), or two (a succession of experiences)? Or even perhaps three: the hearing of each bang plus the experience of hearing one *after* the other? Consider the perception of any kind of movement or change, e.g., a ship moving downstream.[12] The perception of succession is not just a succession of perceptions, for one can have the latter without realizing that there has been a change, and also without having the distinctive experience of perceiving something changing. One can successively see a ship of a certain kind in two positions without knowing whether it is the *same* ship that has moved (for there could have been two similar ships, perhaps not moving at all). With memory and probabilistic inference, one can see *that* one and the same ship has changed its position, without having *seen* it moving. One can see the second hand of a clock moving, but usually not the minute hand, and certainly not the hour hand. The general principle involved here is:

> Succession. A perceptual experience of succession is not reducible to a succession of
> perceptual experiences, even if they occur in the time-order of the events perceived.

There is here a temporal Gestalt phenomenon—the perception of a whole event that is more than the sum of the perceptions of the temporal parts. Consider hearing a lecture or a symphonic movement, seeing a dance or film, or feeling a slow, well-orchestrated massage. If one hears a sentence uttered with long pauses between the words, one's attention may wander and one may not understand the meaning of the complete sentence. If a series of musical notes is played or sung with time intervals between them, they may no longer hold together as a recognizable tune, especially if interspersed with other sounds. Conversely, when one *is* aware of a whole sentence or tune or pattern of movement, as shown in comprehension of its meaning or emotional significance, one need not be similarly aware of the constituent parts.

There is also the phenomenon of *seeming* to see movement where in fact there is none. If a cinematic film is slowed down sufficiently, one loses the experience of movement and sees a mere succession of static images. We see text messages as moving across electronic bulletin boards, when all that is happening is that each bulb in an array is briefly lighting up. Two alternately flashing bulbs can look like one light jumping back and forth, and we see waves on water as something moving across the surface. In each case a *pattern* can be said to move although no material object moves (in the case of the waves, no water moves horizontally).

In most perceptions there is a temporal stream of sensory stimuli coming in over a period of time (measured in seconds or minutes), and often through more than one sense. There are of course practically instantaneous perceptions of single bangs, screams, flashes, touches, stings, or kisses—unrepeated, and perceived through only one sense. But we have to ask what exactly is perceived in such cases. The object of perception may be described merely as a bodily sensation, e.g., a tickle or scratch, or "stars in the eyes"—with no claim about anything outside the body of the subject (in line with Kant's conception of sensation). If there *is* a claim about the public world, that might involve only an instantaneous or very short-lived event (e.g., a flash of light, an audible thud, something tickling one's neck). But there may also be a claim about some persisting object (e.g., a light that flashed, a falling book that thudded, a spider that tickled one's skin), or at least a public state of affairs (e.g., a smell or buzz in the surrounding spatial region). When our perceptual judgments represent persisting objects, states of affairs, or processes, they usually involve the integration of temporally separated sensory signals into judgments about such persisting entities. And such judgments often involve the integration of signals from different senses into judgments about the objects of our cross-modal perception.

In many psychological experiments, highly artificial conditions are contrived in which very short reaction times are imposed, and often to a single stimulus in only one sensory modality. Such experiments may elucidate some interesting facts about our perceptual mechanisms, but they do *not* cast much light upon the complex problem of how the temporal stream of data from our various senses is synthesized in ordinary perceptual experience. Rather few real-life perceptions are instantaneous, or involve only one sense, uninformed even by proprioceptive awareness of bodily orientation. Most human perception is not a succession of static "snapshots" of certain perceivable aspects of the subject's environment, for the instantaneous signals or raw unconceptualized sense impressions are somehow integrated into representations of persisting objects that also change their properties or relationships, and usually we perceive the changes "in real time" as they happen.

IV. THE INDIVIDUATION OF SIMULTANEOUS EXPERIENCES

Interesting questions can also be asked about the unification of *simultaneous* aspects of conceptualized experience. Is Fred's total experience at a particular moment to be understood as the co-occurrence of several experiences, e.g., of hearing the lecturer drone on, seeing a fly zoom about the room, feeling the hardness of the bench, remembering how Jane reacted last night and wondering whether she might be amenable to another approach? How far can such subdivision of simultaneous experience be taken? For example, does Fred's seeing written sentences or diagrams consist of his simultaneous perceptions of individual words, letters, or lines? There is a Gestalt phenomenon here too, in that the subject can be aware of a whole without being aware of its parts. (As primary school teachers know, reading is a complex skill depending on many different cues, especially in a language with spelling as idiosyncratic as English.)

Alan Millar broached this theme when he wrote that an experience of a complex state of affairs is a complex experience, but it should not be conceived as a mere complex of experiences (1991: 19). Consider his simple example of seeing a spoon in a cup: this cannot consist merely in two simultaneous experiences of seeing the spoon and seeing the cup, for one could of course have two such experiences simultaneously without seeing the spoon as *in* the cup. The principle that an experience of a complex is not reducible to a complex of experiences applies to many other sorts of cases. Consider the perception of several features of a single object within one sensory modality. If Olga is presented with a red square, does she have one experience of seeing something red, and another of seeing something square, or does she have a single unified experience of seeing a red square? If she hears the reedy timbre of an oboe playing fifths in 6:8 time, staccato and crescendo, does she enjoy five aural experiences or one, or does she have a complex experience that contains five simpler experiences as its parts?

Obviously, to see a red square does not consist just in seeing something red and seeing something square, but in seeing *one* thing that is both red and square. This point holds even if we apply it to two-dimensional items in the "private" visual field, such as afterimages: to seem to see a green circle is not the same as seeming to see something green and something circular. Articulate subjects will give different verbal reports in the two cases, and less articulate ones may draw different pictures.[13] The oboe may be heard as reedy, high-pitched, and crescendo, but it is heard as one sound with those three properties. It would be a different musical experience to hear them simultaneously instantiated in different instruments—and the difference can be manifested in discriminatory speech or behavior (e.g., by the conductor of the orchestra). I suggest that the general principle here is:

> Object. The experience of perceiving an object as having several features in one sensory modality is not reducible to a conjunction of perceptual experiences of those features, even if caused by the same object.

An analogous principle applies to cross-modal perception (which may sound rather exotic, but you may be relieved to know it is something we all enjoy every day). Many recognitions and descriptions of things or events involve more than one sense, e.g., "I just heard that little brown bird burst into song." If one sees, hears, and feels a slap administered to part of one's anatomy, it is one event that is triply perceived. If Arabella sees and touches the lucky man to whom she delivers a kiss, does she have a visual experience plus a tactile one (and maybe an emotional one, and God knows what else), or does she have one single experience rich in features? For an experience involving all five traditional senses (plus some kinesthetic experience thrown in for good measure), think of crunching into a pungent apple.

Even what might be thought to be *purely* visual experience usually involves our bodily sense of the direction of gravity (which depends on the semicircular canals in the inner ear). For example, if I see a man sitting on a chair, the pattern of light input to my retina might be just the same if both I and he-on-his-chair are inverted, but my experience will then be different (and not just because I feel less comfortable!), for I will then see him as miraculously suspended upside down from a chair. One might not get this effect in weightless conditions in space, but our perceptual systems have been evolved to suit our earthly environment, and we should beware of drawing conclusions about our experience from cases that depart so radically from the biological norm. And even in space, there will surely be effects that depend on orientation relative to the perceiver's body; for example, if one sees a face upside down it is more difficult to recognize the person or their facial expressions.[14]

When two or more senses are coordinated, for example sight and touch in catching an oncoming ball, the experience is not reducible to the conjunction of a visual experience and a tactile one, for they have to be of *the same* ball. It is not sufficient that there are single-sensory experiences caused by the same object at the same time: if the experience is to be genuinely cross-modal, the information from different senses must be integrated in a way that can manifest distinctive behavioral effects.[15] An animal or infant has to learn to coordinate sight and touch in action, without propositional judgment. But in the case of conceptualized experience there will be an ability to assert, as well as to act upon, the perception of one thing in two modalities (e.g., to think or say: "I saw the ball and caught it," "I cuddled the child who was crying," "I smelled the perfume before I recognized its wearer"). To sum this up:

> Cross-modal. A cross-modal perceptual experience of an object cannot be reduced to a simultaneous conjunction of single-modality perceptions of the same object.

There are abnormal cases in which a brain-damaged patient cannot integrate sensory impressions (whether from one sense, or more than one), and thus cannot recognize familiar kinds of objects as such (Sacks 1985: 13). In one subject, there was impressive conceptual articulacy about shape—"a continuous surface infolded upon itself, with five outpouchings," he said, attempting to identify what was in his hand—together with astonishing inability to recognize it as a glove. There was some synthesis going on in counting the "outpouchings," but not the normal (higher-level?) synthesis involved in recognizing the function of the object. Such clinical cases illuminate the complexity behind our normal mental functioning.

V. THE UNIFICATION OF PERCEPTIONS OF THE WORLD

There is yet more to be said about how our conceptualized experiences are synthesized, unified, and individuated. We do not just represent particular objects and states of affairs, we represent all perceived items as related together in one world. When one sees two objects at the same time, one must see them as standing in some spatial relation or other, e.g., that the spoon is in the cup, or behind it, or a few inches to its left. As Merleau-Ponty put it:

> When Gestalt theory informs us that a figure on a background is the simplest sense-given available to us, we reply that this is not a contingent characteristic of factual perception.... It is the very definition of the phenomenon of perception.... The perceptual "something" is always in the middle of something else, it always forms part of a "field."
>
> ([1945] 1962): 4)[16]

Phenomenologically, there is a single two-dimensional visual field containing the whole content of one's present visual experience. Those with some skill in perspective can draw a picture of how things look from one's spatial location. Even a set of simultaneous afterimages or "spots before the eyes" must be spatially related in the plane of the visual field, and the articulate subject can describe such relations. More typically, however, one sees worldly objects as located at various distances from oneself and from each other in *three*-dimensional space. So there is also a *public* concept of visual field, meaning the view of the world that anyone can see by looking in a given direction from a certain position in space.

To put the point in a sense-neutral way without the usual bias toward vision, all the public objects, events, and states of affairs one perceives through any of the senses are represented as existing in one world, a single all-embracing system of spatial and temporal relations. Admittedly, not every perceptual experience unambiguously represents a spatial relationship. Hearing indicates the approximate direction of the source of sound (when both ears are functioning), but it does not usually indicate distance without appeal to collateral information. Touch gives an indication of the spatial relation between the touched or touching object and the perceiver's body, but if one is in an unusually contorted bodily position, one might be somewhat unclear about the spatial relation of two things touching one's elbow and toe. Although we usually see objects as related in three-dimensional space, we cannot always tell at sight whether one thing is farther away than another, e.g., in fog, or when they are both distant (though right-left and up-down relationships are usually more determinate). But for anything one perceives and conceptualizes as distinct from oneself, one has to think of it as belonging to the public world, even if one is unsure about the details in particular cases.

All spaces are represented as parts of one space, Kant said at A25/B39. Analogously, all events are represented as happening in one system of temporal relations (A31–32/B47, B224–25, B275–76). And if Kant is right, these spatiotemporal relationships must also involve causality, at least potentially and indirectly: "All substances, in so far as they can be perceived in space as simultaneous, are in thoroughgoing interaction" (B256).[17] Hallucinations and dreams betray themselves by their lack of connection with this total world-system: we are occasionally deluded, but usually only briefly. Merleau-Ponty echoes Kant in saying that the world has, necessarily, a certain unity (([1945] 1962): 327), which involves spatial, temporal, and interpersonal integration:

> The tacit thesis of perception is that at every instant experience can be co-ordinated with that of the previous instant and that of the following, and my perspective with that of other consciousnesses—that all contradictions can be removed, that monadic and inter-subjective experience is one unbroken text.
>
> (([1945] 1962): : 54)

I claim that we have to recognize a whole extra level of mental synthesis that is involved in our representations of all perceived items as existing in one spatiotemporal world. As so often, Kant has been here before us. In the middle of one of his most intricately difficult expositions (in the A Transcendental Deduction) we find the following passages:

> Just this transcendental unity of apperception, however, makes out of all possible appearances that can ever come together in one experience a connection of all of these representations in accordance with laws.
>
> (A108)

> There is only *one* experience, in which all perceptions are represented as in thoroughgoing and lawlike connection, just as there is only one space and one time, in which all forms of appearance and all relation of being or non-being occur. If one speaks of

different experiences, they are only so many perceptions insofar as they belong to one and the same universal experience. This thoroughgoing and synthetic unity of perceptions is precisely what constitutes the form of experience, and it is nothing other than the synthetic unity of the appearances in accordance with concepts.

(A110)

Andrew Brook has argued that there is a neglected insight here that is vital for contemporary cognitive science and philosophy of mind (1994: Ch.2.2, Ch.6.I). However, it is perhaps an understatement to say that the point could benefit from some elucidation, so let me now attempt some. As we have seen, for Kant "synthetic unity" means unity produced by mental processes of synthesis, and I have elaborated on the temporal and cross-modal aspects of this. My point now is that over and above those, there must be another kind or level of synthesis by which perceptions of particular objects or events are integrated into "one single (or general) experience," "a global representation" of the world. There are perceptual and conceptual aspects to this, however, which need distinguishing.

In perception, the total set of incoming information from the various senses typically gets synthesized into a representation of a single perceived scene (a part of the world as it appears to the subject from her position in space and time). We should not confine this notion of scene to the visual. Sounds, smells, and heat are often referred to particular physical sources localized in space, and tactile qualities are ascribed to stuff in contact with the body. This synthesis is usually as unconscious as that involved in the conceptualization of particular objects and events. Admittedly, we sometimes ask questions such as "What's that noise? What and where is that blob that appears to be on the horizon? Who is responsible for this smell?"—and we may arrive at answers to them by conscious inference, and of course by further investigation. But most of one's perceptual experience comes to consciousness already synthesized, presenting a set of objects and events as located and mutually related in space and time. To sum this up:

> Scene. Incoming perceptual information gets synthesized into a single *scene*—a perceptual representation of part of the world as perceived by the subject from her present position in space.

It is an interesting question for cognitive science: Is some sort of schematic representation of the overall background scene synthesized *before* the synthesis of representations of particular items within it, or might the two be interdependent in various ways? A research program opens up here, largely empirical, but involving conceptual questions in its foundations.

There are of course many *nonperceptual* representations that contribute to one's total set of beliefs about the world—maps, time charts, guidebooks, history books, news reports, testimony, and gossip. There are also the contents of perceptual memory, which are perceptual, but not *presently* so. Every representation that one accepts as veridical, whether a present perception, a memory, a piece of written or verbal testimony, or pictorial information, should be integratable with all one's other accepted representations of the world. Of course, we may have isolated memories, and snippets of geographical and historical knowledge, which we can't place very determinately (one may have heard that Caesar crossed the Rubicon, without having the foggiest idea when he did so, or where or what the Rubicon was); but if one believes that what is thus represented is part of reality, one must accept that it has a local habitation and a time, even if one is ignorant of the details. However, the means by which one builds up one's representations of the world beyond the presently perceptible are more conceptual than perceptual, and lie beyond the scope of this essay (see essays 4 and 5).

VI. THE UNITY OF REPRESENTATIONS OF ONESELF

To connect this topic with the next, let me elaborate on Strawson's example of watching the antics of a dog in the garden, while reidentifying it as one encountered before.[18] This involves conceptualizing the perceived item as a beast of canine kind, which one sees moving around against a perceived background. One can think, synchronically, of everything one presently perceives—the garden and townscape, the noises from the street, the clouds in the sky, and even distant events that one hears reported on the radio—as part of a single world, within which one may be focusing on this intruding dog. Diachronically, one can think of the creature as a persisting entity with its own spatiotemporal history, of which one may have some knowledge.

But over and above all this there is a certain sort of unification *within one's own experiences*. Synchronically, one can be aware that one's recognition of the dog, one's revulsion at its smell, and one's hearing of the radio are all part of one's present experience. And one can also think of oneself diachronically, as having had previous perceptions of this particular dog, and as about to risk a closer encounter with it to chase it away. We return here to the Kantian principle that all the conceptualized experiences of a person can be thought of by that subject as his or her experiences. This can now be divided into two aspects, about simultaneous experiences and temporally separated ones.

To explicate what the first involves, consider the "indexed agglomeration principle," delightfully named as such by Hurley (1994): If S is conscious at time t that p, and simultaneously conscious that q, then S must be conscious (at t) that p and q. Clearly this principle can be iterated to yield consciousness that p and q and r and…for everything that the subject is aware of at t (remember the various perceptions, sensations, memories, and fantasies of Fred in the lecture room). But it is very implausible to say that at every moment one is aware of a long conjunction containing everything one experiences at the time, if that is taken to mean that one consciously formulates some such capacious propositional conjunction.[19] We surely need to reinterpret the agglomeration principle as saying only that for any two simultaneous experiences one has, one *can* become consciously aware that one has both. And if so, one can also become aware of *relations* between one's simultaneous experiences, whether they involve representations of the outer world, or of one's own mental states, or a mixture of the two. The relations of which one can become aware are many and various—e.g., that the music from next door is disturbing my concentration on this work, that fulfilling my promise to pick up the children must soon interrupt what I am doing, or that Joan's tone of voice reminds me of that notorious occasion on which Granny spoke her mind. But there are always *temporal* relations of simultaneity or successiveness, and often one is consciously aware of them: indeed in some cases it is precisely the temporal conjunction that is so annoying or so pleasing, and forms part of the reason for the emotional reaction. If one is irritated by an interruption, or pleased to receive help just as one needed it, one's mental state has a content that involves a temporal relation between two aspects of one's experience ("How annoying—or how lucky—it was that that person happened along just as…"). I suggest the following principle:

> Synchronic Experience. Any two of the simultaneous experiences of a subject S can be thought of together by S, so that the content of S's experience can involve relations between them.

Exceptions to this sort of unification or integration can be found in commissurotomy (split-brain) patients, especially in controlled experimental conditions in which sensory inputs are carefully restricted to one half of the divided brain.[20] Precisely how we should describe the experiences of such people, whether indeed we can still talk of a single subject of experience or whether the application of our usual mental concepts begins to break down in such cases, are subtle questions that I will not address here. My present point is to emphasize their dramatic differences from the normal sorts of synthetic unity in human experience.

There is a diachronic synthesis of conceptualized experience in memory, which is rather more familiar. I suggest formulating it as:

Memory. Many of the experiences of a subject S can be remembered by S at later times, as part of his or her history of experience.

To assert this as a normal and normative condition on human experience is not to deny that (mercifully!) we forget many of our experiences, so that their contents, although synthesized at the time and available to short-term memory, do not get "laid down" over the longer term. The principle implies that there is no logical bar to remembering any particular experience: to put the point in modified Kantian terms, it is possible for the "Once upon a time, I experienced" to accompany a representation of any of my past experiences. But more than bare logical possibility is implied, for our practical rationality depends on our being able to remember, in the long-term sense, the most relevant bits of our previous experience Clinical cases of various kinds of memory loss demonstrate vividly just how central to our ordinary experience, action, and interpersonal relationships is the usual functioning of memory (both short- and long-term) to keep track, however fallibly and incompletely, of what one has experienced and done over the past minutes, hours, days, weeks, and years. When this breaks down, there is a very radical and tragic loss of capacity to live a normal human life involving projects and relationships sustained and developed over time.[21] Normal human experience involves the ability to remember a good deal of one's previous experience and integrate it into a coherent story of one's life. The word "many" in the Memory principle is vague, but substantive.[22]

Further kinds of unity in human experience may involve ethical and aesthetic considerations: we sometimes talk of a well-integrated person, of a disintegration of character, or of aspiration to live a life that displays something like the unity of a work of art. But I will not enter into those deep waters here.

VII. RELATIONSHIPS BETWEEN EXPERIENCE AND THE PRECONCEPTUAL LEVEL

We have seen that normal human experience (in both a statistical and a normative sense) involves some distinctive kinds of integration or unification that I have tried to elucidate. The reader will have noticed that these various principles of unity are variations on a common theme:

NCE. An experience of a complex is not a complex of experiences.

But how does all this relate to the subpersonal preconceptual level? Information processing or synthesis, somehow embodied in the central nervous system and brain, has to create these synthetic unities at the level of conceptualized experience. Sellars claimed that for Kantian sense impressions (the *non*conceptual mental states that are the raw material for perceptual synthesis), precisely the opposite of NCE holds (1968: Ch.1*69):[23]

> CI. An impression of a complex is a complex of impressions.

In principle, this can be reconciled with everything I have said about the synthetic unities of experience, by noting that CI applies at the preconceptual level of sense impressions, and NCE at the level of conceptualized experiences. But let us explore how the details go.

According to Sellars's usage of the term, which derives from the Kantian use I have been following, "sense impressions" do not involve concepts, and they are not available to introspective discrimination or report.[24] So they cannot constitute justification for beliefs, for they are not "in the space of reasons." They have only a *causal* role in perception, and they are postulated on theoretical grounds to explain our capacity to discriminate (and describe) various features of the world (Sellars 1968: Ch.1*42–43). Animals can have sense impressions just as much as we can, for they discriminate certain things and features even if they do not describe them.

It is crucial to note that according to this Kantian/Sellarsian conception, an impression of a red rectangle is not itself either red or rectangular, but is a state of the perceiver, a state of a type normally caused by a sighted subject being visually confronted with something that is red and rectangular on the facing side, and which, in a subject who already possesses concepts of color and shape, typically results in a judgment that there is something red and rectangular in front of him (Sellars 1968: Ch.1*23,*52). Paradoxical as it may seem, sense impressions do not literally have sensory properties such as color, shape, loudness, smell, hardness, or warmth, but as events in the nervous system of the perceiver they must have ranges of intrinsic properties that in some way *correspond* to the ranges of perceptible properties that physical objects have. Sellars describes these as "analogous" or "counterpart" properties (1968: Ch.1*45).

What goes for properties also goes for relations. Physical objects and events are related in space, and as we have seen, perceptions of them typically represent them as spatially related. An impression of a green circle to the left of a red rectangle is a state typically caused by being visually confronted with such an array, and it must itself be a complex state containing as discernible parts an impression of a green circle and one of a red rectangle, mental states that can be separately caused by green balls and red bricks, respectively. Those two component impressions must as mental states stand in *some* relation to each other, but hardly that of being one to the left of the other (mental states as classically conceived by Descartes and

Hume do not stand in spatial relations at all). So despite what Kant wrote, space is not *literally* the form of outer sense, if "sense" means raw unconceptualized sensibility; space can however be said to be the form (along with time) of *conceptualized* perceptual representation[25] (see essay 3). As Sellars puts it: "receptivity provides us with a manifold of representations, but not with a representation of a manifold" (1968: Ch.1*19).

However, we must be ready to identify sense impressions with states or events in the nervous system (at least in a token-token way), and *as such* they will presumably stand in some sort of microspatial relations to each other within the sense organs, nervous system, and brain. Philosophers and psychologists have long been fascinated by the fact that the immediate impacts of light on the retina are arrayed in two dimensions,[26] while our typical visual perception of the world represents it as in three: there is usually a "depth" to our seeing things, a third dimension to our representation of the spatial world. When at the level of experience one sees A as behind B, one's retinal stimulation caused by A will stand in some relation to one's retinal stimulation from B, but not that of being literally *behind* the other, though this could be true of the *tactile* stimulations in one's two hands, if one hand is behind the other. How is the visual experience of depth synthesized out of visual impressions? This is an empirical question, the topic of much recent neuropsychology (complicated cross-modal relations may well be involved). The point I want to emphasize here is that there is no reason to expect the spatial relationships that we represent in our conceptualized perceptual experience to bear any systematic relationship to the microspatial relations that hold between events inside the body. This can be reinforced by noting that when a blind or blindfolded person explores the shape of a large object by feeling around it, there must be a very different sort of synthesis of tactile impressions going on—in this case over time, since the process of exploration by touch takes a little while—from the case of the person who makes the same judgment about shape at a single glance.

A related point applies to time, although the parallel with space turns out to be only partial. If one has a visual impression of a movement, e.g., of a hand going up, that is an impression of an event that has distinguishable temporal stages. There will presumably be a succession of impressions, in which each member is an impression of the hand in one position—a state of the visual system that could separately be caused by the hand being statically in that position. But although those impressions are successive in time, that does not, as we noted above, suffice for an impression of movement. If impressions ceased immediately, leaving no trace, there would be no time at which they could collectively contribute to the common effect of perceiving movement. (If one walks through a large puddle, one makes a series of splashes, but leaves no trail of footprints.) And even if some traces are left, that will not suffice for an impression of movement. To see a picture of an Indian goddess with many arms in different positions is not to see her as raising an arm.[27] For there to be an experience of movement or succession, the traces have to be synthesized in a special temporal way into an experience that somehow "contains" them all.[28] Sellars suggests that there must be a counterpart mental dimension, not time itself but something serving to *represent* time relations, within which successive impressions can be related, so that the representation of time and movement becomes possible (1968: Appendix *14). There are deep mysteries here about time and temporal perception.

It may be objected that if we accept the Sellarsian sense in which an impression of a complex is a complex of impressions (a set of impressions standing in counterpart relations to the relations that hold between the relevant worldly items), does it not follow after all that an experience of a complex *is* a complex of experiences, contrary to NCE above? What distinguishes experiences from impressions is conceptualization, their being in the space of reasons and available for inference and justification; but can't it be the case that a conceptualized experience of a complex *consists* in a set of conceptualized experiences standing in counterpart relations to each other? In my example above, isn't Jane's experience of a lecture (which should surely be conceptualized, if anything is!) a set of successive conceptualized experiences of parts of the lecture?

I do not deny that an experience of a complex is *sometimes* a complex of experiences; but I deny that this is always and *necessarily* the case. Jane's understanding a sentence need not be literally composed of experiences of understanding the words. And even if it is in some cases (e.g., if she repeats a sentence slowly to herself and struggles to understand it), our hearing of sentences is not typically like that. At the level of words, our experience of hearing a word will not be composed of experiences of the constituent phonemes (one will not even have concepts of the latter, unless one is a student of linguistics). There will be physiologically distinguishable aural impressions of phonemes, but no conceptualized experiences of them that the typical hearer can report.

VIII. MIND AND BODY

In conclusion, what are the implications for mind-body identity of the unities of experience formulated above? How can these principles of unity be related to the myriad of physiologically distinguishable events in the body and brain? I see no problem of principle here, but rather a suggestion for how to formulate the identity thesis better. The vocabulary of the physical sciences will not suffice for our explanatory purposes. We need to talk of representations, of content, and perhaps even of computation—albeit in subpersonal, nonconceptual interpretations of those terms. So the identities will surely have to be token-token rather than of mental type to physiological type, and more than one kind or level of mental property will need distinguishing (see essay 8).

Within the body anatomists distinguish parts with particular functions, but the body is an interconnected system in which the functioning of one part typically depends on that of others, as physicians need to know. With the yet more intricate workings of the nervous system, that applies even more. On both the mental and physiological sides of the story, we can distinguish various aspects, while recognizing that they are dependent on the functioning whole. Perhaps Joe detects a straight edge in his visual field if and only if a certain set of neurons fire in his visual cortex, but that is not to say that his seeing a straight line *consists* only in the activation of those particular cells (after all, he won't see anything unless his heart continues to supply blood to his brain). If neurophysiology makes more discoveries about the localization of some mental functions, that does not require us literally to identify the relevant experiences with those brain events, but only to say that the latter are necessary for the former, and perhaps sufficient for them in the context of normal functioning in the rest of the person.

To end with a thought that may sound more Aristotelian than Kantian, the soul is the way in which the whole embodied human being (normally) functions. But how does this fit with Kant's own view? In his practical philosophy he wanted to believe in the immortality of the soul as a matter of faith (something that on his own epistemology he could not *know*), and for that reason at least he was hostile to materialism. But most of his theorizing about our mental powers leaves the way open to an appropriately conceived form of materialism, in particular his doctrine that in introspection ("inner sense") we know ourselves only as we appear to ourselves, not as we really are (B66–69, B152–53). In one place he explicitly allows an assumption about how things may be in themselves:

> The very same thing that is called a body in one relation would at the same time be a thinking being in another, whose thoughts, of course, we could not intuit, but only their signs in appearance. Thereby the expression that only souls (as a particular species of substances) think would be dropped; and instead it would be said, as usual, that human beings think, i.e., that the same being that as outer appearance is extended, is inwardly (in itself) a subject, which is not composite, but is simple and thinks.
>
> (A359–60)

I submit that Kant's theory of mind is broadly functionalist and is consistent with a nonreductionist form of materialism.

Three Ways in Which Space and Time Could Be Transcendentally Ideal

In the Transcendental Aesthetic, the first main section of the *Critique of Pure Reason*, Kant treats space and time as "a priori intuitions," and famously but controversially argues for the "transcendental ideality" though "empirical reality" of space and time.[1] A great deal of scholarly ink has been spilled in interpreting, attacking, and defending Kant's argumentation in the Aesthetic. May I be bold enough to hope to cast a little new light on this much-trampled ground?

It seems to me that (1) we readers of Kant have usually taken him as having a *single* conception of space and time; (2) we have too readily assumed we know what he means by "transcendentally ideal"; and (3) we have tended to interpret the Aesthetic without taking much account of the rest of the *Critique* (since it comes first in the book). I suggest, however, that all three assumptions are mistaken.

I

My thinking has been stimulated by coming across the brief chapter on time and space in Nicholas Rescher's early book *Conceptual Idealism*.[2] He distinguishes "bare" or "minimal" temporality and spatiality from what he calls their "full-blooded" versions. The former involve only

1. the conception of different times and places at which various states of affairs obtain; and

2. the ordering of all times in a single one-dimensional sequence, and the relating of all places in a single three-dimensional space.

Rescher's "full-blooded" temporality and spatiality add

3. the conception that different times fall into a sequence in which chronometry (the measurement of intervals of time) is possible, and that for any two places it is in principle possible to measure the distance between them; and
4. the introduction of the observer-relative conceptions of "the present" (or "now"), and "this place" (or "here").

As Rescher notes, these two conceptions, applied to time, correspond to McTaggart's classic distinction between the B-series and the A-series of points in time. It is the "perspectival," "egocentric," observer-relative feature (4) that marks the most obvious difference: whether (3) and (4) must necessarily belong together is a subtle question that we may touch on later. Obviously (2) presupposes (1): speculations about branching time or alternative universes would involve (1) without (2), though whether such speculations are coherent remains to be seen. In referring to the main distinction between (1–2) and (3–4) I will prefer to talk of "global" and "perspectival" conceptions, instead of Rescher's less informative labels.

Both global and perspectival conceptions involve the public physical world, for there surely have to be distinct objects and events to enable us to distinguish places and times, whether egocentrically or otherwise. The perspectival conception may be said to be "subjective" in the sense that (4) appeals to the position in space and time of a particular observer, but that still involves a point of view *on the public world*. Kant seems to allude to the perspectival spatial conception when he talks (at A23/B38) of locating "something in another place in space from that in which I find myself," but he does not systematically invoke the global/perspectival distinction.

The global and perspectival conceptions are both *conceptions*, involving our concepts. So they are expressible in language, when we attribute to objects and events two kinds of properties and relations, depending on whether a subject's position in space and time is invoked. For example:

nonperspectival: in 399 BCE
after the First World War
80 degrees north and 26 west
in the Scotia bar in Glasgow

perspectival: now
                    in one hour's time
                    on my left
                    35 miles south of here

We have a manifold temporal and spatial vocabulary, much of it involving public systems of chronometry and measurement plus knowledge of salient facts of history and geography. We use such vocabulary every day without using the abstract nouns "time" and "space," though we deploy them in designating particular times and spaces, e.g., when we say there is still time to catch the bus, and that there will be space for our luggage.

It is less commonplace and more theoretical for us to talk or think of space and time as unique systems of relationship (or quasi-individuals?) that include all times and spaces within them, in the way that Kant noticed at A25/B39 and A31–32/B47. But we do this occasionally, e.g., if we remark in elegiac mood how time continually passes and swallows up its dead, or when we understand why Darwin's theory needed huge stretches of geological time for species to evolve, or when we believe what astronomers and cosmologists tell us about the vast reaches of intergalactic space and the deep past of the universe. Thinking of the infinity and infinite divisibility of space and time, as Kant does at A25/B39–40 and A32/B47–48, is also thoroughly conceptual, although no doubt based in some way on the pervasive spatiotemporal structuring of our perceptual experience. The same is true of imagining space or time as empty of objects or events, as at A24/B38–39, A31/B46. But it is one thing to conceive of certain *portions* of space or time as devoid of matter or of change, and another to conceive of the whole of space or time as empty. It is not so obvious that the latter makes sense, although it seems to be what Kant was claiming.

Kant was thinking against a background in which Newton had treated time and space as unique all-embracing "absolute" realities that would exist even if empty of objects and events, whereas Leibniz had analyzed them as systems of relations between objects and events. Since Kant's day physicists and cosmologists have developed very different mathematical models of space and time, notably Einstein's relativization of simultaneity and his theory of "curved" space-time, and the more recent conception of space and time as originating in a mathematical "point of singularity" (Hawking et al.). Modern science has gone far beyond the common sense of ordinary perception and Euclidean geometry that Kant was working with (see essay 5).

II

All that I have mentioned so far of temporality and spatiality is conceptual (the scientific theorizing very much so, involving heavy-duty mathematics). Although Kant set out in the Transcendental Aesthetic to discover the a priori elements in *sensibility* by separating them from the synthesizing and conceptual work of the *understanding,* he found himself unable to ignore the latter, and it was surely insight rather than oversight when he wrote of time and space as *concepts* (A22–32/B37–49)[3] even though his official story was that they are a priori *intuitions* (or *forms* of intuition—which doesn't sound like quite the same thing, anyway). In the B Transcendental Deduction Kant recognizes that there is a *conceptual* aspect to most of our representations of space and time (see B160–61, with the important footnote).

This implies that these conceptual aspects of space and time I have so far been talking about are subject to whatever necessary conditions apply to our conceptualized understanding, our making of judgments about the public world. If Kant is right in his main contentions in the Transcendental Analytic, this will involve the application of the categories according to the principles of the Analytic of Principles, including the persistence of matter and the causality of changes. (So much for treating sensibility separately from understanding!) But the main case can be stated independently of Kant's formidable technical vocabulary, as Rescher does when he argues that to set up and operate our systems of dates and timings and spatial coordinates, chronometry, and measurements, and to locate named places and events, we have to rely on the law-governed persistence and changes of public physical objects (especially our technology of clocks and measuring devices), which themselves have to be individuated and reidentified by criteria of identity. Since all this involves what Rescher identifies in the rest of his book as "mind-involvement" or "conceptual idealism,"[4] and which I have tried to explain and argue for in my own terms in essay 1, our conceptions of space and time are just as much subject to *this* kind of "idealism" as every other conception. This then is one interpretation of Kant's thesis of the transcendental ideality of space and time that makes it philosophically plausible.

III

All this applies most obviously to our global, i.e., tenseless and place-neutral, concepts of time and space and times and places. But there is something special about our perspectival conceptions, for they involve our perceptual experiences in a very direct and distinctive way. Ontogenetically and epistemologically our perceptual experiences, conceptualized in perspectival terms, are surely the foundation of all our knowledge of the physical world; though in the order of scientific explanation the global conceptions come first.

It is necessarily true that whenever and whatever one perceives, one occupies a certain point in space and time, and one perceives the relevant objects, events, and scene as *from* that position in space and at that time, so there is always a way or "manner" in which things appear to the perceiver that is not an objective, unchanging feature of them, but is essentially relational. Kant sometimes talks of space and time as "modes" of perception, which suggests that they are adverbial ways of perceiving things rather than contents or objects of perception.[5] But the only passage I know where he explicitly recognizes this egocentric relativity is that already mentioned in which he talks of locating an object at some distance from oneself (A23/B38). I am not aware of any similarly explicit reference to the subject's position in time, and the matter of tense in the content of our judgments.[6] The perspectival conception of space and time is suggested by a passage in the Antinomy chapter (especially if one relies on Kemp Smith's translation):

> We have sufficiently proved in the Transcendental Aesthetic that everything intuited in space or in time, hence all objects of an experience possible for us, are nothing but appearances, i.e. mere representations, *which, as they are represented, as extended beings, or as series of alternations,* have outside our thoughts no existence grounded in itself. This doctrine I call transcendental idealism.
>
> (A490–91/B518–19 in the Guyer/Wood translation, with my emphasis; Kemp Smith has "*in the manner in which they are represented*" instead of "as they are represented.")

It may be tempting to take it that Kant was here thinking perspectivally. Yet I see nothing in the text that prevents it applying to global conceptions too, involving only the first sense of transcendental idealism outlined above. I fear that Kant was not alert (or not consistently so) to the distinction between global and perspectival conceptions, though he may have had a subliminal awareness of it—which could be one reason why he stuck to his guns on the transcendental ideality of space and time.

However, making and enforcing the global/perspectival distinction enables us to discern an extra layer of truth underlying Kant's puzzling claim that space and time do not characterize things as they really are, things "as they are in themselves." For perspectival properties and relations hold of things only as perceivable from a particular position in space at a particular time, so they are dependent on our mental perceptions in a way that global conceptions are not. In Rescher's terminology, the "full-blooded" perspectival conceptions are "mind-dependent," which is something *over and above* being "mind-involving" in the way that the "minimal" global conceptions are.[7] This gives us a second, stronger interpretation of transcendental ideality that applies only to the perspectival understanding of space and time.

IV

There is a third, less conceptual and more radically subjective kind of temporality and spatiality that is involved in Kant's account of perception, for he seems to be committed to there being spatial and temporal relations between the elementary sensory data that are "given" to us in perception. As I explored in essay 2, he needs a theory about how we (or our unconscious mental processes) synthesize or combine these subjective data in our individual minds to arrive at our conceptions of the physical world, including our judgments about the ordering of events in time and the layout and movement of things in three-dimensional public space.[8]

However, there are some remarkably fundamental disagreements between Kant's interpreters about basic features of synthesis. According to Lorne Falkenstein, in his very substantial book on the Aesthetic,[9] "the problem of knowledge for Kant reduces to the problem of how, from an array of matters splayed out over time and space and occurring over time in a progressive intuition, the mind is able to produce a unified thought (1995: 11). He goes on to say, even more trenchantly, that

> no interpretation that takes spatiotemporal form to be dependent on 'thought', that is, on imaginative or intellectual processing, can be a correct representation of Kant's position. Kant is an intuitionist about space and time. He believes these forms are *given*, not *made*. He believes, moreover, that they are given through the sensory cognitive faculty.
>
> (Falkenstein 1995: 26)

Falkenstein would agree that judgments about public objects and events in public space and time have to be synthesized out of these data (so in *that* sense spatiotemporal form *is* dependent on intellectual processing), but his point is that there are subjective temporal and spatial relations between the "raw data" of perception, the unconceptualized sensations or sense impressions that are simply "given" at the very first stage of perception, before the mind has begun its processes of synthesis. Falkenstein thus understands Kant as assuming a perceptual "manifold" in which elements are ordered in time (in both inner and outer sense), and arrayed in space, or at least in *quasi*-spatial relationships (in outer sense). Sellars (1968: Ch.1*21ff) agrees. This reading would seem to be directly supported by Kant's saying that "every intuition contains a manifold in itself, which however would not be represented as such if the mind did not distinguish the time in the succession of impressions on one another" (A99), and "the manifold for intuition must already be *given prior* to the synthesis of understanding and *independently* from it" (B145, with my emphasis).

However, in another long and intricate book Wayne Waxman has argued[10] that Kant's transcendental idealism should be understood in "the strictest possible manner":

> All spatial and temporal relations must then be supposed to exist only in and through
> imagination, and in no way to characterize sensations; there can be no "flux" of represen-
> tations in inner sense, and not even color "patches" can be regarded as genuine *data*.
>
> (Waxman 1991: 14)

Waxman's view that "for Kant, imagination is constitutive of space and time" (1991: 15) depends heavily on Kant's story of threefold synthesis in the A Transcendental Deduction:

1. The synopsis of the manifold a priori through sense;
2. The synthesis of this manifold through the imagination; finally
3. The unity of this synthesis through original apperception (A94/B127).[11]

Waxman takes quite literally Kant's talk of a third mental faculty, *the imagination*, that plays an intermediate role between sensibility and understanding, sandwiched in the middle of the three levels of mental processing that are supposed to be involved in all perceptual knowledge.[12] So he is committed to saying that not only are conceptions and judgments about public space and time synthesized out of subjective spatial and temporal representations (as almost all interpreters of Kant would agree), but even the latter are themselves synthesized, at an earlier or more primitive level, by a rather mysterious power of the mind labeled "the imagination," out of private data that do *not* stand in spatial or temporal relationships in *any* sense.[13]

I fear I will hardly be able, in this short survey, to resolve this dispute between highly learned Kant scholars.[14] I suggest however that what is involved here is not just a question about how to interpret Kant, but also about what is the best theory in the philosophy of mind and cognitive science—which is a large, tangled, and fast-changing area, with unclarities about what is a priori and what is empirical. On the matter of interpreting Kant, it seems to me that he was continually breaking new ground as he went along, that he never got his terminology under consistent control,[15] in particular his division of mental faculties and the problematic addition of the imagination.[16] Moreover he showed some awareness of this when he said at Axvi–xvii that the "subjective deduction" is not essential to his main purpose and when he revised the Transcendental Deduction so radically in B—which suggests a reason not to give decisive weight to the elaborate theorizing about a three-fold synthesis he offered in A. If so, I suspect that any hope that some sufficiently deep interpretation can eventually be found that would make consistent sense of every word Kant wrote on the philosophy of mind[17] is chimerical. (How many of us would pass such a test applied to what we have written over the years?)

V

That need not stop us from asking which parts of Kant's thought offer us insight even now about how best to understand the extraordinarily complicated processes of human perception. That is an enormous ongoing project. All I hope to do in this final section is to take a look at the implications of treating our sense impressions physically as "irritations of our sensory surfaces."[18] What if we understand the "raw data" of perception as the immediate physiological impacts of the world on our sense organs—our skin, eyes, ears, nose, and palate? Falkenstein adduces evidence from the *Anthropology* that Kant moved in this direction, identifying sensations as physiological states of the body of the perceiver (1995: 119–123), though somewhat unwillingly, being worried about the prospect of "a soulless materialism." But if we distinguish materialism from reductionism, and recognize that there is much of enormous importance to be said about people that cannot be reduced to talk of their physical inputs and neural processing, I suggest we need not be so nervous about the physiological nature of perception.

However, there are (as always) philosophical problems about how the physical relates to the mental. Sellars argued that sense impressions are *neither* purely physical nor conceptual (1968: Ch.1*41) but nonconceptual states of consciousness (1968: Ch.1*24), whereas Falkenstein suggests they are physical while also being in some sense mental, playing a role in people's perceptions and perceptual judgments. I suggest there is no inconsistency here: we can agree that sense impressions are physical in that they are located in time and space (in the sense organs, of course) and have physiological descriptions, but they are also mental in virtue of their functional role in perception. (The pulsing of the blood, and the digestive processes in the stomach are equally physical, but they have no role in perception, and do not count as mental, though they may have *indirect* effects on mental functioning.)

But we need to avoid confusions between content and embodiment. The spatial properties of the physiological stimulations may bear little relationship to the spatial content of the resulting perception. For example, the differences in the vibrations stimulating our two spatially separated ear-drums often enable us to judge the approximate direction of the sound source; and similarly, the slightly different patterns of light arriving at the two retinas assist us in the perception of depth, at least over short distances. As for time, changes within our perceptual experience do not necessarily imply any awareness of change in what is perceived, as in Kant's example of surveying a large house (A190–91/B235–36); and for a case of involuntary motion, think of looking out of the window of a moving train. Similar distinctions apply to the storage of information in computers: the content may be spatial as in a photograph, or temporal as in music, or both as in a video, but the information is stored in the electronic circuitry, and though this involves tiny wires and changes in them, the spatial and temporal properties and relations at that microphysical level bear no direct relationship to those represented in the content.

What tends to cause confusion is the seemingly much more direct relation between the patterns of light stimulation on the two-dimensional (though curved) surface of the retina (ignoring the somewhat marginal binocular effect mentioned above) and the two-dimensional visual field beloved of sense-data theorists, of which we can be in some way aware, for example when we make perspective drawings. The stimulations of touch are spatial in a different way, being located on various parts of the body, and thus occupy a certain portion of three-dimensional space and bear an obvious relationship to our awareness of the three-dimensional arrangement of the things touched. So for sight, touch, and hearing, certain microspatial properties of the immediate stimulations of our sense organs carry information about macrospatial properties of their sources. But for all that we have seen so far, this is information only in the sense that tree rings carry information about past weather: there is no implication that the subject can formulate judgments expressing it.

However, many of our sense impressions can be said to have a *nonconceptual*, nonjudgmental content of which we can obviously be aware. Players of ball games manifest almost instantaneous reactions to fast-changing visual stimulation without having time or words enough to report what they see. The same goes for wrestlers and lovers and the data of touch. In musical perception, many of us, having heard a rhythm drummed or a melody played, can give an approximate rendition of it by tapping the rhythm or humming the tune, without any of the conceptualization involved in writing them down in musical notation. Indeed, much the same applies in animal perceptions, manifested not in language but in behavior (dogs can catch balls, chimps threaten, groom and copulate, some birds have musical imitative abilities).

At the very end of his long and subtle book, Falkenstein (1995: 360) seems to me to overintellectualize our more elementary perceptions (or stages in perception) when he sums up four levels of unification: (1) judging that various "data points" stand in certain spatial and temporal relations to each other; (2) judging that they are qualitatively similar or dissimilar, and make up various homogeneous patches; (3) judging that such patches refer to particular objects; and (4) judging that all the objects belong in single world. This is reminiscent of the "construction of the world" offered by sense-data theorists of the first half of the twentieth century. It might apply to scientists watching incoming data on their computer screens and theorizing about what such data might represent, but it surely does not describe what the ordinary perceiver is doing (including the scientists recognizing their screens as physical objects, not to be bumped into, in the room). We do not ordinarily make *judgments* at these levels at all. So maybe there is point after all in Waxman's defense of Kant's notion of a middle stage in perception, but I doubt if it can be elucidated by exclusive communion with Kant's sacred texts. I recommend a dialogue between Kant and neuroscience in which inspiration might flow both ways, though I am not qualified to conduct it myself.

In summary, I have argued that we need to make a distinction between *public* conceptions of space and time, both perspectival and global, and the very different sorts of temporality and spatiality that characterize the physical inputs to our sense organs and our *unconceptualized* perceptions. The latter offers us a third kind of "transcendental ideality" of space and time.[19]

ESSAY 4

The Given, the Unconditioned, the Transcendental Object, and the Reality of the Past

Please forgive the unwieldy title of this essay; I hope to demonstrate the connections between these four apparently disparate topics in the *Critique of Pure Reason*.

I. CONDITIONS, THE UNCONDITIONED, THE GIVEN, AND SYNTHESIS

In the lengthy Antinomy chapter Kant offers an elaborate diagnosis of a kind of "transcendental illusion" to which he argues we are prone when we try to think about the world as a whole. But he begins and ends the whole Dialectic section by saying that our faculty of reason has a *valid* use in seeking to organize and unify our knowledge of the world:

> Reason, in inferring, seeks to bring the greatest manifold of cognition of the understanding to the smallest number of principles (universal conditions), and thereby to effect the highest unity of that manifold.
>
> (A305/B361)

In Kant's conception, human reason is by nature "architectonic," i.e., we regard all our knowledge as belonging to a possible system (A474/B502); and in the appendix to the Dialectic he suggests (though rather sketchily) how this search for system legitimately guides our scientific theorizing.[1]

However, the main body of the Dialectic is devoted to showing how our systematizing reason tends to lead us *astray*. If we subsume an observed fact *n* under a general causal law, and explain it by deduction from that law and a preceding condition *m*, we may then go on to explain m by some further condition *l*, and so on. We are tempted to suppose there must be some endpoint to such a series, and Kant offers a grand-sounding formulation of what he thinks lies behind our naive thinking:

[P1] The proper principle of reason in general (in its logical use) is to find the unconditioned for conditioned cognitions of the understanding, with which its unity will be completed.

(A307/B364; see also Bxx)

But what does that gnomic statement *mean*? One interpretation would be that "the unconditioned" should be an ultimate truth that can start the chain of explanatory conditions and does not itself need explanation—but another interpretation is that it is the whole series, as suggested below. Kant says here that it is the function of reason to *find* the unconditioned—but presumably he means "*try* to find," for people can look for something that does not exist (such as the Loch Ness monster), or even for something that cannot exist (e.g., a geometrical construction to square the circle). Indeed, much of Kant's discussion in the Dialectic concerns what we are or are not entitled to assume in our search for explanations, and immediately after stating principle P1 he adds:

[P2] But this logical maxim cannot become a principle of pure reason unless we assume that when the conditioned is given, then so is the whole series of conditions subordinated one to the other, which is itself unconditioned, also given (i.e. contained in the object and its connection).

(A307–8/B364)

The labeling of these two principles as P1 and P2 is due to Michelle Grier, who gives them a central place in her illuminating book on transcendental illusion (Grier 2001).[2] P2 differs from P1 in making a more definite claim about the objective existence of "the unconditioned," and in identifying it with the whole (perhaps infinite?) series of explanatory conditions rather than a first member. But despite Grier's valiant efforts, I fear some unclarity remains about their relationship, for she ends rather mysteriously by suggesting that they "express the very same unifying function, or the *very same act of reason*, viewed in different ways" (2001: 274). I hope to throw some more light on this by examining Kant's notion of the given.

Kant offers these extremely abstract formulations P1 and P2 right at the beginning of the Dialectic, in the (debatable) assumption that there is a common structure behind the various illusions about soul, world, and God that he goes on to diagnose at length. I will focus attention on the relevance of P1 and P2 to the First Antinomy, which consists of plausible arguments to the apparently contradictory conclusions that the world is finite or infinite in time and space. Kant begins his analysis of what goes wrong here by insisting on a sharp distinction between empirical science, where "much must remain uncertain and many questions insoluble," and transcendental philosophy, in which "there is no question at all dealing with an object given by pure reason that is insoluble by this very same human reason" (A477/B505).[3] In the sciences we often have to say that we do not know the answer to a certain question, and must await further evidence; but for metaphysical issues Kant asserts that the solution can always be *demanded*. But this does not mean that we are forced to choose between the antinomial alternatives; rather, Kant holds, we need to take a conceptual step back to a position from which we can see that both sides are wrong, since they both rest on an illegitimate assumption about the world as a complete totality, and an associated ambiguity between appearances and things in themselves (Bxx).

What exactly is the illegitimate assumption, then? Kant's suggestion is that when we try to theorize about the universe as a whole, we run into special problems about the relation between our concepts and their supposed object:

> The cosmological ideas alone have the peculiarity that they can presuppose their object, and the empirical synthesis required for its concept, as given; and the question that arises from them has to do only with the progression of this synthesis, insofar as it is to contain an absolute totality, which, however, is no longer empirical, since it cannot be given in any experience.
>
> (A479/B507)

This is hardly the most limpid of sentences! To make sense of it we need to get clear about what Kant means by "given" and "synthesis." He defined synthesis early in the Analytic:

> By synthesis in the most general sense...I understand the action of putting different representations together with each other, and comprehending their manifoldness in one cognition.
>
> (A77/B103)

If synthesis is an act (or rather a process) that we perform, it presumably takes a certain amount of time. In the A Transcendental Deduction Kant tells some elaborate quasi-psychological stories about various stages or processes of synthesis (as noted in essay 3). But what is it that is synthesized? He is not thinking of material processes in factories or kitchens that construct furniture or produce synthetic cream. As I understand Kant (see essay 1), synthesis does not literally synthesize *objects*; rather, we synthesize our *representations* of objects—or more precisely it is our unconscious mental processes that do so (essay 2). Neuroscientists now study the very rapid "syntheses" that take place whenever information is processed through our sense organs and brain, measuring reaction times in fractions of a second (as noted at the end of essay 3). But in the case of a large object that cannot be surveyed in a single glance, the perception of the whole of it may take longer, e.g., inspecting a large house room by room, listening to a symphony, or climbing a mountain.

However, in the First Antinomy Kant is clearly concerned with "synthesis" in a wider sense that seems to mean any sort of geographical, historical, or scientific research, seeking knowledge of larger and larger extents of the world in space and time, and even, in cosmology, of the whole physical universe. The antinomies arise "when we apply reason to the objective synthesis of appearances, where reason thinks to make its principle of unconditioned unity valid with much plausibility" (A406–7/B433). We can search for causes, or for effects:

> I will call the synthesis of a series on the side of the conditions, thus proceeding form the condition proximate to the given appearance toward the more remote conditions, the *regressive* synthesis, and the synthesis proceeding on the side of the conditioned, from its proximate consequence to the more remote ones, the *progressive* synthesis.
>
> (A411/B438)

So "the regressive synthesis" involves inquiries about the past in history, archeology, evolutionary biology, paleontology, geology, and cosmology, which are social processes taking much longer than individual perceptions, though of course ultimately dependent on them. The notion of synthesis is here widened to empirical knowledge gathering in general.

Let us now ask what Kant means by "given." This is a very ordinary little word that takes on more than ordinary depths of meaning in the critical philosophy, but I am not aware of any systematic study of its use in Kant. At the end of the Introduction he says:

> There are two stems of human cognition, which may arise from a common but to us unknown root, namely sensibility and understanding, through the first of which objects are given to us, but through the second of which they are thought.
>
> (A15/B29)

So "given" primarily means "given to the senses" or "given in perception," and this is immediately confirmed when Kant says in the very first paragraph of the Aesthetic that an object can be given to us only in so far as it "affects the mind in a certain way," and that there is no other way that objects can be given to us (A19/B33). This message may seem to get muddled by his going on to describe space, time, and the objects of mathematics as "given a priori" (A4/B8, A23/B38, A31/B46, A77–78/B103–4). But that is in the context of his theory of a priori *intuition*, so the connection of "the given" with sensibility, albeit sensibility of the supposedly a priori kind, remains. Kant's terminology is flexible, but not contradictory.

When we get to the Dialectic, "the given" seems to take on a wider reference still. In section 6 of the Antinomy chapter, where he introduces transcendental idealism as the key to the solution, Kant writes:

> The objects of experience are never given in themselves, but only in experience, and they do not exist at all outside it.
>
> …Nothing is really given to us except perception and the empirical progress from this perception to other possible perceptions.
>
> (A492–93/B521)

By way of example, he says that the existence of inhabitants of the moon, unperceived by human beings, can only mean that "in the possible progress of experience we could encounter them," i.e., if we could get to the moon, they would be given to us in perception. Kant is making a sharp distinction between perceptual givenness and the notion of things being "given in themselves," which he rules out.

An important feature of his analysis is his extension of "the given" beyond individual, time-bound perceptions. What I have perceived in the past is, in the strictest sense, no longer "given" to me, but provided that I can remember it, it can be said to remain "given" to me in a wider sense. Something that somebody *else* has perceived and reported can similarly be described as "given" to those who receive the report; and Kant must intend this when he talks of what is given to "us" in the plural. And if testimony is thus admitted as a potentially reliable (though fallible) means of transmission of knowledge, then chains of testimony extending over centuries can "give" us such distant historical facts as the assassination of Julius Caesar.[4] Moreover, inductive argument can inform us of facts that, although perceptible in principle to suitably placed observers, are beyond the reach of all human perception, such as the existence of dinosaurs long before the evolution of human beings, and of "stars a hundred times farther from me than the most distant ones I see" (Kant's example at A496/B525). Back in the Postulates he said:

One can also cognize the existence of the thing prior to the perception of it, and therefore cognize it comparatively *a priori*, if only it is connected with some perceptions in
accordance with the principles of their empirical cognition (the analogies).

(A225/B273)

There he cites our knowledge of "magnetic matter" from our perception of
its effects on iron filings, and the implication is that the existence of magnetic
fields is thus indirectly "given" to us (though he rather spoils the point by
suggesting that it is only the grossness of our senses that prevents us from
perceiving magnetism itself). Theoretical science now claims to justify
belief in atoms, chemical bonds, genes, quarks, black holes, and even the
big bang, as the best explanation of observed phenomena, but without any
implication that the sense organs of any possible creature could perceive
such things directly. I suggest that wherever we have good empirical evidence (i.e., ultimately based on perception) about unperceivable entities,
Kant would accept that these are "given" to us in an extended sense.

II. THE TRANSCENDENTAL OBJECT

With this understanding of "the given," it comes as a shock when in section
6 of his resolution of the antinomies, Kant suddenly indulges in a quite different, nonperceptual talk of being "given." He says that the nonsensible
cause of our representations is entirely unknown to us, but that

we can call the merely intelligible cause of appearances in general the transcendental
object, merely so that we may have something corresponding to sensibility as a receptivity. To this transcendental object we can ascribe the whole extent and connection of
our possible perceptions, and say that it is *given in itself* prior to all experience. (A494/
B522–23, with my emphasis)

This is in apparent contradiction to what Kant has so firmly laid down about
nothing being given to us except in perception. He is notorious for his terminological wobbles, and this is a particularly egregious example. However,
I think there is a way of rendering him consistent. As far as I know, he never
talks of transcendental objects in the plural, so I suggest that for "the
transcendental object" we can simply read "reality."[5] Then his point there
would be that we have to believe that reality remains distinct from all our
perceptions of it, and all our talk of it. This seems to fit with his introduction
of the mysterious phrase "transcendental object" in the first version of the
Transcendental Deduction:

The pure concept of this transcendental object (which in all of our cognitions is really one and the same = X) is that which in all of our empirical concepts in general can provide relation to an object, i.e., objective reality. Now this concept cannot contain any determinate intuition at all, and therefore concerns nothing but that unity which must be encountered in a manifold of cognition insofar as it stands in relation to an object. (A109)[6]

In the light of this, we can endorse the fundamental Kantian claim that we can only have any *specific* knowledge of reality insofar as our representations of it are synthesized through our perceptions and concepts, involving the processes of historical and scientific research and the extended sense of "given" discussed above. Yet reality still remains distinct from all our representations of it. Perhaps then we can accept Kant's rather incautiously worded statement that the transcendental object is "given in itself prior to all experience," noting that he immediately insists that "*appearances...are given not in themselves* but only in experience, because they are mere representations" (A494/B523, with my italics). But let us not be misled (as so many readers have been) by that phrase "mere representations." "Appearances" are the objects of perception (A20/B34), or of empirical knowledge more generally. Kant's view is not that appearances are mental states (Berkeleian idealism), or that they can be defined in terms of mental states (phenomenalism), but rather that everything we perceive or know about the world must be represented by us, through our perceptions and our conceptualization (see essay 1). Kant's "transcendental" idealism is perfectly consistent with his empirical realism.

III. THE REALITY OF THE PAST

In resolving the antinomies Kant has some interesting but rather obscure things to say about our knowledge of the past:

The real things of past time are given in the transcendental object of experience, but for me they are objects and real in past time only insofar as I represent to myself that, in accordance with empirical laws, or, in other words, the course of the world, a regressive series of possible perceptions (whether under the guidance of history or in the footsteps of causes and effects) leads to a time-series that has elapsed as condition of the present time, which is then represented as real only in connection with a possible experience and not in itself, so that all those events which have elapsed from an inconceivable past time prior to my own existence signify nothing but the possibility of prolonging the chain of experience, starting with the present perception, upward to the conditions that determine it in time. (A495/B523)

I take the first line of this gargantuan sentence to mean that we all know a priori that the world has a past, in other words that reality (or "the transcendental object") includes the past history of everything in the world. This offers an interpretation of Kant's mysterious earlier statement about the whole of the past being "given necessarily": "According to the idea of reason, the whole elapsed past time is thought of as given necessarily as the condition for the given moment" (A412/B439). But this is not to know (it is not to be "given") anything *in particular* about the past: for that, we have to depend on the details of our perceptual experience. Kant's talk of "a regressive series of possible perceptions" here is ambiguous. It might mean that in representing to ourselves that X happened before we were born, we imagine that if we *had* been around at that earlier time we would have observed X, or perhaps that if we could travel back to that time we would observe X; though it would involve less dramatic counterfactuals to say that anyone who was there at the relevant time could have observed X and reported it. But this is only to elucidate the *meaning* of statements about the past; it does not tell us how specific claims can be empirically "given" and acquire the status of knowledge. Kant's mention of "the guidance of history or causes and effects" indicates that they must be based on presently available evidence, via testimony, induction, and of course memory. When he talks of "prolonging the chain of experience upward," I suggest he is not thinking of time travel into the past, but rather of inference to past events as the best explanation of present evidence.

The mere possibility of perception by anyone in the right place at the right time applies to past and future events equally, yet Kant sees an asymmetry between past and future in respect of being "given":

> Thus one necessarily thinks of the fully elapsed time up to the present moment as also given (even if not as determinable by us). But as to the future, since it is not the condition for attaining to the present, it is a matter of complete indifference for comprehending the present, what we want to hold about future time, whether it stops somewhere or runs on to infinity. (A410/B437)

The difference cannot be that we have knowledge of the past but none whatsoever of the future—for there is much about the past that we do not know, and we do know *some* things about the future with as much certainly as anything empirical, for example future days, years, and eclipses. I take it Kant's point is that we are entitled to think of there being a vast multitude of determinate facts about the past (about many of which the various historical and scientific disciplines can tell us, though there is undoubtedly more that we will never know), whereas we are *not* entitled to think of there being a similarly complete and determinate set of facts about the future. We thus think that the truths or facts about the past are completely fixed, even where unknown to us, whereas we are not so constrained in how we think about the future: as far as the present argument is concerned, we may think of the future as indeterminate or open, at least to some extent (though the issue of determinism remains to be addressed—see essay 9). Kant says that the whole series of antecedent, regressive conditions of any given condition has to be presupposed as "given," whereas its consequent, progressive conditions "cannot be regarded as given, but only as *dabilis*" [i.e., capable of being given] (A410–11/B437).

In section 7 Kant at last offers his "critical decision" of what he takes to be the common logical form of all four antinomies. He diagnoses an ambiguity in principle P2, and hence a fallacy in the cosmological syllogism:

> If the conditioned is given, then the whole series of conditions for it is also given;
> Objects of the senses are given as conditioned;
> *ergo*: The whole series of conditions for objects of the senses is also given.

He first remarks that it is clear and certain that "if the conditioned is given, then through it a regress in the series of all conditions for it is given to us as a problem" (A497–98/B526). This can be readily agreed, for the phrase "given as a problem" only means that when we are "given" any particular fact, there is an intellectual challenge to *try to find* as many as possible of its antecedent conditions, as Kant's principle P1 stated at the outset. Kant calls this a "logical maxim" or "regulative principle" of reason, he suggests (rather implausibly) that it is analytic, and he goes on about it at some length in the pages that follow. But the main point of his diagnosis is that we tend to assume that "given" in the major premise means *given as things in themselves*, whereas in the minor premise we take it as *given as appearances*:

> If the conditioned as well as its condition are things in themselves, then when the first is given not only is the regress to the second *given as a problem*, but the latter is thereby really already *given* along with it.... Here the synthesis of the conditioned and its conditions is a synthesis of the mere understanding, which represents things *as they are* without paying attention to whether and how we might achieve acquaintance with them. (A498/B526)

To talk of a synthesis *of the understanding* is another startling terminological twist, at this very late stage! But once again, we can be reassured that Kant is not going back on anything already laid down; I suggest that when he speaks here of a "synthesis of the understanding" and a corresponding sense of "given," he is thinking of mathematics, and purely mathematical models of the universe. Despite his occasional verificationist-sounding formulations, Kant does not want to deny all meaning to thought that goes beyond testing by observation. He recognizes mathematical knowledge based on geometrical and arithmetical constructions in pure intuition, and it is relevant to note that we also use the word "given" in such contexts, e.g., "Given two circles, construct the line joining their centers; given a prime number, prove that there exists a larger one." Such mathematical constructions do not represent any particular facts in the physical world; they involve a purely abstract or imaginative sense of being "given." They yield a special kind of synthetic a priori knowledge, but Kant denies that such purely mathematical thinking can, on its own, give us any knowledge of the physical world, for that requires appeal to our perceptions:

> If I am dealing with appearances, which as mere representations are not given at all if I do not achieve acquaintance with them...then I cannot say with the same meaning that if the conditioned is given, then all the conditions (as appearances) are also given.... For the *appearances*, in their apprehension, are themselves nothing other than an empirical synthesis (in space and time) and thus are given only *in this synthesis*.
>
> (A498–99/B527)

Let me finally apply this to the case of *past* conditions for present facts:

> If the conditioned is given, then the whole series of conditions for it is also given;
> Present states of affairs are given as conditioned;
> *ergo*: The whole series of past conditions for present states of affairs is also given.

Our discussion of the given now reaps dividends. The main distinction we have made is between being *given empirically* (i.e., known to exist in the physical world, on the basis of some combination of perception, memory, testimony, induction, and inference to the best scientific explanation) and *given necessarily, but utterly indeterminately* (in the way that reality as a whole, including the reality of the past, is known to exist, as discussed above). So if the major premise is taken to mean: "If a present state of affairs is empirically given, i.e., known about on the basis of perception, then the whole series of past conditions for it is also empirically given," it is false. However, if it is taken to mean: "If a present state of affairs is empirically given, then the whole series of past conditions for it is necessarily given, i.e., we know that some such series exists, but we have no determinate knowledge of it, we can have no empirically justified conception of how far it stretches and what it contains," it can be accepted. But then of course it does not generate any conclusion about the whole series of past conditions being given empirically.

What then should we make of the well-attested twentieth-century cosmological theory that asserts that the universe does after all have a finite history? This involves difficult mathematics and arcane observational evidence; the claim is that we can extrapolate every ongoing process in the universe back to a mathematical point of origin in "the big bang" some very large but finite time ago. I offer some amateur thoughts on this in essay 5.

A Theory of Everything? Kant Speaks to Stephen Hawking

Theoretical physicists have recently described themselves as aspiring to a "theory of everything." But over two centuries ago Kant offered, in the Dialectic of his *Critique of Pure Reason*, a systematic diagnosis of a certain kind of illusion to which we are prone when we try to think about the world as a whole. I propose to look afresh at Kant's thought in the Antinomy chapter and ponder its implications for contemporary cosmo-logical theorizing; and conversely, to ask whether modern science can throw any light on his dark musings. This may amount only to a confronta-tion of one species of unintelligibility with another, since I can claim only a modest competence about Kant and an immodest incompetence about modern physics—but I will try.

I. KANT'S FIRST ANTINOMY

At the beginning of the Antinomy chapter Kant claims to show how our naive reasoning leads us into apparently *contradictory* claims. Much of the discussion in this lengthy chapter can be understood without appeal to anything that comes earlier in the *Critique*.[1] In this essay I will focus on the First Antinomy. Here are the contradictory pro-positions, with my summary of the arguments for them that Kant presents:

Theses:

(A) The world has a beginning in time: for otherwise there would have been infinitely many events before the present, but an infinite series "can never be completed through successive synthesis."

(A426/B454)

(B) The world is limited in space: for if one is to think of an infinite whole "the successive synthesis of the parts of an infinite world would have to be viewed as completed, i.e, in the enumeration of all coexisting things, an infinite time would have to be regarded as having elapsed, which is impossible."

(A428/B456)

Antitheses:

(A´) The world has no beginning in time: for there cannot have been a first event, for "no arising of any sort of thing is possible in an empty time," since there would be no reason why the world should start at that time rather than any other.

(A427/B455)[2]

(B´) The world has no limits in space: for there cannot be a sphere in space outside which there is no matter, for a relation of the whole material world to empty space would be "a relation of the whole world to *no object*. Such a *relation*, however, and hence also the boundedness of the world by empty space, is nothing

(A429/B457)[3]

Kant is here thinking not so much of a succession of pure temporal moments— "times" in the abstract, as it were—but of the series of all *events*, i.e., changes in material objects and states of affairs. And similarly his topic is not spaces considered merely as geometrical segments of empty space, but rather the matter that occupies portions of space. This Antinomy concerns *the whole material world*, the universe, the sum total of all the matter and energy in space and all the changes occurring in time.

There is some ambiguity between ontology and epistemology in Kant's presentation of the supporting arguments. Is he concerned with the conceptual and metaphysical conditions for something to *be* the case, or about the epistemic conditions for our *knowing* it? The argument for (B) refers to conditions for our *thought* (representation) of the past ("successive synthesis," etc.); but the other arguments may appear at first sight to concern pure ontology. Interpreted as such, the support for (B´) may seem particularly weak, for what is the problem about the mere *conception* of a finite amount of matter existing in infinite space? But as we will see, much depends on how we interpret "synthesis."

Having presented this clash of arguments, Kant goes on to claim that only his "critical" solution can pinpoint where we are led astray, and his diagnosis of the first two antinomies is that the rival conclusions are dialectical rather than analytic contradictories, i.e., they can't both be true, but they can both be false. That is because they rest on a questionable assumption about the universe as a complete totality, and a resulting ambiguity between taking it as phenomenon or noumenon, appearance or thing in itself. However, I propose to approach this topic while postponing as long as possible any consideration of Kant's controversial theory of transcendental idealism, despite the fact that in section 6 of the Antinomy chapter he presents that doctrine, which he claims to have already proved earlier in the *Critique*, as the *key* to the solution (A491–507/B519–35). My justification for such disregard for that bit of the text is that in the very next section Kant claims that the antinomies provide "indirect proof of the transcendental ideality of appearances—a proof which ought to convince any who may not be satisfied by the direct proof given in the Transcendental Aesthetic" (A506/B534). Since many readers may remain unconvinced by that "direct proof" from his treatment of space and time (even as reinterpreted in essay 3), my hope is that careful examination of the issues raised by the First antinomy may throw some light on transcendental idealism, rather than the other way round.

II. AN APPROACH TO KANT'S SOLUTION OF THE FIRST ANTINOMY

As he begins his elaborate diagnosis of what goes wrong in our antinomial thinking, Kant draws a sharp distinction between empirical science and philosophy. No new evidence or experience is needed to solve *philosophical* problems: all the relevant pieces are already before us; the difficulty is to see how they fit correctly together, and to arrive at what Wittgenstein called "a perspicuous representation." As Kant puts it: "the answer to the transcendent cosmological question cannot lie anywhere else save in the idea. We are not asking what is the constitution of the object in itself" (A479/B507). So he is not merely being agnostic about whether the world is finite or infinite in space and time. His point is that there is a *conceptual* problem that if we are careful we can diagnose and remedy a priori, before we appeal to any a posteriori scientific investigation of the world.[4]

Kant's main point here is that when we try to theorize about the universe as a whole (the cosmos), we run into special problems about the relation between our concepts and their supposed object:

> The cosmological ideas alone have the peculiarity that they can presuppose their object, and the empirical synthesis required for its concept, as being given; and the question that arises from them has to do only with the progression of this synthesis, insofar as it is

to contain an absolute totality, which, however, is no longer empirical, since it cannot be given in any experience.

(A479/B507)

In the Antinomies Kant is concerned with scientific research rather than simple perception. His talk of a regress of conditions (see, e.g., A331–32/B 388–89) involves a series of "Why?" or "What before?" questions, so "synthesis" surely means the process of reaching answers to such questions by inquiries in history and the sciences. Such research involves much more than the syntheses involved in perception (though of course it all ultimately depends on perception): it is social rather than individual. The elaboration, testing, and confirmation of a scientific theory can take decades; the building up of a collective body of human knowledge in geography, history, geology, and scientific theory (and its passing on by education) involves most of human history.

Let us now ask what Kant means by "given"? We can talk of something being "given" in several different ways:

i.   Actually perceived by a certain observer (given to the senses)
ii. Perceivable by any observer who is, was, or will be in the right place at the right time (given – or givable - to the senses in an extended sense)
iii. Known to exist, though not presently perceivable (e.g., "Given that there is an island to the West, as the map shows…," or "Given that the colonel was knifed in the back…," or "Given that there are elements heavier than aluminium…"). In such cases the speaker is appealing to knowledge of the world already established on the basis of many observers' perceptions
iv. Conceived of as a purely hypothetical or abstract example (e.g., "Given five people and a boat that only takes two, how would you get them all across the river," "Given two numbers, find their greatest common divisor")

Among our representations of facts in the world, some are based on present perceptions, some on memory of previous perceptions, and some on testimony, i.e., on what one has learned from other people. We each acquire most of our historical, geographical, and scientific knowledge in this secondhand way, but if it *is* to count as knowledge, other people must have justified the relevant claim by perception, or reasoning based on perception. Theoretical science thus claims to justify belief even in *im*perceptible entities such as elements, atoms, chemical bonds, genes, collapse of wave functions, and black holes, as the best explanation of observed phenomena. This would seem to be the sort of thing that Kant has in mind in these passages: "Nothing is really given us save perception and the empirical advance from this to other possible perceptions" (A493/B521). This is not yet to resolve the First Antinomy; but in outline, it looks as if Kant's proposal is going to be that we can be "given" (i.e., acquire by "synthesis" empirical knowledge of) lots of particular facts about the contents of space and time (past time, at least), but we can never be similarly "given" empirical knowledge of the universe as a complete totality. However, at this point I propose a break from Kant, to take an amateur look at some relevant science before we return to the peculiarly Kantian mysteries.

III. REINTERPRETING KANT IN LIGHT OF THE PROGRESS OF SCIENCE

I will here try to relate Kant's highly abstract philosophizing to our scientifically informed contemporary views. Let us take a concrete example, to clarify our thinking. Consider the birth of a baby, a tender event that can be perceived by those privileged to be there. But we know that the mother must herself have been born of another mother. Thus a regress starts, and we are led to say that there must have been a whole series of ancestors, going back into the mists of prehistory. But there is no corresponding pressure to say that there *must* be a series of *descendants* of today's baby: for there can be no guarantee that it will live long enough to have progeny, or choose to have any. Indeed, humans as a species may become extinct (God forbid). (The example is in effect Kant's own at A512–13/B540–41, though to allow for contemporary sensibility I have added the bit about birth and motherhood.) This confirms that sense iii of "given" yields the asymmetry between past and future events that Kant is talking about. We know that our ancestors must have existed, even if we know nothing specific about them (which is presumably what Kant meant by the phrase "not determinable by us"). But future generations are not yet known to exist, and in this climate-changing and nuclear-armed world there is no guarantee that they will.

I have been proceeding cautiously, holding on to the leading strings of common sense. But conceptual problems lurk. When we talk of "the whole series" of ancestors that have led up to the baby before us, what do we mean? In what sense can such a series be a *whole*? The regress of ancestors soon disappears into the unknown mists of past time. Of course, it is logically possible to stop the regress with a postulated first pair of humans. Such is the view of those who take traditional creation stories such as those in *Genesis* literally. That would imply serious inbreeding from the third generation onward—though perhaps the Creator could turn the trick again, and enhance the gene pool by creating new people (or arranging virgin births?).

For those who hold that the laws of biology allow no such miraculous exceptions, the regress may seem mind-bogglingly infinite. Do we have to believe that it is humans "all the way down"? But if we really want to *know* anything about the distant past, we will have to take on board some serious science.

In the early 19th century, geology made a revolution in the prevailing worldview that literal readers of the Bible found deeply disturbing, for it involved recognizing that our earth has had a hugely longer past than anyone previously imagined.[5] The geological revolution provided enough past time for the evolution of new species by natural selection.[6] Biology now believes neither in a first human, nor in an infinite series of past humans, but rather that we have evolved from creatures that were not human, and ultimately not even mammals. But if all humans are born from humans, how can humans have evolved from something else? A sorites paradox threatens here, but it can be seen off by the Darwinian reflection that species are mutable, so that species terms are vague in their application over evolutionary time. There was no First Pair, but we can put a temporal lower bound on humans: there have *not* been infinitely many humans (you may be relieved to know!), but there hasn't been any determinate finite number of them either.

This solution to what we might call "the Human Antinomy" takes the logical form Kant envisaged for his first two antinomies, namely, the rejection of both alternatives. It is not a *skeptical* solution: there is no relevant fact of the matter that lies beyond our ken. Rather, it is a *critical* solution in that it involves conceptual considerations that show why we should reject both alternatives. Of course Kant himself, writing in the century before Darwin, did not have those theoretical resources, so this is not a Critical solution with a capital "C."[7] It may be said at this stage that these evolutionary considerations only push the problem further back, for we now have to extend the series of our ancestors through an even longer series of life forms on earth. But if a living thing can only come from another living thing, how did life get started? To suggest that it may have come from elsewhere in space (as Fred Hoyle used to do) only puts the question back a further stage: how did extraterrestrial life get started? There may be a scientific stop to this regress, if it can be shown that simple forms of life can emerge from inanimate matter in certain conditions. Besides, there may be room for some conceptual vagueness and elasticity about what exactly to count as life, and whether there are borderline cases.

But we are in a metaphysical frame of mind here, and we can hardly confine our thought to biology. Even if science does lead us to believe that there was a first emergence of life from inorganic matter, this would not be conceived of as creation *ex nihilo*. Nothing can come of nothing—so a very ancient saying goes.[8] In the envisaged scientific account of the origin of life, what we are imagining is a special kind of organic structure with self-maintaining and self-replicating powers somehow appearing for the first time, presumably in some rich and well-heated primeval soup. Yet in any such set of chemical reactions we believe that at least the atoms themselves are conserved: exactly as many atoms of each element must come out of the process as went into it.

But are the atoms themselves eternal? The ancient Greeks thought so, and so did most chemists (though not the alchemists) until the advent of atomic theory. Since then physicists have told us that protons, neutrons, and electrons are themselves composed of still smaller and more mysterious entities rejoicing in the name of quarks and bosons, which hardly count as "particles" at all. And we are now reliably informed that all the contents of the whole universe originated in a mathematical singularity, the "big bang," which occurred a finite time ago. We have now gone far beyond common sense; we have instead been holding the hand of science. But let us see what bearing Kant's philosophical considerations have on these cosmological issues.

IV. STEPHEN HAWKING SPEAKS TO KANT—AND KANT ANSWERS BACK

We have seen how we can get an empirical grip, so to speak, on some very large totalities of past entities. Evolutionary theory and the fossil record enable us to put a lower bound on our human ancestors. For the origin of life itself, physics and chemistry may one day show how that was possible. For the origin of the observed material universe, our best contemporary theories and observations enable us to extrapolate back to a mathematical point of origin some very large but finite time ago. In each case, there is no question of anyone ever *perceiving* such huge totalities, or their limiting points, so they can never be "given" in sense i or ii above. But (so we are told) we can get to know something about them by indirect means, since the scientific theories we appeal to are well-confirmed by a wide variety of observations; if so, these totalities can be "given" in sense iii.

It may therefore sound very much as if contemporary cosmology has now provided scientific justification for the *theses* of the First Antinomy—that the universe has indeed had a beginning in time, and presumably has a finite extent in space at each stage of its expansion. So have Kant's elaborate philosophical reflections simply been made redundant by scientific progress? Certainly, theoretical physics has gone way beyond anything that he conceived of. We hear of non-Euclidean space, of space-time as a four-dimensional continuum, of curvatures in space-time itself, and of space-time being finite but unbounded—though hearing is one thing, and understanding is another! We have also heard confident predictions from theoretical physicists like Stephen Hawking (1998) that they are getting close to a Grand Unified Theory, covering both the very large and the very small, and uniting the four fundamental forces in a so-called Theory of Everything. It would be easy to conclude that Kant's discussion in the Antinomies chapter is of merely historical interest. But I beg leave to question that, although doing so may strain my limited understanding of modern physics to the breaking point.

In the first place, a paradox lurks behind that tempting phrase "a Theory of Everything." Suppose at some stage physicists come up with some single formula—no doubt very complex in its meaning and its implications—that they claim is the Ultimate Law of Nature, the explanation of everything.[9] If this were right, each single event in the history of the universe could be explained in terms of this Ultimate Law, applied to the conditions preceding that event - for there must always be a particular case to which to *apply* the general law. What then about explaining the existence of *those* preceding-states of affairs? This sets us off on a familiar regress. We are told that we can now take the regress back to a singular first event, the big bang. Physicists also say that the laws of nature break down at a singularity: when there is infinite density and zero size, nothing can be predicted. But in that case, we do not have a theory that explains literally *everything*.

Theologians tend to take a metaphysical jump here, and say that it is God who decided on the Creation, and lit the touch-paper for the big bang, as it were.[10] But that just moves the regress further back—or rather *sideways*, into a different kind of theorizing or language game in which some us may want to ask *why* (with what purpose) God created the universe, particularly such a universe as we are burdened with; but it is not clear how such questions can be answered except by appeal to theological authority.

Maybe the latest theory of space-time as itself finite but unbounded will allow us to sidestep such awkward questions about the causation of a *first* event—but if mathematical singularities such as black holes occur at various places within the universe, as is now confidently asserted, it still seems that the laws (or Law) of physics will break down at those points. And even if such singularities can be avoided, the Ultimate Law will still surely be an a posteriori, not an a priori truth. Its epistemological role is to explain all the other empirical truths, including all the observed ones—and to be supported by the fact that it explains all observations so far. But there lies an inductive rub, for we can never exclude the logical possibility that new observations may one day turn up that will *not* fit our so-called Theory of Everything. Of course, if centuries had passed without our finding any such counterevidence, we would say that it had been proved beyond all reasonable doubt. But the logical fact would remain that even such an extremely well-evidenced theory could not explain *itself*: it could not be literally a theory of *everything*. It would always be open to new generations of ambitious young physicists to ask why the so-called Ultimate Law takes the form it does, and to search for a deeper level of physical theory to provide an explanation of it. If they succeeded, that would invite yet further regress. I submit that the continual search for explanations is fine, but the thought that there is a particular place where it must stop is *not*—which is very much what Kant said:

> The principle of reason is only a *rule*, prescribing a regress in the series of conditions for given appearances, in which regress it is never allowed to stop with an absolutely unconditioned.
>
> (A508–9/B536–37)

And perhaps there is still more to be learned from Kant. In my attempt to review contemporary cosmology, I was careful to use the phrase "the whole *observed* material universe," and I suggest that there remains a crucial gap between that and the whole material universe, period. Cosmologists tend to remain silent about what (if anything) happened before the big bang. Some of them may say that the question makes no sense, since time itself began with the bang. That invites a counterquestion: what sense does it make to talk of time *beginning*? And if piles of stuff can fly out from the initial singularity, a mathematical zero-point in the equations, couldn't stuff stream *into* such a point, too? (Isn't that what is supposed to happen in black holes?) It may be replied that no structure, and hence no information, can survive a big bang, so that if the universe has had a pre-bang history, we can never know about it. So how can empirical science ever be in a position to say anything about the *whole* history of the *whole* universe? It looks as if the empirical synthesis cannot be completed, as Kant said.

I suggest that Kant's instinct was right, even if some of his details are outdated or dubious. Despite the confidence of Stephen Hawking and his ilk, it is not clear that anyone could ever be in a position to make claims about the universe as a totality, a completed whole. This is not a contingent limitation on our knowledge, not something that might be overcome by the progress of science and technology. When physicists talk, with their sublime arrogance, of "a Theory of Everything," I make bold to suggest that they do not literally mean what they say. It is not part of the ambition of physics to explain why Mozart's Piano Concerto no. 21 is so ravishingly beautiful, how Hitler was able to rise from the gutters of Vienna to become chancellor of Germany, or why Asha eventually consented to marry Ahmed.

Physics abstracts in its lordly way from all such wonderful or terrible details of the world. Physical theories are not about such humanly important stuff, but about more boring but measurable quantities of mass, length, time, charge, and radiation.

And even when confined to such physical facts, there are still deep problems in the notion of a Theory of Everything. A scientific theory, as Hawking himself admits (1998: 11), is a humanly constructed model that exists only in our minds, but tries to economically explain a large class of past observations in terms of a small number of assumptions, and to accurately predict future observation. Up till now, all physical theories have been partial; they have only tried to explain a large but limited class of physical phenomena. Moreover, the computing of the observational implications of a physical theory always involves making approximations and simplifying assumptions, as Hawking also concedes (1998: 187,204). Adjudicating the fit or lack of fit between a theory and reality is a somewhat messy business, both conceptually and technologically. So is there any real possibility of a theory that is complete rather than partial, and that fits observations with utter exactness.[11]

Hawking famously concluded his best-selling book with the line that if we ever find out why it is that we and the universe exist, we would know the mind of God. But that little word "why" is crucially ambiguous: are we talking of causes, or of purposes? Purposes, intentions, values, and humanly intelligible meanings lie completely outside the domain of physics. No doubt Hawking just wanted a memorable phrase with which to end his book (and in that he succeeded), but if we really assume that there must be a single true answer to the question about causes, a theory of everything waiting to be discovered by sufficiently clever scientists, an ultimate truth already known to God in His omniscience, then we would be committed to that theocentric transcendental realism that Kant did so much to undermine.

V. DOES ALL THIS THROW ANY LIGHT ON KANT'S TRANSCENDENTAL IDEALISM?

I hope these reflections may do something to elucidate an interpretation of Kant's transcendental idealism that is intelligible, and even acceptable (and will fit with the arguments of essays 1 and 4). We have found reason to doubt that any race of finite beings, however intelligent and technologically sophisticated, could ever get an empirical grip, in terms of well-confirmed scientific theory, on the universe as a whole. If so, the universe cannot be "given" in sense iii. But now we meet some classic issues of Kant-interpretation. If he is not saying that the universe has an age and a size but

we can never know it, is he saying that these questions *are not even meaningful*? In twentieth-century terms, if he is not an epistemically pessimistic
realist, is he a verificationist?

Paul Guyer has argued that Kant is a verificationist in the *Critique*, though
at earlier stages of his thinking he restricted himself to a thesis of epistemic
modesty.[12] As we have seen, Kant's arguments for the thesis and antithesis
of the First Antinomy are essentially epistemic, since they rest on the possibilities of "synthesis," which I have interpreted in terms of our processes of
acquiring empirical knowledge. Guyer argues that an explicitly verificationist premise is needed to derive the conclusion that there can be no fact of
the matter about the age and size of the universe, and he concludes that
since Kant does not justify this verificationism, he fails to support his metaphysics of transcendental idealism (1987: 407–9).

I suggest this misses something vital in Kant's thought. Of course there
are plenty of empirical cases in which epistemic modesty is the right attitude to take: we do not know whether there is intelligent life elsewhere in
the universe, though it is a perfectly realistic possibility (Kant allowed that
the moon may be inhabited, at A493/B521). We might find evidence of
alien intelligence by picking up meaningful radio signals, or one fine morn-
ing bug-eyed creatures might drop by in their spaceships (though we could
never have decisive proof of the negative proposition that there is *no* intelligence anywhere else in the universe). It is important to note, however, that
epistemic modesty about a proposition involves a conceptual presumption
about its determinacy of sense. To say that there may be life elsewhere is to
presuppose that we know what would *count* as life in all manner of exotic
locations, i.e., that *our* concept of life would have determinate application,
true or false, to whatever strange stuff there may be out there.

But in some cases we can see that our lack of knowledge is not merely
contingent. When we discussed whether there has been a finite or an infinite series of human ancestors, we concluded that there is no fact of the
matter either way, since we have had to reconceptualize our understanding
of species terms as involving vagueness of application over long periods of
evolutionary time. We now realize that in the evolution of primates, there
will have been many hominoid creatures about which there is no determinate fact of the matter whether they count as human beings. Our concept of
humanity does not reach out with clean-cut yes-or-no application into the
deep past. (And our concept of a *person* might get similarly stressed by
whatever alien life forms there may be out there in deep space.)

Analogously, but more radically, Kant's diagnosis of the First Antinomy
is that there is a *conceptual* defect in the very idea of the universe as a
complete totality of which it would make *sense* to say that it must be either
finite or infinite, even if we can never know which. At A506–7/B534–35 he

says it is "false that the world (the sum of all appearances) is a whole exist-ing in itself." He sometimes sounds like a verificationist, but there remains for him some sense in which we *can* meaningfully talk about the whole uni-verse. And this is a point where his distinction between appearances and things in themselves comes in. Remember his "principle of reason"[13] that generates all this trouble:

> The principle that if the conditioned is given, the entire sum of conditions, and conse-quently the absolutely unconditioned (through which alone the conditioned has been possible) is also given.
>
> (A409/B436)

At A498–99/B526–27 he says that if the conditioned and its conditions are understood as things in themselves, then if the former were given, so would the latter. But if the conditioned is only an appearance, "given" in an empirical synthesis in space and time, a regress to its explanatory condi-tions is not given in the same sense, but only set as a task (as we saw in essay 4). In terms of the varieties of "the given" that we distinguished above, we can say that the universe can be given to thought only in sense iv, not in senses i through iii. As Kant puts it, "we can have the cosmic whole only in concept, never, as a whole, in intuition" (A519/B547). But he does *not* say that all talk of the cosmic whole is meaningless: he was not an eighteenth-century logical positivist (Hume is a much better candidate for that label).

The concept of the whole universe, the sum total of all matter and events, is a paradigm case of what Kant calls a transcendent "idea," something that can be conceived of, but cannot be exemplified in experience. There is no corresponding completed, synthesized totality of which we can have any empirical knowledge. So there is no fact of the matter about whether the universe has a definite size or temporal extent, whether finite or infinite:

> Because the world does not exist at all (independently of the regressive series of my rep-resentations), it exists neither as *an in itself infinite whole* nor as *an itself finite* whole. It is only in the empirical regress of the series of appearances, and by itself it is not to be met with at all.
>
> (A505/B533; see also A518/B546ff.)

This is one of those Kantian sayings that raises hackles in realists (which means most of us, most of the time) and leads many readers to conclude that he is really a Berkeleian idealist. His use of the singular possessive pro-noun "my"[14] makes it sound as if he is saying that the world does not exist outside *his* mental states, which would make him "Master of the Universe" in a sense that not even Stephen Hawking would aspire to! He should surely

have used the *plural* pronoun "our," for we have seen how his notion of synthesis implicitly embraces our collective knowledge gathering. But that still
leaves him open to the robustly realist objection that the world is not a
product of our scientific activity (after all, the sun, the earth, and the dinosaurs long predated the advent of humans). I suggest that Kant means only
that *our conceptions of the world* are a product of human cognitive and
scientific activity, so I would propose rewriting the passage as follows:

> Any conception of the world is a product of our human cognitive activity; and any
> theory about the universe is a result of science as it has progressed in terms of theory and
> observational evidence up to that time, so it will be fallible and incomplete. We can
> never know for certain that we have arrived at a theory that represents the world exactly
> as it is ("in itself")—that is an impossible ideal. In particular, our conceptions of
> finitude and infinity depend for their application on principles of individuation and
> counting, which have changed in the progress of science, and may change again. So we
> will never be in a position to say for certain that the whole universe itself is finite, or that
> it is infinite; we can only know that some of our fallible theories represent it as such.

However far into the future we may try to imagine, at any stage of scientific
research programs, the best that scientists can say is only that this is how
they presently believe the world to be, on the basis of all the evidence and
all the theorizing known to them so far. In making those claims about the
world, they assert what they believe to be *true*, and in putting them forward
as justified by the available body of evidence, they assert them as *knowledge*.
Scientists have to admit that new evidence or arguments may at some future
time rationally require the modification (or even the rejection) of some of
what they now believe, so some of what we presently *take* to be knowledge
may turn out not to be. But such acknowledgment of fallibility, the logical
possibility of the defeat of current assertions, does not mean they now must
cease making claims to justification, truth, and knowledge.

Another ambitiously philosophizing scientist, the sociobiologist
E. O. Wilson, proclaimed his faith that we can "devise a universal litmus test for
scientific statements, and with it eventually attain the grail of objective truth":

> Outside our heads there is freestanding reality. . . . Inside our heads is a reconstitution of
> reality based on sensory input and the self-assembly of concepts. . . . The alignment of
> outer existence with its inner representation has been distorted by the idiosyncrasies of
> human evolution. . . . The proper task of scientists is to diagnose and correct the misalign-
> ment. The effort to do so has only begun. No one should suppose that objective truth is
> impossible to attain, even when the most committed philosophers urge us to acknowl-
> edge that incapacity.

(Wilson 1998: 65)

Now I do not dispute for a moment that science has dramatically widened and deepened our understanding of the physical world, but I want to question the philosophical gloss that Wilson puts on this universally accepted truism.[15] If there are "misalignments" between reality and the way it is represented, and if we are to diagnose and correct them, then we will need to have knowledge of the two things that are misaligned—some particular aspect of reality on the one hand, and the way it is misrepresented by some person or community, on the other. But whoever is making such a diagnosis is *assuming that he himself knows the relevant facts about that aspect of reality*, that his representation of it is correct, i.e., true. And how is he to justify *that* assumption? To talk of "objective" truth adds nothing to talk of truth. As we saw in essay 4, the notion of "reality" (or Kant's notion of "transcendental object") is only a sort of unspecified stand-in (the unknown = X); any particular claims we make about reality have to be justified by our fallible processes. If by "objective truth" is meant representations that exactly correspond to reality as it is "in itself," independent of the human mind (even the most well-informed scientific minds)—that is an ideal that Kant has shown is empty.

ESSAY 6

༺❦༻

Opinion, Belief or Faith, and Knowledge

In the B Preface to the *Critique of Pure Reason* Kant famously said he had "to deny knowledge (*Wissen*) in order to make room for faith (*Glaube*)," and he indicated that the primary objects he had in mind for faith are God, freedom, and immortality (Bxxx). Two questions arise: How does he differentiate between faith and knowledge; and what are the appropriate topics for faith? In this essay I will try to answer the first question: What exactly is Kant's conception of *Glaube*, and how does it fit into his epistemology?[1]

It is not until the concluding Method section that Kant explicitly addresses these issues, when in the Canon of Pure Reason at A805/B833 he poses three questions that for him sum up "all interest of my reason":

1. What can I know?
2. What should I do?
3. What may I hope?

Kant here put *hope* on the agenda of philosophy. In his essays on history he argued that we can hope for secular progress in the development of human culture and politics; but in his moral and religious philosophy he also expressed eschatological hope that in a life after death we can perfect our characters and that the Moral Governor of the universe will ensure that happiness is eventually proportionate to virtue. About immortality and the existence of God, his constant refrain is that we cannot have theoretical knowledge, only a practical kind of *Glaube*. His treatment of freedom (i.e., free will) is officially similar, but somewhat different in detail; I will discuss it in essay 9. How are we to understand this distinctively Kantian attitude of practical, moral "belief" or "faith"? (As we will see, both words have been used to translate *Glaube*). In the Canon Kant introduces a threefold classification of ways of holding a proposition to be true—*meinen, glauben,* and *wissen*—usually translated as opinion, belief, and knowledge. This trio of propositional attitudes seems to have been part of the conventional wisdom of Kant's day.[2] It reappears in the various versions of his "Logic" lectures, with some interesting variations.[3] In this essay I will start by systematically scrutinizing what he has to say about *meinen, glauben,* and *wissen.*

I

We need to proceed with due sensitivity to some tricky matters of translation. At A822/B850 Kant explains his use of *meinen* (believing, or holding an opinion),[4] *glauben* (believing, or having faith), and *wissen* (knowing). He presents these as three different "stages" (degrees, or ways) of "taking something to be true" (*fürwahrhalten*), which he equates with "the subjective validity of judgment," so this holding or taking to be true is the genus, the basic concept that he assumes as undefined. Here we come up against a first possibility of confusion, for it has been common for philosophers writing in English to use the word "believe" (or "assent") in this wide sense, meaning *any* sort of holding a proposition to be true, however confident or hesitant, rational or irrational, justified or unjustified. It would thus be tempting to translate Kant's verb *fürwahrhalten* as "believe." In that usage, knowledge implies belief; and "mere" belief, without any sufficient justification, will then be the kind of belief that does *not* amount to knowledge.[5]

But if we are to translate *fürwahrhalten* as belief in this very wide modern sense, we obviously cannot also translate Kant's *glauben* or *meinen*, which are subspecies of it, as belief without creating confusion. Kant's English interpreters are in some disarray over this point. Guyer and Wood allow that it would be natural to read *Glaube* as "faith" when Kant is thinking of religious topics (as at Bxxx), but since he also uses the term in many contexts where it can only be translated by "belief," they decide to use "belief" throughout.[6] Pluhar in his translation of the *Critique of Judgment* decides to render *Glaube* usually as "faith," on the grounds that this fits better with the mutual exclusiveness of *wissen* and practical *glauben*.[7] This warns us that Kant's conception of *Glaube* requires very careful interpretation. We should not assume one English word as its universal translation and conduct all our subsequent discussion using our selected word in its contemporary meaning. That is a likely way of missing what Kant may have to teach us.

A further question to settle at the outset is the relation between Kant's trio of propositional attitudes and the notion of judgment that he uses throughout the main body of the *Critique*. The ambiguities of the noun "judgment" are well known:

1. An object (or possible object) of an act of judging, i.e., a *proposition*— A6–9/B10–13 (in this sense, a hypothetical judgment contains two judgments, linked by the "if... then" connection—A73/B98, B141)
2. A *mental act* of judging, in which someone judges a proposition—A69/ B94, A130/B169 (this means judging it to be *true*—not merely entertaining it, as in a question or a command, or as a component in a complex proposition)
3. The *mental power*, ability, or faculty of judging—A130/B169, A133/ B172

The distinction between 2 and 3 provokes the question whether *meinen, glauben,* and *wissen* are occurrences or dispositions. There obviously are such dispositions, for we describe people as retaining their opinions, beliefs, and knowledge when they are thinking about different matters or are asleep. But these dispositions are actualized in particular mental events, so Kant must be prepared to distinguish three corresponding types of mental acts, which will be subspecies of judging in sense 2. For *meinen* we can suggest conjecturing or guessing; but the English words "believing" and "knowing" do not ordinarily stand for occurrent mental events or acts (and as applied to mental dispositions we have yet to address the question how far these words correspond to Kant's intentions). And of what disposition is the whole genus of judging an actualization? Holding to be true (*fürwahrhalten*) is the obvious answer, and the logic lectures made this fairly explicit.[8]

A philosophically challenging question can be raised here. If judgings actualize dispositions of holding-to-be-true, are they passive events that "just happen" in us, or are they under our voluntary control? Describing judgings as mental *acts* might be taken to entail the latter, but it need imply only that they are occurrent mental *events*: the question remains open whether judgings are voluntary. That is the topic of essay 7, in which I examine what Kant and his early modern predecessors have to say about whether the will can influence the formation of belief.

In this essay my first main business is to examine Kant's explanations of *meinen, glauben,* and *wissen.* The method section may seem rather late in the day to be defining epistemological concepts, but Kant has not made any significant use of the trio earlier on, and his introduction of them at this point is connected with his foray into "moral theology" in the Canon of

Pure Reason, where he sketches how he intends (in his yet-to-be-written moral philosophy) to make good on his promise to put faith (*glauben*) into the empty place of theological knowledge.[9]

Kant begins the third section of the Canon with some general logical and epistemological definitions. He first distinguishes "objective grounds" and "subjective causes" for judgments (A820/B848). If someone's judgment is valid for everyone "merely so long as he has reason," its ground is "objectively sufficient," and Kant calls it "conviction" (*Überzeugung*). If however it "has its ground only in the particular constitution of the subject," it has mere "private validity"; such a taking to be true "cannot be communicated" and is called "persuasion" (*Überredung*). Kant then says that persuasion cannot be distinguished from conviction subjectively; we have to test whether "the grounds that are valid for us have the same effect on the reason of others" in order to reveal "the merely private validity of the judgment, i.e., something in it that is mere persuasion" (A821/B849).

Kant's "objective sufficiency" is surely an epistemological concept, distinct from truth. He assumes a correspondence account of truth as the agreement of a judgment with the relevant facts ("truth rests upon agreement with the object"); but as he acknowledged back at A58/B82, this is mere analysis of the concept of truth, not a criterion that can be used to find out what is true. Agreement between people is a "touchstone" or presumption of truth, a useful though inconclusive way of finding out (A820–21/B848–49). It is fallible because others might agree or disagree for bad reasons ("subjective causes") such as politeness, credulity, ignorance, shortsightedness, prejudice, or sheer cussedness. So when Kant says that private validity cannot be communicated, he surely does not mean that one can never communicate *that* one believes a proposition; or that one can never get others to agree (perhaps by arousing subjective causes in others, as rabble-rousing politicians do). What he must mean is that if one has only subjective causes for a belief (mere "private validity"), one cannot communicate any publicly recognizable justification for it—for one has no such justification to transmit.

It is now high time to quote, in full, Kant's official explanation of his trio of propositional attitudes:

> Taking something to be true (*fürwahrhalten*), or the subjective validity of judgement, has the following three stages in relation to conviction (which at the same time is valid objectively): *having an opinion, believing* and *knowing. Having an opinion* (*meinen*) is taking something to be true with the consciousness that it is subjectively *as well as* objectively insufficient. If taking something to be true is only subjectively sufficient and is at the same time held to be objectively insufficient, then it is called *believing* (*glauben*). Finally, when the taking something to be true is both subjectively and objectively sufficient it is called *knowing* (*wissen*). Subjective sufficiency is called *conviction* (for

myself), objective sufficiency, *certainty* (for everyone). I will not pause for the exposition of such readily grasped concepts.

(A822/B850)

We have already seen reason to suspect that Kant is being over-hasty in assuming that this is all so obvious as to need no further explanation. For one thing, we will want to know whether "sufficiency" and "validity" are synonyms. It does look as if "objective sufficiency" means the same as "objective validity"; but in the first sentence of the quotation, "subjective validity" is identified with holding to be true, whereas "subjective sufficiency" in *glauben* and *wissen* must mean something else. Maybe this is just a slip—he could have kept "subjective validity" as a synonym for "subjective sufficiency" ("private validity" is different, for it involves some kind of illusion). There is another worry, however, about Kant's use of "conviction": for in the penultimate sentence he calls subjective sufficiency "conviction (for myself)," yet in the first sentence he talks of conviction being valid objectively, and a couple of pages back at A820/B848 he said its ground is objectively sufficient. It sounds as if he recognizes two species of conviction—objective and subjective—but if so, he should have said so more clearly. Kant's interpreters have long had to struggle with his annoying habit of not being consistent in his usage of technical terms, even where he has given explicit definitions. Sometimes the problem is only an editorial one, that can be resolved by more exact definitions and greater care in following them, as perhaps is the case with the above two points. But often Kant's apparent inconsistencies are the result of his subliminal sensitivity to underlying philosophical issues, and the diagnosis of what is going on requires delicate interpretation.

Another question is whether Kant intends *meinen, glauben,* and *wissen* to exhaust the extension of *fürwahrhalten*. They are obviously mutually exclusive, and it is natural to assume that he thinks of them as covering all the possibilities. Throughout his logic lectures, he presents the trio as "the three degrees of holding to be true." If we assume that objective sufficiency entails subjective sufficiency, and we first divide holdings to be true into those that are objectively sufficient and those that are not, and then divide the latter into the subjectively sufficient or not, we get an exhaustive partition into three species.

But if we reread Kant's above-quoted definition of *meinen* with care, we notice that it involves not just the *lack* of objective and subjective sufficiency, but the *consciousness* or awareness of those absences. In the case of *glauben* he says that the taking to be true is subjectively sufficient (with no mention of consciousness), and held to be objectively insufficient. But who is to do this holding—the subject, or other people? Is Kant appealing to a first-person or a third-person point of view?[10] Presumably he would plump for the former, in line with his account of *meinen*. Yet in the case of *wissen*, his definition does not require consciousness at all. Did he intend these asymmetries, or are they a mere verbal accident? Systematic considerations incline us toward the latter view. Overall, the simplest interpretation is that Kant assumes that the presence or absence of objective or subjective sufficiency is reliably discernable by introspection. If consciousness of objective or subjective sufficiency coincides with possession of it, we would have an exhaustive partition of propositional attitudes into three kinds (as above), with the added point that they are subjectively distinguishable. This interpretation is also supported by the logic lectures, in which we find variously worded explanations of *meinen, glauben,* and *wissen* that sometimes mention consciousness, but in other versions omit it, partly or completely.[11]

There is a difficulty for this interpretation, however. For we have noticed Kant saying, just before the definitions at A822/B850, that persuasion (holding to be true on grounds that are not objectively sufficient) *cannot* be subjectively distinguished from conviction (holding to be true on grounds that are objectively sufficient). This suggests that there can be cases of taking something to be true, while thinking or assuming that one's grounds for it are objectively valid, when in fact they are not. That was Kant's point at A822/B850, and he calls such cases *Überredung* (translated, not perhaps very happily, as "persuasion"). They do not count as *wissen* because objective sufficiency is lacking, nor as *meinen* or *glauben* because Kant's definitions of them, as actually worded, require awareness of one's lack of objective sufficiency, whereas persuasion involves the illusory awareness of its presence.

II

We have yet to understand what Kant means by "objective" and "subjective sufficiency," the central undefined concepts in the definitions at A822/B850. An obvious suggestion is to identify objective sufficiency (and objective validity) with the epistemological concept of justification, i.e., reason or evidence that reaches some publicly shared standard of good enough reason to believe the relevant claim.[12] But how then should we interpret "*subjective* sufficiency"? If one comes to this question as a pure epistemologist unconcerned with moral philosophy (and still less with theology), it may be tempting to suggest it means *thinking one has objective sufficiency*, i.e., taking it that one is justified in holding the relevant proposition to be true. This seems to fit with Kant's remark at A821/B849 that persuasion and conviction cannot be subjectively distinguished, which on the present interpretation would mean that one cannot tell by introspection whether what one *takes* to be justification really is justification, valid for everyone. Accordingly, we could define the following three concepts:

Meinen 1 is holding something to be true, thinking one does not have sufficient justification for it, when indeed one does not—i.e., unjustified belief that the subject realizes is unjustified.

Examples of this would be when one expresses or asserts something only as one's own guess, hunch, hypothesis, conjecture, or opinion.

Glauben 1 is holding something to be true, thinking one has sufficient justification for it, when one does *not*—i.e., unjustified belief that the subject takes to be justified.

But as we have seen, this is what Kant usually calls *Überredung*. *Glauben* 1 is obviously not belief in the modern sense. Can we call it faith? Cases of believing something while wrongly thinking one has sufficient justification for it may be described as naive or blind faith (e.g., believing the word of salesmen, government spokesmen, or loquacious strangers one meets on the street). A different conception of faith is where someone has a belief for which he *admits* he lacks sufficient justification: cases where faith goes self-consciously beyond the evidence. This seems characteristic of religious faith (on many people's conceptions of it), but it can also apply to secular faith that someone will keep her promise, or that a certain investment will eventually be profitable. (This is one usage of "belief" in contemporary English.) However, *glauben* 1 is not that concept either: it is, rather, *mistaking* insufficient justification as sufficient. The word for this is "credulity" (but English lacks a single verb for believing credulously).

Wissen 1 is holding something to be true, thinking one has sufficient justification for it, when indeed one *does*, i.e., justified belief that the subject takes to be justified.

"Knowledge" is not quite the right word for this, since knowing p entails the truth of p, whereas justification, on the usual modern conception of it, does not. *Wissen* 1 is the attitude of *thinking* one knows a proposition—but that cannot count as knowledge in cases where the proposition is false.

We have here three epistemological concepts that may be useful wherever we can assume an objective, publicly assessable standard of justification, but are they what Kant intended? There are several reasons why not. As we have seen, his actual definition of *meinen* at A822/B850 involves not just the absence of objective and subjective sufficiency, but the *consciousness* of that fact. On the present suggestion, this definition would imply an iteration to the effect that the subject is conscious that she is conscious of her lack of justification, which is surely not what Kant meant. In the case of *glauben* his definition would also imply an implausible mental iteration.

What then *does* Kant mean by "subjectively sufficient"? There is a wide-ranging and well-known ambiguity in his use of "subjective" that we must face up to here. At A820/B848 what is contrasted with an objective sufficiency is a ground for judgment that is "only in the particular constitution of the subject," and here Kant surely means *the individual subject*—he says that such judgments have only *private* validity, they are mere persuasion (*glauben1*). But in some important contexts elsewhere in the Critical philosophy, "subjective" means *dependent on the constitution of the human species*.[13] Kant holds that ours is a "particular" constitution compared with those of other actual or possible beings, but he also thinks there are philosophically significant features that are common to all humans. One famous place where he uses "subjective" in this way is at the beginning of the *Critique of Judgment* (5:215), in his account of aesthetic judgments as having universal yet subjective validity; another is early in the first *Critique*, where he claims that space and time are "subjective" in that they are dependent on the constitution of human sensibility (A42/B59).

There are wider questions I cannot hope to settle in this essay. What we have to recognize here is that by "subjectively sufficient" in his definition of *glauben* Kant means that the subject can have a ground or reason that she acknowledges not to amount to objective justification, but that she takes to be *good enough in its own distinctive way* to justify her in holding the proposition to be true. Thus the distinction between subjective and objective sufficiency is not between the subject's own view of her justification and the publicly evaluable fact of whether she really is justified, but rather between *two different conceptions or standards of justification*. What, then, are the standards Kant has in mind? They are not explained at A822/B850, so someone who examines this passage in isolation, with a single ("objective") notion of justification in mind, may be puzzled as to how *anything* could count as "subjective sufficiency." But anyone who reads the rest of the Canon of Pure Reason will realize that Kant distinguishes the two standards as *theoretical* and *practical*. At A823/B851, three paragraphs after his definition of *glauben*, he writes, "Only in *a practical relation* . . . can something that is theoretically insufficient to be true be called believing (*glauben*)."

As Allen Wood has pointed out,[14] Kant's *wissen* and *glauben* are based on grounds that are *universally* valid, that have the power to appeal to *any* person. They both involve conviction rather than mere opinion or persuasion, but conviction of very different kinds: *wissen* must be based either on logical proof (deduction) or such strong empirical evidence (induction) as to amount to knowledge beyond all reasonable doubt, whereas *glauben* is based on what Kant sees as morally demanded of all persons. *Glauben* can in its own way be stronger than *wissen*, for as Kant remarked in the second *Critique* and in his logic lectures, people have sometimes been ready to die for their moral or religious beliefs, but not for mathematical theorems or factual claims. The grounds of *Glaube* are not "objective" in the sense of being about the object(s) that the judgment refers to; rather they are subjective in the sense that they involve people's personal commitment. Wood warns against identifying the status of *Glaube* with the subjective universality of aesthetic judgments, for the latter do not rest on concepts, whereas to support *Glaube* Kant appeals to moral considerations or arguments that can be expressed in words. So it seems we have to recognize two different kinds of subjective universality—conceptual and nonconceptual.

Confirmation that this is Kant's conception of *Glaube* comes from other works in which he explains his distinction between *meinen, glauben,* and *wissen*. One is his essay "What Does It Mean to Orient Oneself in Thinking?" published in 1786:

> Every belief, even the historical, must of course be *rational* (for the final touchstone of truth is always reason); only a rational belief or faith (*Vernunftglaubens*) is one grounded on no data other than those contained in *pure* reason. All believing is a holding true which is subjectively sufficient, but *consciously* regarded as objectively insufficient; thus it is contrasted with *knowing*.
>
> (8:140–41)[15]

The second sentence here, with Kant's italicizing of the word "consciously," confirms that by "subjective" and "objective sufficiency" he means two quite different conceptions of justification. Now if we are to interpret objective and subjective sufficiency as theoretical and practical justification, we might expect to do the same in his definitions of *meinen* and *wissen*. The results would be:

> *Meinen* 2 is holding something to be true, while being neither practically nor theoretically justified in doing so.
>
> *Glauben* 2 is holding something to be true, and being practically but not theoretically justified in doing so.
>
> *Wissen* 2 is holding something to be true, and being both practically and theoretically justified in doing so.

But when we look at other things Kant says about *meinen* and *wissen*, they do not fit with this suggestion. The passage from the "Orientation" essay continues:

> On the other hand, when something is held true on objective though consciously insufficient grounds, and hence is merely *opinion*, this *opining* (*meinen*) can gradually be

supplemented by the same kind of grounds and finally become a *knowing* (*wissen*). By contrast, if the grounds of holding true are of a kind that cannot be objectively valid at all, then the belief can never become a knowing through any use of reason.

(8:141)

And there is a very clear passage in the *Jäsche Logic*:

Believing, or holding-to-be-true based on a ground that is objectively insufficient, but subjectively sufficient, relates to objects in regard to which we not only cannot know anything, but also cannot opine anything—indeed, cannot even pretend there is probability, but only can be certain that it is not contradictory to think of such objects as one does think of them. What remains here is a *free* holding-to-be-true, which is necessary only in a practical respect given *a priori*; hence a holding-to-be-true of what I accept on *moral* grounds, and in such a way that I am certain that the *opposite* can never be proved.

(9:67)[16]

So Kant sees *meinen* and *wissen* as different grades *on the same scale* of theoretical justification, so that an accretion of evidence can convert one into the other. But *glauben* is not on that scale at all: it does not compete in the theoretical stakes, for it involves a distinctively practical kind of ground that can be had only in the absence of theoretical justification. So the above conception of *wissen* 2 is incoherent, since for Kant nothing can be both practically and theoretically justified. Anyone who had the attitude of *meinen* 1 to a proposition, hoping to acquire *both* practical and theoretical justification for it, would be in a state of conceptual confusion. The propositions that are the objects of faith are different in kind from empirical claims about the contents of the physical world.

In section 91 of the third *Critique* Kant offers an apparently ontological distinction between three kinds of "cognizable things: matters of opinion (*opinabilia*), matters of fact (*scibilia*), and matters of faith (mere *credibilia*)" (5:467).[17] But the preceding sentence suggests that Kant's distinctions here are not primarily ontological: "The question whether something is a cognizable being or not is not a question concerning the possibility of things in themselves but concerning the possibility of our cognizing them." He goes on to say that *meinen* can only be about empirical matters, and *wissen* about matters of fact that can be either a priori (in logic or mathematics) or empirical (based on experience), whereas *glauben* can only be about topics that are matters of neither *wissen* nor *meinen* nor estimates of probability: "a wholly moral faith is one that refers to special objects that are not objects of possible knowledge or opinion" (5:472).

Actually, we can question Kant's claim that there is no *meinen* about a priori matters—for surely there are mathematical conjectures, based not on proof but on mathematical "intuition" (in a non-Kantian sense of the word), or on verification in a finite sample of an infinite set of cases (perhaps by computer). Perhaps there can even be such a thing as a *philosophical* conjecture, i.e., an opinion that a certain proposition is true a priori, even if one cannot at the time formulate a transcendental proof of it. If we thus allow that there can be *meinen* about the a priori, we can simplify Kant's position as follows: *meinen* and *wissen* would have as their range all matters of possible knowledge (whether empirical or a priori), and *glauben* would have as its range the quite different set of topics—so far unspecified—about which no knowledge is possible. It thus emerges that the distinction between subjective and objective sufficiency has to be differently applied for *glauben* on the one hand, and *meinen* and *wissen* on the other. In view of what we have seen of the overall shape of Kant's critical philosophy we have to interpret his epistemic trio in this mixed way, combining versions of *meinen* 1, *wissen* 1, and *glauben* 2.

Before trying to state exact formulations of these, we should ask how the question of consciousness or awareness of justification, discussed in section II, applies now that we have distinguished practical and theoretical justification. For practical justification it seems natural to assume that its presence or absence is subjectively knowable (as we did for subjective sufficiency). Theoretical justification seems to be the same as objective sufficiency, so we can offer the following revised definitions:

> *Meinen 1'* is holding something to be true, thinking one does not have sufficient theoretical justification for it, when indeed one does not.
>
> *Glauben 2* is holding something to be true, and being practically but not theoretically justified in doing so.
>
> *Wissen 1'* is holding something to be true, thinking one has sufficient theoretical justification for it, when one does have such justification.

III

This is still not the end of our interpretative problems, for Kant discusses various examples of *Glaube* about *empirical* matters, although according to what he has declared about the incompatibility of theoretical and practical justification there should be no such thing. The first line of the above quotation from the "Orientation" essay mentions historical belief or faith without further explanation. In the third *Critique* Kant says more:

> It is true that something that we can learn only from the experience of others, through their *testimony*, is something in which we must have faith (*Glaube*), but it is not yet on

> that account a matter of faith (*Glaubenssache*) but only a case of historical faith (*historische Glaube*), because for *one* of those witnesses it was after all his own experience and a matter of fact, or we presuppose that it was that.
>
> (5:469)

Here he makes a very artificial-seeming distinction when he says that a historical proposition that we accept "on faith," i.e., on the basis of the testimony of witnesses, is a case of historical faith but not a *matter* of faith (*historische Glaube* that is not *historische Glaubenssache*). The verbal puzzle can be resolved if we distinguish between faith and belief, particularly between historical belief and religious faith. That this is Kant's intention is confirmed by what follows:

> Moreover, by following the path of historical faith it must always be possible to arrive at knowledge; and hence the objects of history and geography, and everything whatever that in view of the character of our cognitive powers it is at least possible for us to know, are not matters of faith but matters of fact. Only objects of pure reason can be matters of faith at all; but not if they are merely objects of pure theoretical reason.
>
> (5:469)

Kant (at least when he is careful) makes a strict demarcation between matters of faith (*Glaube*) in his special sense of the word, and all empirical matters of fact in geography, history, and science generally (which can be "given" in the wide sense analyzed in essay 4). In this he comes into conflict (and surely quite self-consciously so) with religious traditions that treat some particular historical claims as matters of faith, such as the Christian dogmas of the bodily resurrection of Jesus or his virgin birth, and Jewish or Muslim claims about divine intervention in history. Kant's late *Religion* makes a sharp contrast between these and religious faith "within the limits of reason alone." This is not the place to debate these issues: all we need note here is that Kant verbally handicaps himself by sometimes using *Glaube* for a degree of belief in empirical propositions that is less than knowledge but more than opinion, when he argues elsewhere that these are quite different concepts.

Is there any philosophical need to distinguish such an intermediate grade of belief or assent? And how exactly would it be defined? Here is a suggestion gleaned from some of what Kant says about historical claims:

> Glauben 3 is holding something to be true on the basis of someone else's testimony, rather than on the basis of one's own perceptual experience.

This is a perfectly intelligible conception, but does *glauben* 3 never amount to knowledge? Sometimes people cautiously say "I *believe* so" when they are reporting what they have been told rather than what they have seen for themselves, yet this usage need not express any serious doubt about the truth of the proposition. Does Kant mean to imply that nobody can ever *know* anything on the basis of what she is told? That would imply a very radical revision of what we take ourselves to know, for the vast majority of what any one of us believes has been received from other people. Kant hardly touches on testimony in his published work, but he discusses it in some detail in his logic lectures, and the notes show that he did not commit himself to such a restrictive epistemology. In the *Jäsche Logic* 9:70–71 he says that knowledge is assent from a reason that is both subjectively and objectively sufficient; this is identified with certainty, which can be either empirical or rational. Empirical certainty is described as "original" when it is founded on the subject's own experience, and "derived" when it is founded on the experience of others (which he calls "historical certainty"). In the Vienna Logic Kant says quite definitely that we can have knowledge of empirical propositions on the basis of testimony (e.g., that Madrid is the capital of Spain).

> To be sure, the testimony that we accept from others is subject to at least as many risks of error as our own experience. But we can just as well have certainty through the testimony of others as through our own experience. Believing is thus the same kind of thing as knowing. If we contradistinguish believing from knowing, then this is only practically sufficient holding-to-be true.
>
> (24:896)[18]

This sounds very modern in its dismissal of Cartesian solipsist methodology; but in saying that believing is the same kind of thing as knowing, Kant appears to be contradicting what he has said elsewhere: the charitable interpretation is that he was working with two different concepts of belief without being explicit about their differences.

The *Jäsche Logic* denies that there can be knowledge of *mathematical* truths by testimony (9:68), but we will surely want to question that. Someone unfamiliar with a proof can be said to lack understanding of *why* the proposition is true, but that does not exclude her knowing *that* it is true. There are quite simple mathematical propositions (e.g., that there are infinitely many primes, or that 2 has no rational square root) that can be readily understood and believed—and why not known?—by someone who does not know their proofs. When a proof has been constructed and checked by mathematicians, it is hard to see why the rest of us cannot be said to know the result on the basis of their testimony, in the same way that we can know historical and geographical and scientific facts on the authority of others.

Of course, there will be many empirical reports, claims, and allegations to which one gives at best only a marginal degree of assent, describable as opinion or conjecture. So *glauben* 3, believing on the basis of testimony, will not make a neat partition of what we hold true into three grades of *wissen*, *glauben* 3, and *meinen*; it belongs to a different family of epistemological concepts, other members of it being

> believing on the basis of one's current perceptual experience
> believing on the basis of one's memory of previous perceptual experiences
> believing on the basis of an inductive argument
> believing on the basis of what seems self-evident
> believing on the basis of a deductive argument

It remains open to epistemologists to question the reliability of these sources of belief, but these issues cannot be settled by terminological stipulation. To formulate them clearly, we need one set of terms to distinguish the sources of belief, and another for the different kinds of normative status that we may attach to beliefs.

IV

In that passage in section 91 of the third *Critique* Kant may seem to be leading us toward a quasi-Platonic distinction between the objects of *meinen* and *wissen* on the one hand and those of *glauben* on the other; indeed, in his *Inaugural Dissertation* he offered a metaphysical theory of two separate realms of objects of sensibility and objects of understanding. But in his mature Critical philosophy he sees the two faculties as cooperating in forming representations of one world of spatiotemporal appearances. He still echoes Plato in reserving a special propositional attitude of faith (*Glaube*) that seems to relate us to a separate realm of things in themselves,[19] but he reverses Plato's epistemological priorities, for according to the critical philosophy we have knowledge about the perceptible world of material things in space and time, but we can only have *Glaube* about "the supersensible."

We know, of course, that Kant has some controversial doctrine about things in themselves. But need the idea of a distinctively practical sort of justification for believing involve anything about that? Can't we make sense of this interesting notion without involving conceptions of anything transcending human experience? Kant sometimes veers in this direction, in contexts in which he extends his usage of *Glaube* to any empirical proposition that is accepted *as a basis for action*. This is a matter not of the justification for a belief, but of the sort of confidence or strength with which it is held. A lengthy footnote to the discussion of belief in the *Jäsche Logic* begins:

Believing is ... a kind of incomplete holding-to-be-true with consciousness. ... it is distinguished from opining, not by its degree, but rather by the relation that it has as cognition to action. Thus the businessman, for instance, to strike a deal, needs not just to opine that there will be something to be gained thereby, but to believe it, i.e., to have his opinion be sufficient for an undertaking into the uncertain.

$$(9:67-68n)[20]$$

Later in that same footnote there is talk of "a holding-to-be-true that is enough for action, that is, a *belief*." Here we seem to have a new pragmatic conception of belief, as distinct from mere opinion. There had already been a formulation of this in the first *Critique*:

Only in a *practical relation*, however, can taking something that is theoretically insufficient to be true be called believing. This practical aim is either that of *skill* or of *morality*, the former for arbitrary and contingent ends, the latter, however, for absolutely necessary ends.

$$(A823/B851)$$

As an example of the former, Kant cites the case of a doctor who is obliged by his profession to do his best to save his patient's life; he can make only a provisional diagnosis while being aware that there may be better explanations of the symptoms; yet the urgency of his unassisted situation makes it reasonable for him to give treatment on the basis of his conjectural diagnosis. Kant calls such contingent beliefs, which ground the use of means to certain actions, "pragmatic beliefs" (*pragmatische Glauben*) (A824/B852). Here we have an implicit suggestion of another grade of assent to empirical propositions intermediate between opinion and knowledge:[21]

Glauben 4 is holding something to be true with a firmness that is less than knowledge (theoretical justification), but is sufficient to ground action, and is thus more than mere opinion.

Anticipating Frank Ramsey, Kant notes shrewdly that the firmness of pragmatic beliefs can be tested by the subject's willingness to *bet* on them:

Sometimes he reveals that he is persuaded enough for one ducat but not for ten ... thus pragmatic belief has only a degree, which can be large or small according to the difference of the interest that is at stake.

$$(A824-25/B852-53)$$

However, a person's willingness to act on a given empirical claim will obviously depend not only on his degree of belief in it, but also on what he thinks may be gained or lost by the proposed action. The rationality of accepting a certain bet will thus be a product of at least two factors: the subject's estimate of the probability of the relevant proposition, and the odds of gain or loss that are offered.[22] For example, if someone is stupid enough to offer odds of more than 6 to 1 against a dice coming up on one particular face, it would be rational to accept. But if I am invited to play Russian roulette with a revolver containing a single bullet in one of its six chambers, I will not put the thing to my head even once, however high the reward, if I don't want to risk my life. Therefore *glauben* 4 is a hopeless conception, for there is no definite degree of belief that justifies action: one-sixth is enough in one case, but not in another. If it is suggested that there is still a viable distinction to be made between the "beliefs" that one would act on in *some* possible context and the "opinions" that one would only express in words, it can be replied that a speech act is after all one kind of action; to make an assertion (or fail to make one) can have serious consequences in certain situations.

There is more hope of arriving at a reasonable estimate of a person's degrees of belief in various propositions (also called "subjective probabilities") by testing their willingness to accept various bets involving different stakes for the same proposition, or different propositions for the same stake. So we can include in our conceptual options a notion of a graduated degree of belief that is comprehensive, rather than some arbitrarily chosen middle segment of the scale:

> *Glauben* 5 is the subjective probability of a proposition, the degree of belief the subject has in it, the strength with which she holds it true.

This may be a reasonably clear concept,[23] but it will not fit into Kant's trio. For the measure of strength that is involved in *glauben* 5 can be applied to all grades of assent, including 1 (complete certainty) and 0 (certainty of the negation) at the two ends of the scale. Propositions that one is sure of beyond all reasonable doubt will be assigned a subjective probability of nearly 1; and those that one is prepared to affirm as one's opinion but not to bet very much on will be assigned a subjective probability of a little more than 0.5. But there is no reason to pick out any particular numbers less than 1 or over 0.5 to divide up the continuous scale into three segments; any such choice of dividing point would be an arbitrary convention.

Kant remarks on the necessity and stability of "moral belief" (A828/ B856). What he means by the latter phrase is *not* (as might be expected) beliefs about what one ought or ought not to do; rather he has in mind certain metaphysical claims—his old favorites about God and immortality—that he thinks one has to accept if one is to be motivated to strive toward one's own moral perfection and the highest good, i.e., the unity of virtue and happiness in the world. The acceptance or belief that he sees as involved here is of a very special kind: the conviction is not *logical* but *moral* certainty, and, since it depends on subjective grounds (of moral disposition), Kant suggests that one should not say "*It is* morally certain that there is a God," etc., but rather "*I am* morally certain." etc. (A829/B857). Here Kant strikes an existentialist note, anticipating Kierkegaard.[24] His distinction between moral beliefs and theoretical beliefs (even those about the things in themselves) is not between different propositions, but different styles of believing the same propositions.[25]

V

Is there any payoff for our contemporary philosophizing from these rather intricate matters of Kant-exegesis? It comes, I suggest, from noting the differences between the various conceptions of belief we have met along the way. My final set of numberings will *not* correspond to those of the varieties of *glauben* distinguished above, for one main lesson we have learned is that believing in modern philosophical English is not synonymous with *glauben* in Kant's eighteenth-century German.

We first noted that one modern usage of "belief" or "acceptance" can be identified with Kant's *fürwahrhalten*:

Belief 1—to hold or take a proposition to be true.

A subspecies of this is "mere belief," as contrasted with knowledge; which would be the union of Kant's *meinen* and *glauben*:

Belief 2—to hold a proposition to be true while acknowledging that one does not know it.

This includes beliefs about the future (which it is also quite natural to describe as "faith") that go beyond the presently available evidence, as in "I believe that Bertram will be faithful to me," or "that the policy of our Party will be vindicated," or "that biotechnology stocks will give a good return over the next five years," where we understand that future evidence may falsify the relevant claim. There can also be beliefs about past matters of fact where no verification or falsification by any new evidence can realistically be expected, e.g., that Irvine and Mallory reached the summit of Everest before dying on the descent, that the last Neanderthals died in a cave in Gibraltar about 30,000 BCE, or that Jesus was born of a virgin. We also noted the rather idiosyncratic usage of "I believe so" to express the acceptance of something on the basis of testimony (*glauben* 3):

Belief 3—to hold a proposition on the basis of testimony, rather than any more direct evidence about the relevant states of affairs.

(This need not be a subspecies of Belief 2, if the person accepts that knowledge via testimony is sometimes possible.) Then there was the Bayesian conception of belief as subjective probability, with degrees that can be estimated by the subject's dispositions to action (*glauben* 5):

Belief 4—to hold a proposition with a certain degree of strength, measurable by the person's dispositions to action (given her values), in particular her willingness to accept bets at certain odds.

This is not so much a subspecies, but a different conception of beliefs in general, or at least of those kinds for which a bet can be laid with a definite condition for payoff.

There are some apparently empirical claims that do not admit of decisive verification or falsification because of their generality or vagueness, but that some people may maintain as a guide to attitude and action (though not with any measureable degree of strength), for example "Every person is capable of recognizing what he or she has done wrong, regretting it, and making a new start," or (more prejudicially) "No white (or black, or brown, or yellow) person is completely trustworthy," or (crazily) "If you step on the cracks in the paving stones, something bad may happen to you." I suggest the following conception, a gloss on Kant's *glauben* 2, to identify this kind of belief or faith:

Belief 5—to hold a proposition, realizing that one can never have sufficient evidence to claim knowledge of it (or of its negation), while maintaining a firm commitment to it as a reason for certain principles of action.

Belief 5 represents, I suggest, Kant's main intention in his talk of *Glaube*. But to identify this rather special propositional attitude is not yet to identify any appropriate objects for it—though my examples above suggest that some distinction between appropriate and inappropriate objects can be made, and I will offer some support for the first example, involving belief in people's freewill, at the end of essay 9. Perhaps Kant's most controversial contribution in this area is his account of religious faith as belief in this fifth sense in claims about nonempirical, transcendent matters, namely, the existence of God and an afterlife, which he argued with dubious plausibility, are necessary presuppositions of thoroughgoing moral commitment. But those are topics for another occasion.[26]

Freedom of Judgment in Descartes, Spinoza, Hume, and Kant

Is our judgment of the truth value of propositions subject to the will? Do we have any voluntary control over the formation of our beliefs, and if so, how does it compare with the control we have over our actions? These questions lead into interestingly unclear philosophical and psychological territory. In this essay I first examine the classic early modern discussions in Descartes, Spinoza, and Hume. Then I review relevant themes in Kant, including some lesser-known material from his lectures on logic. Kant's critical philosophy makes important appeal to the notion of spontaneity, but I think our discussion will enable us to distinguish as many as five different flavors of it. I hope thus to clarify the differences between the freedom of judgments and of actions.

I. THE TEXTBOOK CONTRAST BETWEEN CARTESIAN VOLUNTARISM AND SPINOZEAN/HUMEAN DETERMINISM ABOUT JUDGMENT

Descartes famously claimed that our mental acts of judgment (some of them, at least) are under the control of the will. In his "Method of Doubt," set out in the *Discourse on the Method* and the first Meditation, he proposed the deliberate suspension of ordinary perceptual beliefs as Pyrrho had done in ancient times, though Descartes recommends this skepticism only as a first stage in inquiry, to be overcome later. In the fourth Meditation he diagnoses the cause of our cognitive errors as lying in our "cognitive sin"[1])— our failure to restrain our free power of assent to those cases in which we rationally ought to exercise it, namely, when we have "clear and distinct perceptions":

> When I look more closely at myself and inquire into the nature of my errors...I notice that they depend on two concurrent causes, namely, on the faculty of knowledge which is in me, and on the faculty of choice or freedom of the will; that is, they depend both on the intellect and the will simultaneously. Now all that the intellect does is to enable me to perceive the ideas which are subjects for possible judgments; and when regarded strictly in this light it turns out to contain no error....
>
> If...I simply refrain from making a judgment in cases where I do not perceive the truth with sufficient clarity and distinctness, then it is clear that I am behaving correctly and avoiding error. But if in such cases I either affirm or deny, then I am not using my free will correctly.[2]

Spinoza, writing a generation after Descartes, flatly rejected this alleged freedom of the will, whether in judgment or in action, and embraced a thoroughgoing determinism about everything mental:

> There is in the mind no absolute, i.e., no free, will, but the mind is determined to will this or that by a cause, which is again determined by another, and that again by another, and so on to infinity.
>
> (*Ethics* II.48)

> Human beings think themselves to be free insofar as they are conscious of their volitions and of their appetite, and do not even dream of the causes by which they are led to appetition and to will, since they are ignorant of them.
>
> (*Ethics* Appendix to Part I)

In the next century Hume also denied freedom of the will in judgment, but in the context of a radically empiricist approach to human nature. According to Descartes and Spinoza, the ability to make judgments (i.e., the faculty of "intellect" or "reason") is unique to human beings, so there is no question of ascribing judgments or beliefs to animals. But Hume proposed to deal with human and animal mentality in the same way, treating beliefs as involuntary mental states that are caused by repeated patterns of sensory stimulation, and that in turn cause behavior. In the section "Of the Reason of Animals," which concludes his revolutionary treatment of induction and causation in Book I, Part 3 of the *Treatise of Human Nature*, he wrote:

> No truth appears to me more evident, than that beasts are endow'd with thought and reason as well as men.

> ...'Tis from the resemblance of the external actions of animals to those we ourselves perform, that we judge their internal likewise to resemble ours....
>
> ...When any hypothesis, therefore, is advanc'd to explain a mental operation, which is common to men and beasts, we must apply the same hypothesis to both....
>
> Beasts certainly never perceive any real connexion amongst objects.
>
> ...'Tis therefore by means of custom alone, that experience operates upon them. All this was sufficiently evident with respect to man. But with respect to beasts there cannot be the least suspicion of mistake; which must be own'd to be a strong confirmation, or rather an invincible proof of my system.
>
> (*Treatise* 1.3.16)

And in the Appendix he explicitly rejects voluntarism about belief:

> Belief consists merely in a certain feeling or sentiment; in something, that depends not on the will, but must arise from certain determinate causes and principles, of which we are not masters.
>
> (Appendix to the *Treatise*)

At first sight, then, whereas Descartes ascribes as much freedom to our judgment of propositions as to our choice of actions, Spinoza and Hume ascribe just as *little* freedom to each. The only sort of mental freedom that Hume admits is what he calls "the liberty of spontaniety [*sic*]"—the absence of "violence" or other kinds of external causes such as threats, as opposed to "the liberty of indifference"—the absence of *all* causes, which is the notion of an act of will (a judgment or decision) that is undetermined by its preceding states of affairs (*Treatise* 2.3.2). Spinoza would endorse that. According to Hume, "the union betwixt motives and actions has the same constancy, as that in any natural operations," and there is the same sort of "union" between perceptions and beliefs. In both cases it consists in an experienced constant conjunction of As followed by Bs, which leads to a mental habit of inferring from As to Bs. That, notoriously, seems to be all Hume meant by causal connection—though Spinoza would not agree, having a much stronger account of causation. Yet despite the differences between our three philosophers, they appear to agree on the counterintuitive claim that our beliefs enjoy the same degree of freedom as our actions: a high degree for Descartes, and a very low degree for Spinoza and Hume.

II. A CLOSER LOOK AT DESCARTES'S ACCOUNT

On more extensive reading, however, the contrast between Descartes and Hume turns out to be not quite so stark, for they both make significant qualifications to their bolder statements. Descartes does not merely say that we *ought* to believe what is clearly and distinctly presented to us; he claimsthat we cannot do otherwise, since whatever is thus presented is "irresistible" to our judgment. Admittedly, in Meditation One he seems prepared to apply his method of doubt even to simple mathematical and logical propositions, although these later turn out to be his paradigms of what can be clearly and distinctly presented. Perhaps he is assuming at the first stage of his inquiry that such propositions are not *yet* presented clearly and distinctly (i.e., with their proofs), but have merely been accepted on authority. Even after the *cogito* argument of Meditation Two, he still allows (at the beginning of the third Meditation) the slight or "metaphysical" possibility that "some God could have given me such a nature that I was deceived even in matters which seemed most evident." That doubt does not get finally resolved until after the proofs (later in Meditation Three, and in Meditation Five) of the existence of an omnipotent and benevolent God, who will guarantee the reliability of our faculties when we use them properly.[3]

The relevant point for this paper is that Descartes is committed to saying that at *some* stage of inquiry there is a peculiarly convincing way in which a proposition can be presented to the intellect ("clearly and distinctly," "by the natural light") such that one has no choice but to assent to it. He usually seems to assume that one can always *tell* whether one is perceiving something clearly and distinctly, but in the third Meditation he admits that one might only *think* so, and in the seventh set of Replies he admits that "it requires some care to make a proper distinction between what is clearly and distinctly perceived and what merely seems or appears to be" (AT VII 36 and 461–62). That suggests that one *can* always make the distinction correctly if one pays sufficiently careful introspective attention to the manner in which the proposition is presented. If Descartes were to allow that one can never know for certain whether one is perceiving a proposition clearly and distinctly, the bottom would fall out of his whole epistemology, for he would be unable ever to *apply* his rule that whatever is perceived clearly and distinctly is true. He must be assuming that one can *sometimes know* that one is indeed perceiving p clearly and distinctly, and hence know beyond all possible doubt that p is true. And for the negations of such propositions, if presented equally clearly and distinctly, there will be no choice but to *reject* them. His alleged freedom of judgment can therefore apply only to propositions for which neither they nor their negations are clearly and distinctly perceived (though they may be supported by evidence that is less than conclusive, e.g., by testimony or probabilistic reasoning).

Descartes claims that this mental freedom, limited as it may be in the range of propositions to which it applies, is so "complete" that he cannot conceive that any mind could have any greater freedom, though he can

readily allow that a divine being may possess the mental faculties of understanding, memory, and imagination in greater degree than we do:

> Although God's will is incomparably greater than mine [in virtue of His knowledge and
> power, and the range to which His will applies] it does not seem any greater than mine
> when considered as will in the essential and strict sense. This is because the will simply
> consists in our ability to do or not do something (that is, to affirm or deny, to pursue or
> avoid).[4]

Descartes thus implies that in any situation in which we are deciding what
to do, or what to believe when a proposition is *not* perceived clearly and
distinctly, we have a two-way ability to act or not to act, to assent or not. Yet
in the very same sentence he goes on to say something different:

> Or rather it consists simply in the fact that when the intellect puts something forward for
> affirmation or denial or for pursuit or avoidance, our inclinations are such that we do not
> feel we are determined by any external force.
>
> (AT VII 57)

But this invites the objection that the absence of any *awareness* of "determination by an external force" does not prove the nonexistence of any such
determination. In making our judgments, we may smoothly follow our
rational "inclinations," i.e., our reasons, with no feeling of being pushed
around or forced by anything external to ourselves. Yet this does not show
that we could have made a different judgment: it does not prove that we
have the power *to decide either way*, as Descartes said in the first part of his
sentence.

As if aware of his vulnerability to this objection (soon to be voiced by
both Spinoza and Hume)[5] Descartes then veers off on another track and
suggests that a two-way power is not crucial for judgment after all:

> In order to be free, there is no need for me to be inclined both ways; on the contrary the
> more I incline in one direction—either because I clearly understand that reasons of
> truth or goodness point that way, or because of a divinely produced disposition of my
> inmost thoughts—the freer is my choice. Neither divine grace nor natural knowledge
> ever diminishes freedom; on the contrary, they increase and strengthen it.
>
> (AT VII 57–58)

He seems to be switching notions of freedom here without realizing that he
is doing so, in very much the way that Henry Sidgwick diagnosed in Kant.[6]
Up to this point Descartes has been thinking of what Sidgwick called
"Neutral" or "Moral Freedom," i.e., the two-way power to do something

rational or irrational, good or bad. But now he seems to jump to Sidgwick's "Good" or "Rational Freedom," which is the quite different concept of a one-way ability to do the rational or good thing, with no implication that there is any ability to choose an alternative. A symptom of the switch is Descartes's sudden use of a comparative notion of freedom ("freer"), which is surely inconsistent with his already-noted affirmation that his freedom is so great that he cannot conceive a greater. It fits well, however, with Sidgwick's talk of Rational Freedom as the kind "which a man is said to manifest more of in proportion as he acts more under the guidance of reason" (1901:512).[7]

Descartes continues: "the indifference which I feel when there is no reason pushing me in one direction rather than another is the lowest grade of freedom" (fourth Meditation, AT VII 57). This sounds like what Sidgwick called "Capricious Freedom," which he defined as the power of acting without a motive (1901:512)—though it might be better thought of as the ability to choose between two opposing motives or reasons that are exactly balanced in strength (and thus to solve the dilemma of Buridan's ass by "plumping" for one of two equidistant and equally luscious bundles of hay).

Within this single paragraph Descartes anticipates these three different conceptions of freedom in a compressed, inexplicit way. His retreat from the first to the second suggests some awareness that insistence on a two-way power of judgment is going to be difficult to defend. But elsewhere he insists that we possess Neutral Freedom of judgment for all propositions for which neither they nor their negations are presented clearly and distinctly. As we have noted, he proposes as a crucial part of his method the suspension of all beliefs based on perception, memory, and testimony, and he reaffirms this as *epistemically obligatory* in Meditation Four (AT VII 59–60). In at least one place he went so far as to say it is *self-evident* that we have such freedom:

> That there is freedom in our will, and that we have power in many cases to give or withhold assent at will, is so evident that it must be counted among the first and most common notions that are innate in us.[8]

This statement contains the rather vague qualifying clause "in many cases," but if those cases include paradigm factual beliefs based directly on perception, I can only say that this is an example of one philosopher finding self-evident what others think false, and even self-evidently false! If on the other hand the "many cases" are restricted to those in which the evidence for and against a proposition is finely balanced, then Descartes's claim about freedom of judgment becomes less counterintuitive, but less striking. I think we are finding that his extreme voluntarism about judgment tends to moderate or evaporate under pressure.

Before leaving Descartes we should also note how he carefully adjusted the presentation of his thought to the real-world political and religious context in which he lived. The "Dedicatory Letter" and opening sentences of the *Meditations* make it clear that his project of freeing himself temporarily from all practical concerns and conducting the very unusual kind of theoretical exercise of subjecting all beliefs to the method of doubt is not something that he recommends to everyone. Nor does he intend it to affect his own practical life: this is made explicit in the *Discourse*, where he sets out a "code of morals" by which to live while pursuing his research program:

> The first was to obey the laws and customs of my country, adhering firmly to the faith in which, by the grace of God, I had been educated from my childhood, and regulating my conduct in every other matter according to the most moderate opinions.[9]

Thus in framing his inquiry Descartes conspicuously places the dogmas of the Catholic religion outside the scope of his method of doubt. Although he later tries to prove the existence of God and the immateriality of the soul by reason alone, he here accepts the revealed articles of Christian faith on authority. After the Papal condemnation of Galileo's sun-centered astronomy, Descartes was very cautious, even somewhat devious, in the presentation of his own scientific system, which contained a similar heliocentric cosmology. Whenever dispute with the Church threatened, he offered a nonrealist interpretation of his scientific theories as merely explanatory *hypotheses*, descriptions of possible worlds, not competitors for belief as literally true.[10]

In the *Discourse*, Descartes shrewdly goes on to say that to ascertain people's real opinions one ought to take notice of what they *do* rather than what they say, thus recognizing a conceptual tie between belief and action that is not apparent on the radically first-person approach he takes when laying the foundations of his philosophy. In the second of his provisional maxims he resolves to be firm and resolute in action: although one often has to act on beliefs that are probable rather than certain, it does not follow that one should act hesitantly, for indecision and wavering are unlikely to achieve anything at all. On these pragmatic points (though obviously not on religion) Descartes's thought approaches nearer to Hume's.

III. SPINOZA ON JUDGMENT AND FREEDOM OF THE WILL

Spinoza differs radically from both Descartes and Hume. His thought-world is obviously alien to that of Hume in its deeply entrenched rationalism. This involves more than the common view that the human mind is capable of rational insight (or "intuition") into the necessary truth of logical and mathematical propositions. Hume would agree with that, while adding that mere relations of ideas (Kant's analytic truths) do not tell us anything about the world. Spinoza maintains an extreme form of rationalism that is very implausible to us contemporary readers who take for granted the empirical basis of all factual and scientific knowledge. In this he went beyond Descartes, who allowed that science must appeal to observation and experiment, as well as the systematic use of reason. In the *Ethics* Spinoza systematically expressed his ultra-rationalist faith that if we properly conceive all the contents of the world (attaining what he calls "adequate ideas" of things), then we would be able to "perceive" (i.e., to understand) why everything *must* be as it is, how each state of affairs follows, not just by contingent causal laws but *by logical necessity*, from the preceding state of the world (*Ethics* I.29, I.33, Scholium 2 to II.40). The thought is that our reliance on perception, memory, and testimony for knowledge of particular states of affairs, and on inductive reasoning for our knowledge of laws of nature, could *in principle* be replaced by rational insight plus purely logical or mathematical reasoning.

Spinoza differs from Descartes in being a monist rather than a dualist about mind and a thoroughgoing determinist about everything mental. He holds that there is no mental act or event without a sufficient preceding cause, whether inside or outside the mind (*Ethics* II.48). My business here is to examine his position on the question of voluntary control over judgment and belief. As we have already seen, if that is taken to involve uncaused mental acts, he denies any such possibility. Spinoza's arguments for his position involve certain peculiarities of his philosophy of mind. In the Scholium to II.48 he says that by "will" he understands "the faculty by which the mind affirms or denies what is true or what is false, and not the desire by which the mind desires things or has an aversion to them"; and the eccentricity of this view comes out dramatically when he states that "will and intellect are one and the same thing" (Corollary to II.49). This is so counter to the standard understanding of mental faculties that one wonders what can be going on! Is Spinoza using the term "will" with a different meaning? Could his difference from our usual conception more than verbal?

Spinoza cannot deny that we desire things that are not the case, and may be averse to something that *is* the case. But we can desire something without actually *willing* it, for we can have idle wishes that we do not or cannot act on; and we may have *some* desires that we resolve *never* to act on! Is Spinoza implying that the everyday concepts of forming an intention, trying to do something, choosing one course of action from several options, and with them the notion of human action itself, have no proper application? Surely not: in the fascinating Scholium to III.2 he writes of "decrees of the mind."

I take it he is not denying that we make choices and decisions and do things intentionally, but is claiming that all these familiar mental events or acts or actions have causes of which we are unaware, so they are not free in the sense of being uncaused, i.e., we *never* have the two-way power of "Neutral Freedom," even when we think we do.

Spinoza applies this to *all* mental events, including judgments on propositions as well as decisions to act: all such "volitions" are determined by preceding causes. Moreover he is committed to a mind-body identity thesis, according to which all mental acts are identical with bodily events (which may now be identifiable in the brain and central nervous system, in the light of progress in neuroscience whose general direction Spinoza foresaw):

> The decree of the mind, and the appetite and the determination of the body, are simultaneous in nature, or rather are one and the same thing, which when it is considered under the attribute of thought and is explained through the same we call a decree, and when it is considered under the attribute of extension and is deduced from the laws of motion and rest, we call a determination. (*Ethics* Scholium to III.2; see also Scholium to II.7)

A crucial question this raises is how such thoroughgoing materialism and determinism about the *causation* of judgments can be consistent with our having *reasons* for them.[11] Spinoza will not allow that we have two-way "Neutral Freedom" in judgment; in his view, we can only have "Rational Freedom," the ability to judge as the reasons direct us. Even to call this an "ability" can be misleading, for his claim is that on each particular occasion of judging a person has no ability to judge in any other way than as she does, though of course she might have thought differently had the circumstances been relevantly different. Each particular act of judgment is determined by the subject's preceding mental and physical states.[12] Spinoza must be committed to thinking of each act of judgment as both rationally determined by the subject's awareness of the reasons for it and causally determined by the physiological states that embody her awareness of those reasons—these being the two sides of the mental/physical unity that we are.

Spinoza has an eccentric understanding of judgment itself, for one of his theorems asserts: "There is in the mind no volition, or, no affirmation and negation, apart from that which an idea involves in so far as it is an idea" (*Ethics* II.49). His proof of this begins: "There is in the mind...no absolute faculty of willing and being unwilling; there exist in it only particular volitions, namely, this and that affirmation, and this and that negation." As noted, he draws the corollary that "will and intellect are one and the same," and in another of his extended "scholia" or comments (which tend to reveal more of his thinking than the very abstractly stated "propositions" and "demonstrations") he tries to refute a series of objections to that counterintuitive claim. Part of our puzzlement can be reduced by realizing that Spinoza uses the term "idea" for an *activity* of the mind, rather than its object. But we still have to ask what he means by "volition." If he understands volitions as acts or exercises of will, his definition of the will as the faculty of affirming and denying would imply that volitions are acts of affirmation or denial. Indeed, he uses as an example of volition the "mode of thinking by which the mind affirms that the three angles of a triangle are equal to two right angles" (Demonstration of II.49).

But to identify mental judgments (which have propositions as their objects) with nonpropositional concepts is to invite confusion. Spinoza goes on to claim that the affirmation that the three angles of a triangle are equal to two right angles involves the idea of a triangle, and conversely that that the idea of a triangle must involve that affirmation. Even allowing his eccentric usage of "idea" to mean a mental action, there is a problem here. The first involvement is indisputable; but the second is very questionable, for someone can have the concept of a triangle (and thereby affirm—or have a "volition"—that it has three angles) *without* realizing that those three angles add up to two right angles; similarly, one can have the idea (or "volition") of a right-angled triangle without knowing Pythagoras's theorem, or of a prime number without knowing that there are infinitely many primes.

In general, we have concepts without realizing all their logical implications. Otherwise there could be no such thing as mathematical or logical discovery, finding a proof that nobody else knew (or at least that one had not seen for oneself). Spinoza may want to say that an "adequate" or perfect conception of something would involve knowing or affirming *all* its logical entailments (which are infinitely many)—but then it would follow that no human mind, being finite, has an "adequate" conception of anything! At this point we have to acknowledge that his ultra-rationalist ideal of basing all knowledge on intuitive insight into the essences of things is humanly impossible. For in the very citadel of rationalism—the practice of mathematical or logical reasoning itself—there lies an inherent limitation on our mental powers to attain the kind of completely adequate conception that Spinoza sought. His fundamental claim that "the order and connection of ideas is the same as the order and connection of things" (*Ethics* II.7) thus comes into doubt.

Spinoza bites the rationalist bullet when he denies that we have "Capricious Freedom," and predicts that not just an ass, but even a man, placed exactly equidistant from food and drink, will perish of hunger and thirst (Scholium to II.49). So a Spinozean rationalist, confronted in the supermarket by two cans of beans of equal quality and price, will find himself paralyzed, totally unable to choose between them! This is a *reduction ad absurdum* of rationalism in action: we obviously need to make some such arbitrary choices in many practical matters. If Spinoza had been more cautious, he might have said that we do not have "Capricious Freedom" *in judgment*, i.e., when the available evidence is equally balanced for and against a proposition, what we are rationally and causally determined to do is to *withhold* judgment. Presumably that is how we *should* judge such cases, but in practice the influence of emotion has to be taken into account, for there certainly seems to be such a thing as wish-fulfilling judgment.

IV. A CLOSER LOOK AT HUME'S ACCOUNT OF BELIEF
AND REFLECTION

Let us now return to Hume, to examine the qualifications he makes to his apparently behaviorist and involuntarist account of belief. In a less frequently cited section of the *Treatise* entitled "Of the Probability of Causes" (1.3.12) he acknowledges that in human beings "reflection" *as well as* the association of ideas by animal-like habit can influence the formation and strength of our beliefs.

> A contrariety of events in the past [Hume means a mixed course of experience, in which As have sometimes, but not always, been followed by Bs] may give us a kind of hesitating belief for the future after two several ways. *First,* By producing an imperfect [i.e., weaker] habit and transition from the present impression [of a new A] to the related idea [of a new B].[13]

He claims, however, that this first "principle" is not what most often influences our mind in our probable reasonings; rather,

> We commonly take *knowingly* [my italics] into consideration the contrariety of past events; we compare the different sides of the contrariety, and carefully weigh the experiments, which we have on each side: Whence we may conclude, that our reasonings of this kind arise not *directly* from the habit, but in an *oblique* manner; which we must now endeavour to explain.
>
> (*Treatise* 1.3.12)

Hume goes on to give one of his imagistic or associationist accounts of how the human mind works, suggesting that a number of agreeing images render an idea more lively, while dissimilar ones weaken it. He then says (with dubious consistency—for his quasi-automatic account of these mental processes does not make them sound very like *reasoning*) that this is "the second species of probability, where we *reason with knowledge and reflection* from a contrariety of past experiments." In a contrast of

10,000 cases on one side and 10,001 on the other, it must be the judgment rather than any discernible difference of "liveliness" of images that gives a slight preference to the latter. And near the beginning of the section he says that

> the mind, having form'd another observation concerning the connexion of causes and effects, gives new force to its reasoning from that observation; and by means of it can build an argument on a single experiment, when duly prepar'd and examin'd.
>
> (*Treatise* 1.3.12)

Indeed, he had already written:

> 'Tis certain, that not only in philosophy [by which Hume means natural science], but even in common life, we may attain the knowledge of a particular cause merely by one experiment, provided it be made with judgment, and after a careful removal of all foreign and superfluous circumstances.
>
> (*Treatise* 1.3.8)

Thus the Hume who so famously places such emphasis on the nonrational effects of past experience ("custom"), and the similarity between animal and human mentality in this respect, does after all admit that there is a limited but nonzero role for reasoning in human belief formation. This allows him to treat some scientific and ordinary life inferences as genuine reasoning rather than the blind association of ideas. At several points elsewhere he admits that "reflection" does have some influence on human belief: it can *correct* the influence of mere custom (*Treatise* 1.3.13, 1.4.6), or detect the *fallacy* of a previously accepted opinion (1.4.2). This use of rationally normative language makes a very substantial qualification to the purely naturalist account of belief usually attributed to Hume, which he likes to present in iconoclastic, headline-grabbing form:

> The truth of my hypothesis, that all our reasonings concerning causes and effects are deriv'd from nothing but custom; and that that belief is more properly an act of the sensitive, than of the cogitative part of our natures.
>
> (*Treatise* 1.4.1)[14]

But his admissions about the rational role of reflection surely require him to qualify that last statement, to say that "the sensitive part of our natures" has a more fundamental and more common role in belief formation than "the cogitative part"—but *not that the latter has no role at all.* Where Hume makes a quiet (and often unnoticed) qualification to his strident empiricism, Kant puts the role of reason at center stage, as we shall see.

In the *Enquiry concerning the Human Understanding*, Hume again assimilated human inductive reasoning to animal learning:

> Animals, therefore, are not guided in these inferences by reasoning: Neither are children: Neither are the generality of mankind, in their ordinary actions and conclusions: Neither are philosophers themselves, who, in all the active parts of life, are, in the main, the same with the vulgar, and are governed by the same maxims.[15]

Notice, however, that the qualifying phrase "in the main" allows that philosophers (and scientists) do perform *some* reasoning even in the "active" parts of their lives! There is a lengthy footnote to this section, in which Hume asks how "men so much surpass animals in reasoning, and one man so much surpasses another," and lists nine ways in which one person's mental abilities, education, and dispositions may differ from another's; after this, he says, "the reason of the difference between men and animals will easily be comprehended." But that sounds like a putting of the human cart before the animal horse. Descartes and Spinoza would have objected (and we who have read Chomsky are likely to agree) that the gulf between reason in humans and its absence from animals dwarfs the differences between the various degrees of human intelligence and education. By "reason," Descartes meant that degree of intelligence that is manifested in the language use and activity of all mentally normal humans.[16] Just how a normative account of human reasoning can be integrated with a scientific, causal account of the mind's operations is of course a fundamental question for Hume and for any subsequent form of naturalism. (We have seen it arising for Spinoza's rationalist monism, too, and we will find Kant addressing it in his own peculiar way.)

Hume has his own normative recommendations about what, in the light of philosophical reflection, we should and should not believe: though we cannot resist our natural tendencies to form beliefs on the basis of our experience of constant conjunctions,[17] we can and should control our equally "natural" tendencies[18] to believe whatever people tell us[19]—especially the dogmas of religion.[20] In these areas at least, Hume takes it that we have some power to moderate our credulous dispositions by rational reflection.

We can carry forward the thought that there is a difference of kind rather than degree between human beliefs and belief-like states in animals. The use of language and the capacity for conscious reflection are obviously connected with this distinction. Any concept of a representational state in a creature that lacks language must be based on its dispositions to nonlinguistic behavior. And there is nothing to prevent the ascription of this kind of mental state to creatures that *also* have language.

As noted in essays 2 and 3, we humans have many animal-level perceptions manifested in our behavioral and emotional reactions, e.g., the
tennis player's seeing the ball coming from a certain direction at a certain
velocity, an infant's perception of a facial expression or tone of voice as
loving or as angry, and our adult awareness of other people's emotions,
moods, and attitudes to which we are behaviorally sensitive, but for which
we may lack words (or *precise* words). Animals obviously do not evaluate
reasons or evidence for their belief-like representational states, and there
is no question of their having rational control over them; and we do not
seem to have any direct voluntary powerover those of our mental states
that are like animal perceptions. To that extent, Hume was right. But
Descartes and Spinoza were surely also right to emphasize that human
language, rationality, and self-consciousness give us distinctively rational
kinds of belief formation and belief assessment, over which we have some
degree of control—though hardly the wide-ranging suspension of judgment that Descartes claimed to practice.[21]

V. JUDGMENT AND THE WILL IN KANT'S LOGIC LECTURES

In his published works Kant rarely touched on the question whether the
will can influence judgment or belief. But in his "Logic" lectures,[22] from
which student notes from various years have come down to us,[23] he
addressed the topic explicitly. In the *Blomberg Logic* (from the early 1770s),
there is, as far as I know, his most extensive treatment of our topic. He poses
the question

> Whether our free choice has an influence on whether we *give* our approval to a cognition
> [i.e., judge it to be true], or *withdraw* it from it [i.e., judge it to be false], or whether we
> even *withhold* it [i.e., suspend judgment].
>
>   Answer. In most cases, such a procedure of giving our approval, or withdrawing it, or
> holding it back, does not rest at all on our free choice, but rather is necessitated through
> and by the laws of our understanding and our reason.[24]

Kant says that someone who sees from his accounts that he owes more than
he possesses cannot believe otherwise (much as he might like to), for he is
"too evidently convinced of the correctness of the arithmetic." We cannot
quite so *easily* avoid painful truths by choosing to believe the opposite, when
faced with manifest evidence; though people are prone to form wish-fulfilling beliefs in situations in which the evidence is not so manifest. The qualifying phrases "in most cases" in the above quotation, and "if not utterly
impossible" in the next, suggest that the will can *sometimes* influence belief:

This free *arbitrium* in regard to approval...disappears entirely, and in the presence of certain degrees of the grounds it is always very hard, if not utterly impossible, to withhold one's approval.

(24:157–58)

In this last statement a further qualification is suggested, namely, that it is only very *high* degrees of evidence such as simple mathematical reasoning (or Cartesian "clear and distinct perception"?) that absolutely rule out voluntary control over judgment. But Kant also cites situations in which the subject cannot but believe an *empirical* proposition (e.g., when your employer has just personally dismissed you, you can hardly doubt that you have lost your job); so he is not setting the standard of certainty quite as high as Descartes did: Kant does not doubt short-term memory, nor does he dally with the possibility that one might be dreaming.

The will can certainly have an *indirect* influence on belief formation:

Although approval does not depend *immediately* on men's choice, it nevertheless often does depend on it *indirectly, mediately*, since it is according to one's free wish that he seeks out those grounds that could in any way bring about approval for this or that cognition.

(24:158)

In any deliberate investigation (whether in science, detective work, or the mere opening of an envelope) it is our actions (the paradigms of free choice) that causally contribute to our acquiring evidence that may result in our making judgments and forming beliefs. This indirect influence of the will through choice of investigative actions obviously has to be agreed on all sides, but it is not at the center of our philosophical inquiry.

Kant explicitly mentions the possibility of wish-fulfilling belief, which would explain why he kept a chink open for a more direct influence of the will:

It is certain, of course, that in the human soul there occurs an arbitrary direction of the powers of mind towards what we would like to see and what we wish for.

We give our approval at once to a cognition that is agreeable and pleasant to us, without even taking the trouble to investigate more closely the proper, true grounds for taking it to be true.

If something is very weighty for us and of very great importance, so that a great part, indeed, even the greatest part of our peace of mind and of our external well-being and happiness depends upon it, then in this case the mind is just not free enough to consider the matter indifferently and impartially from both sides....And, on the other hand, we soon reject and disapprove what could cause us harm or sickness.

(24:158–59)

Kant hazards some further generalizations about human dispositions to form beliefs irresponsibly. There is, he says, "an insatiable desire that prevails among many so-called philosophers or dogmatists to decide every question without the slightest investigation" (this remark confirms his strong antipathy to the empty controversies of the schools). And in all of mankind, there are what Kant calls "affects" (i.e., sudden rushes of emotion that threaten rational self-control):

> These perverters of man, which in common life produce so much disorder, are in no less a position to confuse man's understanding and lead it into errors. Now these affects of man direct the grounds of certainty concerning a thing solely to one side, and they do not allow him to consider the other side as well. Thus we can of course blame someone who has given approval to a false cognition, namely, when the responsibility actually lies with him for rejecting those grounds that could have convinced him of the object of the cognition he has, and could have freed him from his error.
>
> (24:160)

In these last two passages we can discern between the lines Sidgwick's concept of Rational Freedom. When someone has strong desires or emotions about something, they may prevent him "considering the other side as well," and he may be described as "not free enough to consider the matter indifferently and impartially." Kant sees our more violent emotions (the "affects") as *disturbing* causes that tend to stop us following the lead of evidence and reasoning, whereas Rational Freedom would seem to imply a disposition to consider matters according to evidence and reasons, and hence imply the absence of two-way Neutral Freedom. Yet in allowing that we may *blame* someone who makes a false judgment through partiality, Kant seems to think of the subject as misusing his Neutral Freedom by rejecting or failing to consider relevant evidence. Should we blame the subject, if we think that his emotional state made it *impossible* for him to judge the evidence properly? That would seem to go against our notion of justice. Or does Kant mean we should not blame him for his particular errors, but rather criticize his disposition or character that results in such partial and erroneous judgments? But can we *make* this distinction in practice? How can we decide whether a given person was *capable* of considering a certain matter impartially? Kant was skeptical about the possibility of knowing people's motives for actions, including our supposed *self-knowledge* (footnote to A551/B579), so we might expect him to be equally chary of making judgments about people's mental capacities on the theoretical side.

If all this is to be consistent with what Kant says about how "in most cases" we have no choice but to judge as the evidence directs, he will have to set some standard of evidence against which wish-fulfilling belief is impossible. In one place he tries to do this:

> Only mathematics and pure and immediate experience are of such a kind that they leave us no grounds for their opposite.
>
> All of our other cognitions, on the other hand, are of such a kind that they quite frequently offer us grounds of proof for maintaining the opposite of a thing that are just as great as the grounds of proofs for accepting the thing.
>
> (24:160)

But what is to count as "pure and immediate experience"? It sounds very like Cartesian "clear and distinct perception," but we have already seen that Kant must have had a less demanding standard in mind. In a slippery slope of degrees of empirical evidence, it is not obvious where to put in a marker and say that below it our emotional states can influence our judgments and above it they cannot. But perhaps we can help Kant out with the suggestion that a non-Cartesian conception of "pure and immediate experience" can include the evidence of the unimpeded senses, of confident memory, and of unanimous testimony that there is no reason to impugn, i.e., "the given" in the wider sense considered in essay 4.

Lecture notes from Kant's later years touch again on the relation between the will and judgment. In the *Vienna Logic* he investigates again to what extent our judgments depend on the will (24:859). And he is reported as saying:

> To withhold one's judgment is a faculty of a practiced power of judgment, and it is not to be found in beginners or youths, but only with increasing age. For our faculty of cognition is so desirous of extending itself that it tries with the greatest impatience to extend itself as soon as an opportunity offers itself. In young minds this inclination to accept the seeming as true is so great that they find it very hard to withhold their judgment. When they see, however, how one can be misled into making a judgment that one has to retract, i.e., when they are made more clever by much experience, then they suspend judgment more.
>
> (34:860)[25]

As we foresaw, Kant strongly emphasizes the power of our rational faculties, which can overcome the effects of imitation, custom, and desire, though it is very much up to us whether we actively use our reason rather than passively "go with the flow":

> All reason, as to its nature, is a self-active *principium* of thought, and even when I take experience as the ground in thinking, reason nonetheless makes universal rules of experience. The use of reason consists in self-activity, then, but the laziness of men makes

them prefer to proceed passively, rather than raising their power of cognition so far as to make use of their own powers.

(24:866)

This fits both with what Hume said about the power of reflection to correct our unreflectively formed beliefs, and with Spinoza's claim that our tendency is to believe in whatever we conceive of, unless counteracted by other considerations.

VI. KANT ON THE FREEDOM AND SPONTANEITY OF JUDGMENT

In his well-known but obscure discussion of freedom in section 3 of the *Groundwork* Kant appeals at one point to considerations about theoretical as well as practical reason. This passage might at first glance be taken as a robust statement of the freedom of judgment:

> One cannot possibly think of a reason that would consciously receive direction from any other quarter with respect to its judgments; since the subject would then attribute the determination of his judgment, not to his reason but to an impulse. Reason must regard itself as the author of its principles independently of alien influences.[26]

It is not obvious what Kant means by the phrases "from any other quarter,"[27] "impulse," or "alien influence." It is of course a well-known view of his that we should not accept things just because they are asserted by a supposed authority, whether political or religious or even academic: he vigorously asserts the right to think for oneself in defending the spirit of the Enlightenment.[28] But here in the *Groundwork* he is surely touching on the problem of relating reasons and causes, and is insisting on a more basic kind of autonomy, spontaneity, or self-directedness of human reason. His central point is that when one evaluates the truth value of a proposition, one cannot conceive of one's judgment as being brutely *caused* by preexisting states of affairs (whether inside or outside one's own mind) irrespective of what one is prepared to recognize as *reasons* for or against the proposition. We standardly conceive of our bodily *sensations* and *sense impressions* (pain, strain, heat, tickles, light, sound, etc.) as being caused[29] by physical events and states (whether inside or outside the body), so it makes no sense to talk of reasons for a sensation or sense impression. But beliefs have propositional contents, and when one makes a judgment, one commits oneself to the truth of a proposition, and (at least normally) to there being reasons for believing it.

There is, alas, plenty of empirical evidence that people can be induced by peer-group pressure, advertising, hypnosis, political reeducation, or torture to believe all sorts of things, against what would in more benign circumstances be their better judgment. But Kant's point is that reason cannot be *consciously* directed from outside: insofar as any such brainwashing succeeds, it has to make people think they have reasons for their new beliefs. When hypnotic subjects are asked why they believe or do something weird, they typically make some attempt at giving a reason, which observers may dismiss as "mere rationalization." Tyrants will hardly be satisfied if their victims say "I now believe p, but only because your minions have caused me to believe it," for that is to imply that one has no good reasons for the belief. Really effective mind controllers want their subjects to end up not only believing the preselected propositions but also thinking they have good reason to do so.

So far this seems to be robust realistic sense. But could Kant also mean (as Descartes tried to maintain) that even publicly available testimony or evidence counts as "direction from outside" that can be rejected by voluntary suspense of judgment, using our free inner power of will (two-way Neutral Freedom)? No, I take his view to be that when one has rational grounds (empirical evidence or reasoning) presented to one's attention, one's judgment should be based on the rational strength of those grounds, and not on any other sort of "decision" that, although sometimes possible, would be arbitrary or "capricious." A reason, far from being an "alien influence" on the mind, is precisely what *ought* to influence it. I submit that Kant's analysis shows us the defect in Descartes's view of the freedom of the will in judgment. The rational force of a ground or reason for believing p (a relation of logical entailment or inductive support between two *propositions*) must be compatible with a causal connection between the presentation of that reason to someone and their coming to believe p (a relation between two mental *events*). As against Spinoza, conceptual and causal connections need to be distinguished, though they had better be compatible.

On the other hand, as against Hume, Kant gives a much more conspicuous and central role to reasoning and conscious reflection in belief formation. He redraws our picture of the powers of the mind, replacing the manifestly inadequate Humean conception of "ideas" as faded copies of impressions by a sharp distinction between concepts and sensory impressions, and hence between judgment and mere sensory stimulation ("affection"). At crucial points in the first *Critique* Kant emphasizes the "spontaneity" or "self-activity" of conceptual thought, as opposed to the passive "receptivity" of sensibility:[30]

The combination of a manifold in general can never come to us through the senses...for it is an act of the spontaneity of the power of representation, and, since one must call the latter understanding...all combination...is an action of the understanding which we would designate with the general title synthesis.

> (B129–30; see also A97, A127, footnote to B158)

He writes in the *Prolegomena*:

> When an appearance is given us, we are still quite free as to how we should judge the matter. The appearances depend on the senses, but the judgment on the understanding; and the only question is whether in the determination of the object there is truth or not.[31]

Here he is not, I think, endorsing Descartes's alleged freedom to suspend all judgments based on perception. I suggest he is making the point that our judgments involve concepts as well as intuitions: so a judgment about what we perceive will depend not only on the present input to our senses, but on what concepts we have acquired (and in many cases, what else we know or believe about the situation). In *that* sense, the judgment is spontaneous, i.e., not determined by the sensory input alone.

However, Kant had more than one use for his term *Spontaneitat,* and therein lie some deep ambiguities in his philosophy. In his moral philosophy he lays enormous and ever-repeated stress on the distinction between two kinds of motives: our natural inclinations, and our recognition of moral duties. He vigorously defends the spontaneity or freedom of our will, both in particular practical decisions and in adopting or "incorporating" general principles of action ("maxims"). These themes recur throughout his critical philosophy. But he also talks of the spontaneity of the *understanding* in synthesizing the input from the senses, applying concepts, and making judgments. These are surely quite different kinds of "spontaneity," belonging to the philosophy of action and to epistemology, respectively. In making judgments we do not have the same sort of freedom that we have in deciding what to do, and the difference should not be swept under the carpet with a broad-brush notion of "spontaneity."

Introducing his proposed solution to the third antinomy between freedom and determinism, Kant writes:

> Freedom in the practical sense is the independence of the power of choice from necessitation by impulses of sensibility. For a power of choice is sensible insofar as it is pathologically affected (through moving-causes of sensibility); it is called an animal power of choice (*arbitrium brutum*) if it can be pathologically necessitated. The human power of choice is indeed an *arbitrium sensitivum,* yet not *brutum* but *liberum,* because sensibility does not render its action necessary, but in the human being there is a

faculty of determining oneself from oneself, independently of necessitation by sensuous impulses.

(A534/B562; see also A548/B576 and A803/B828–31)

Obviously this passage is about our power of choosing actions, not our propositional judgments. "Impulses of sensibility" here means natural desires or inclinations, which are bodily-based and connected with survival and reproduction. We share such desires with the animals, but unlike them we have choices whether and when and how to act on them: our actions are not necessitated by them.

But when Kant talks of reason as "a self-active *principium* of thought," and emphasizes how reason cannot be consciously directed "from outside," i.e., by mere sensibility and sensible affections, he is making a different point, about judgment and belief rather than action. He can be interpreted as saying that only a *belief* can be a reason for another belief, i.e., that justification cannot extend outside the space of reasons. "Sensibility" in this context refers to sensory *stimulation*, the causal foundation of the process of perception, and his contrast is between the conceptual and the sensory, rather than duty and desire. In both cases there is a kind of independence of the intellectual element from the sensuous one—hence the tendency to categorize both as "spontaneity." Kant's famous contrast of "the intelligible world" and the "sensible world" suffers from a parallel ambiguity, because there are two ways of interpreting the word "sensible"—as sensory stimulation, or as bodily-based desire—and also two ways of taking the word "intelligible"—as applying to reasons in general (for beliefs or actions) or to specifically *moral* reasons for action.[32]

There are still more uses of the term "spontaneity" in Kant. In stating the thesis of the third antinomy, he talks of "an absolute causal spontaneity beginning from itself a series of appearances that runs according to natural laws, hence transcendental freedom" (A446/B474). This is the notion of an uncaused cause—an event that, although it may be preceded by other events, is not caused by any of them, yet can itself be the cause of subsequent events. Kant notoriously claimed that the notion of practical freedom cannot be satisfied by a merely compatibilist account,[33] but requires absolute spontaneity (hence Neutral Freedom) at the unknowable noumenal level. But it is not so obvious that he has to give a parallel account of freedom of judgment: there Rational Freedom would seem to suffice. It has to be acknowledged, however, that there are ambiguities and obscurities in Kant's philosophy of mind; he was plainly reluctant to embrace anything like Spinoza's thoroughgoing determinism,[34] and he wanted to keep open the option of some sort of noumenalist metaphysics of mind, even if he maintained (most of the time!) that we cannot know anything about the noumenal aspects of ourselves (A379–80, B420).

Kant surely did philosophy a service by alerting us to the distinct explanatory roles of causes and reasons, when he distinguished between "causality in accordance with laws of nature" and another causality, that of "freedom" (A444/B472), i.e., "a mechanical causality...through bodily movements" and "a psychological causality through conceptions."[35] But he bequeathed to us the problem of how we are to make overall philosophical sense of the distinction between justification by reasons and explanation by causes—a problem with which we are still struggling. A lesson of the present discussion is that this problem arises just as much for propositional judgments as for practical decisions.

In chapter 3 of the *Groundwork* Kant alludes to yet another conception of spontaneity or "self-activity" in his critical philosophy:

> Now, a human being really finds in himself a capacity by which he distinguishes himself from all other things, even from himself insofar as he is affected by objects, and that is *reason*. This, as pure self-activity, is raised even above the *understanding* by this: that though the latter is also self-activity and does not, like sense, contain merely representations that arise when we are *affected* by things (and are thus passive), yet it can produce from its activity no other concepts than those which serve merely *to bring sensible representations under rules* and thereby to unite them in consciousness, without which use of sensibility it would think nothing at all; but reason, on the contrary, shows in what we call "ideas" a spontaneity so pure that it thereby goes so far beyond anything that sensibility can ever afford it.
>
> (4:452)

Here Kant distinguishes sharply between "understanding" and "reason." The former is the faculty for making judgments, and the most basic sort of judgments are those in which particular perceived items are brought under general concepts. The understanding can equally be called the faculty of concepts, since all judgments involve concept application, and the only use of concepts is in the making of judgments (A68/B93). In contrast, "reason" here emerges as the faculty of "ideas" in Kant's nonempiricist, indeed rather Platonic, sense of the term, namely, concepts that are so pure or ideal that they *cannot* be exemplified in experience (A546–47/B574–75). The making of judgments involves the basic sort of spontaneity, namely, the independence of the concepts thereby applied from the sensory stimulation received at the time (they may have been previously learned, or some of them may be innate, and some are a priori). But in those levels of thought that involve *ideals* Kant finds an even stronger kind of independence from sensory experience.

We are now in a position to list five different Kantian conceptions of spontaneity:[36]

1. The spontaneity that characterizes the distinctively human level of thought (whether theoretical or practical—in judgment or in action), merely in virtue of the *language-based conceptualization* involved
2. The spontaneity that applies to the *reflective control* of judgment by the conscious evaluation of reasons, as opposed to the unreflective, quasi-automatic, primitive kind of belief formation
3. The spontaneity that characterizes *reason* in Kant's sense, where *ideal concepts* are employed, either in the scientific explanation of observed phenomena (the pure theoretical use of reason), or in deciding what one is morally required to do, or to strive toward (the pure practical use of reason)
4. The spontaneity or Neutral Freedom of choice that is a *two-way power*
5. The absolute spontaneity of an *uncaused* event (including exercises of Capricious Freedom)

Our practical choices are sometimes between two equally attractive or unattractive options (e.g., Shall I order pizza or lasagna? Shall I pay an insurance premium, or take the risk of an accident?), and in many such cases, both trivial and serious, there is a need for "Capricious Freedom" or "plumping." Other practical choices are between moral obligations and self-interest, and more generally, they involve conflicting inclinations, reasons, values, or ideals, thus taking the following form: I have a reason to do X and another kind of reason not to do X, so what, all things considered, shall I do? In practical decisions there thus seems to be a stronger sense of voluntariness or freedom than there is for judgments, even in the most reflective cases. When one tries to "decide" which of two propositions is true, one has to think of one's judgment as rationally guided by all the reasons one is aware of (and by nothing else). And if the reasons are equally balanced, the rational response is to suspend judgment. But in practical decisions, there is often no realistic option of postponing the choice, one has to act or refrain here and now, and one can quite reasonably think of the choice one makes as undetermined by everything one knows (and perhaps by anything one may ever come to know). It thus appears that practical decision is often free or spontaneous in the fourth sense involving a two-way power, and sometimes even in the fifth sense involving "Capricious" choice—but neither of these seem to apply to judgment or belief formation.

ESSAY 8

Six Levels of Mentality

This essay will depart further than the others from Kant into twentieth-century philosophy, but it connects with the themes of (1) the contrast between animal and human mentality, and between conceptualized and unconceptualized mental states in essays 2 and 3; (2) the varieties of propositional attitudes in essay 6; and (3) the various kinds of mental freedom or spontaneity in essays 7 and 9. (May I indulge in the fantasy that if Kant in his afterlife is keeping an eye on philosophical developments, he might approve the direction in which I am taking his philosophy of mind?)

Some forty years ago Ronald de Sousa wrote:

> At the core of our lives, there is, no doubt, something of a mess. We are incoherent in our choices, inconsistent in our beliefs, falsely persuaded that we know ourselves. But at the core of all such self-deprecation, there is the concept of Belief; and it too is something of a mess. (1971: 52)

I rather fear that the mess about belief has still not been cleared up. In this essay I review various proposals to split the concept into two, and I will argue that when we distinguish the distinctions involved, we can recognize at least six levels of mental functioning. (The question as to which of these deserves the term "belief" may then be seen to be only verbal.)

I. BELIEF AMONG THE BRUTES?

Davidson (1975) claimed that to have beliefs, a creature must have the *concept* of belief, and for that it must be a member of a speech community.

His argument was that one cannot have a belief unless one understands the possibility of being mistaken, which requires grasping the contrast between truth and error, which he argues can emerge only when interpreting others' use of language. But it seems too strong to say that to have beliefs a creature must itself *understand* the possibility of being in error—isn't it sufficient that there *be* such a possibility?—manifested, for example, in a dog barking up the wrong tree (one that does not contain the escaping squirrel)?[1]

At the opposite extreme, Dennett suggested that we should distinguish "opinions" from beliefs, and that "belief, the lower brutish state, is best considered divorced from language" (1978: 305). But confining the term "belief" to the brutes seems a perversely counterintuitive bit of linguistic legislation: why can't we say that both animals and humans have beliefs, while acknowledging that nonlinguistic belief is importantly different from the linguistically expressible kind?

Segal argued that the issue cannot be settled, because to have an adequate philosophical account of belief we need some idea about which *non*-human beings have beliefs, yet our views about that are erratic and fallible: we can hardly trust them without a theory into which to fit them, but we cannot test any such theory except by seeing how well it accords with our intuitions (Segal 1994: 146–52). The method of reflective equilibrium has been proposed in response to similar difficulties in other areas in philosophy;[2] it does not guarantee an agreed result, but Segal has hardly shown that no progress is possible.

The messiness of this situation may seem to support the eliminativist proposal to abandon the concept of belief along with the rest of folk psychology, at least for serious scientific purposes (Churchland 1981; Stich 1983). But that raises the question of what is meant by those honorific but eminently contestable terms "serious" and "scientific." I suggest that however much scientific theory or popular conceptions change, we will always have a need to say (seriously, and literally) things of the form: "S believes that p, but p is not true," "A believes that p, but B doesn't," and "I used to believe that p, but I don't believe it now."

The concept of belief may well be vague in crucial respects, reflected in Stich's proposal that "S believes that p" means that S is in a mental state that is like the state the utterer is in when he or she is prepared to assert that p—where the respect and degree of similarity are left unspecified (Stich, 1983: Ch.5). Belief might even be a family resemblance concept, based on a network of overlapping similarities and differences, with some of its application left undetermined by preceding usage. But it does not follow that it is not a legitimate concept for certain purposes, nor that nothing illuminating can be said about its logical geography. Since none of the four above-mentioned positions are incontestably in possession of the field, I will now examine a succession of proposals to split the concept of belief into two.

II. THE DISTINCTION BETWEEN NONVERBAL AND VERBAL BELIEF

De Sousa (1971) argued that there are two conceptions of belief that we tend to confuse. We explain behavior in terms of beliefs and desires, and thus we attribute beliefs (at least about their present environment) to dumb animals. Yet we express our own beliefs in words, and we attribute beliefs to other people on the basis of what they say. This distinction between the behavioral attribution of belief and that based on language use seems to coincide with that between the Bayesian and classical accounts of belief. According to the classical (and more commonsense) conception, belief is an all-or-nothing affair—one either believes a proposition or one doesn't. But according to the Bayesian conception, belief is a matter of degree: anyone who believes p to degree d must thereby believe not-p to degree1 – d; and for every proposition one must believe it to some degree (if one suspends judgment, or has no opinion, that degree is 0.5). Since these "subjective probabilities" are defined in terms of dispositions to act, Bayesian decision theory can be applied to animals.[3] De Sousa therefore suggested that

> our verbalized reasoning abilities may be different in kind from those pre-linguistic deci-
> sion-making mechanisms which we share with the animals. Might the two be func-
> tioning at different *levels*? The Bayesian theory provides us with a way of describing the
> mechanism of nonverbal deliberation in humans and other animals. At a more sophisti-
> cated level, our own reliance on language adds incalculably to the scope and complexity
> of our deliberations, by providing us with a stock of sentences accepted as true. This is
> what the classical notion of belief is designed to capture....it seems beyond doubt that
> verbalized reasoning, using sentences taken as true, exhibits a kind of belief which exists
> and is peculiar to humans.
>
> (de Sousa, 1971: 57–58)

I shall later be developing this suggestion that humans have *both* nonverbal and verbal kinds or levels of mental functioning. De Sousa calls the corresponding kinds of mental states "confidence" (or "subjective probability") and "belief proper" (1971: 63).[4] Some empirical studies suggest that humans can act in unconscious conformity with Bayesian theory, their actions being explicable in terms of probabilities and utilities of which the subjects have no awareness; if so, the degrees of confidence that explain some of our actions are different from our conscious, linguistically expressible beliefs.[5]

Dennett (1978: Ch.16) proposed a change in terminology, arguing that the cases that distinguish the human kind of mental functioning are decisions in which we "make up our mind." One sometimes has to choose from a range of things that meet one's requirements: e.g., when choosing a sloop, one has somehow to move from the *de dicto* state of wanting relief from slooplessness (one of Quine's most memorable quips) to the *de re* state of purchasing a particular boat. There comes a stage when, having reviewed all the pros and cons one can think of, one "plumps" for one item, and one may not be able to say why one chooses precisely *that* one (if there are two of equal attractiveness and price tag, one may have to exercise what Sidgwick called "Capricious Freedom," as we noticed in essay 8). This existentialist theory of shopping leads Dennett to relabel de Sousa's two concepts:

> The parallel remark to make regarding all cases of making up or changing one's mind is that changes of mind are a species of judgment, and while such judgments arise from beliefs and are ultimately to be explained by one's beliefs, such judgments themselves are *not* beliefs ... but *acts*, and these acts initiate states that are also not states of belief, but of something rather like commitment, rather like ownership.... I suggest that we would do quite well by ordinary usage if we called these states *opinions*, and hence sharply distinguished opinions from beliefs.
>
> (Dennett 1978: 303–4)

Dennett thus says "animals may have *beliefs* about this and that, but they don't have *opinions*. They don't have opinions because they don't *assent*", and in his view they don't assent because they don't have language."[6] There are signs of strain in his account, however. When he distinguishes belief from opinion, his criterion seems to be that opinions are arrived at by conscious changes of mind, but he goes on to talk of opinions being acquired by other means that seem much less conscious, free, or rational:

> There are ... many ways of adding to one's collection of opinions.... One can inherit them, fall into possession of them without noticing, fail to discard them after deciding to discard them, take them on temporary loan and forget that this is what one has done. For instance, one's verbal indoctrination as a child—as an adult too—certainly has amongst its effects the inculcation of many ill-considered *dicta* one will be willing to parade as true though one has never examined them.
>
> (Dennett 1978: 307–8)

Something seems to have gone wrong in Dennett's account of "opinions." My next section may help identify the problem.

III. THE DISTINCTION BETWEEN PRIMITIVE CREDULITY
AND REASONABLE ASSENT

Henry Price noted a tendency in human nature to believe any proposition that is put to us, unless it is obviously contradicted by experience. Labeling this our "primitive credulity,"[7] he distinguished beliefs formed in this way from those arrived at by considered judgment or assent:

> The human mind has a spontaneous (unacquired) tendency to accept without question any proposition which is presented to it; and this tendency operates as a matter of course, unless there is something else to hold it in check. The power of suspending judgement, of asking questions and weighing evidence, the power on which reasonable assent depends, is not something we possess from the beginning. It is an achievement, which has to be learned, often painfully....We have to acquire this attitude of being "objective" and impartial, much as we have to acquire the power of controlling our instinctive desires.
>
> (Price 1969: 214)

As Price saw it, every normal adult has acquired this power of suspending judgment, but it does not extend to all topics or all occasions, and it can be affected by tiredness, illness, emotion, or stress.

This distinction between primitive credulity and reasonable assent was anticipated by Kant two centuries earlier (as we saw in essay 7):

> To withhold one's judgment is a faculty of a practiced power of judgment, and it is not to be found in beginners or youths, but only with increasing age. For our faculty of cognition is so desirous of extending itself that it tries with the greatest impatience to extend itself as soon as an opportunity offers.
>
> (Kant 1992, the *Vienna Logic* 24:860)[8]

William James made a similar distinction: "All propositions...are believed through the very fact of being conceived, unless they clash with other propositions believed at the same time....The primitive impulse is to affirm immediately the reality of all that is conceived" (James [1890] 1950: 290).[9]

We can now see that the distinction between nonverbal and verbalizable beliefs need not coincide with that between primitive credulity and reasonable assent. The latter distinction subdivides human verbally expressible beliefs into two classes: either primitively formed and unreflective, or reasoned and reflective. We can thus distinguish *three* kinds of beliefs. Dennett's apparent confusion over the acquisition of "opinions" can now be resolved. Many of our linguistically expressible beliefs are formed by primitive credulity. Nonverbal, Bayesian beliefs (in us, or in animals) can be described as more primitive still.

Price went on to connect his notion of reasoned assent with the question of our freedom of judgment, claiming that on those (perhaps rather rare) occasions when we reflect, and use our powers of reasoning and critical judgment, we have a crucial degree of mental freedom:

> It is in our power ... to become self-conscious and clearly aware of what is going on in us ... and to criticize and evaluate it; to ask ourselves what reason there is for believing something we find ourselves believing, or what good there is, either moral or pruden-tial, in some action we find ourselves doing or about to do. And then, if we see fit, we can decide, at least sometimes, to give up this belief and either suspend judgment or adopt some other belief instead; and similarly, to abandon this action, and either do nothing, or do something else instead. Moreover, these decisions are sometimes effective.
>
> ... It is as if we had the power of intervening, consciously and rationally, in our own mental processes, and of altering the course they take. And this is one of the excuses for the talk about "two selves," a "higher" and a "lower" self, which bothers some philoso-phers so much.
>
> (Price 1969: 230)

Deep philosophical issues are raised here, and they connect with our list of five Kantian kinds of spontaneity at the end of essay 7. We are on the track of big game—perhaps nothing less than a reconceptualization of human nature. But if we are to make any progress on these elusive and long-standing questions, we must take things slowly and patiently. Price finds an impor-tant role for conscious decision. Let us next examine proposals to distin-guish voluntary acceptance from involuntary belief.

IV. THE DISTINCTION BETWEEN BELIEF AND ACCEPTANCE

a. Belief as Involuntary, and Acceptance as Voluntary

Keith Lehrer proposes to distinguish "acceptance" from belief in terms of the subject's direct voluntary control over it:

> Belief is more like a habit than an action. A person may strive to change his habits and he may strive to change his beliefs, but such changes often take time and are not momen-tary transformations. By contrast, a person can change his mind in a moment about what to do or about what to accept. A person may decide whether or not to accept a statement

just as he may decide whether or not to perform an action. Acceptance, unlike belief, is
a matter of choice.

(Lehrer 1990a: 148–49)

Lehrer adds that acceptance is a *context-relative* reliance or trust in the truth
of a statement. When one accepts something one does so in a certain
situation, and for certain purposes only (e.g., one might accept that a mush-
room is of an edible species for the purpose of including it in one's collection, without being prepared to add it to one's cooking pot).[10] But a change
of conversational or institutional context does not usually involve a change
in one's *beliefs*, though it may affect whether and how one expresses them or
acts on them.

When Lehrer lays out his theory of knowledge he uses a more specific
notion of acceptance, which he defines (somewhat inelegantly) as
"acceptance for the purposes of obtaining truth and eschewing error with
respect to just the thing one accepts" (Lehrer 1990a: 228; 1990b: 10–11,
26–27, 113–15). This is a *sub*species of the above more general notion of
acceptance, a subspecies that Lehrer still wants to distinguish from belief,
for he suggests that people can believe things—for the sake of felicity or
piety—that they do not accept in this purely epistemic sense. But whether
people should really be described as *believing* in such cases is debatable;
indeed, ordinary usage can put it the other way round, and say that people
sometimes accept (e.g., for purposes of public statement or policy) what
they do not really believe.

In his *Essay on Belief and Acceptance,* Jonathan Cohen puts his own
spin on this distinction.[11] He urges epistemologists to explore the differing
roles of active and passive cognition, and he explains his distinction as
follows:

> Belief that p is a disposition...normally to feel it true that p and false that not-p, whether
> or not one is willing to act, speak, or reason accordingly. But to accept the proposition or
> rule of inference that p is to treat it as given that p. More precisely, to accept that p is to
> have or adopt a policy of deeming, positing, or postulating that p—i.e. of including that
> proposition or rule among one's premises for deciding what to do or think in a particular
> context, whether or not one feels it to be true that p.

(Cohen 1992: 4)

Belief for Cohen is not a disposition to *say* something, nor is it a disposition
to act, though that is a reliable *sign* of belief. It is for him a disposition to
"feel" that p, where such feelings are occurrent mental events. But what are
these "credal feelings" supposed to be? Can we ascribe them to animals and
infants? Cohen says so (1992: 8), but it is very doubtful that a tendency to

credal feelings is what we *mean* when we ascribe beliefs to languageless creatures. And what exactly are such feelings in ourselves? We sometimes talk of "having a feeling in one's bones" that p, without believing p. In a case of perceptual illusion in which one knows that the appearances are deceptive, one *might* be said to feel that p even though one knows that not-p (though I do not find the locution very natural). People sometimes feel that their deceased spouse is still around the house (and for that combination of the emotional and the quasiperceptual, the word "feel" feels right). But such feelings do not amount to belief; they seem to be passive states, in which the feeling "comes over one." Mental acts of *judging*, in which a more active and conscious mental power is involved, do imply belief. It seems that in his talk of credal feelings, Cohen has failed to sort out the active from the passive elements in cognition as he hoped to do.

Acceptance for Cohen is something mental, not the outer act of assertion; yet it is conceptually tied to the possibility of verbal formulation, so there is no question of dumb animals accepting anything (Cohen 1992: 2). Acceptance is more like an action than a mental disposition: both Lehrer and Cohen emphasize how it is voluntary in a very strong sense, and changeable in a moment; though if one accepts something, one presumably continues to do so in the relevant context unless and until one makes a new decision: as Cohen says, acceptance is a *policy*. But his claim that "the standard way to discover whether you yourself believe that p is by introspecting whether you are normally disposed to feel that p when you consider the issue" (Cohen 1992: 4) is implausible in comparison with Evans's view (following Wittgenstein) that when one judges whether one believes p, one's attention is on whether p, not on oneself.[12] However, the point (which Cohen shares with Lehrer) that we can distinguish acceptance from belief as a voluntarily adopted, context-relative policy seems solid.[13]

b. Belief as Mental, and Acceptance as Metamental

Lehrer later put a rather different gloss on the difference between belief and acceptance:

> The human mind is a metamind. Human freedom, rationality, consensus, knowledge, and conception depend on metamental operations and would not exist without such operations.... What is a metamental operation? It is a thought about a thought, about a feeling or about an emotion. The intentional object of a metamental operation is itself a mental operation. Moreover, the intentionality of the metamental operation is crucial. A thought causing another thought is not a mentamental operation. A thought

about a thought is. Intentionality is not causality. So a being might have thoughts that caused other thoughts without having metamental operations.

(Lehrer 1990a: 2)

In the next paragraph he suggests it is useful to think of the metamental in terms of a computational model of the mind. In the terminology of cognitive science, there is an evaluation of lower-level information by a higher-order "central system."

Lehrer was surely influenced here by Jerry Fodor's distinction between input systems and central systems (Fodor 1983). Fodor presented his view of the mind as a high-level *empirical* theory "of the structure of the causal mechanisms that underlie the mind's capacities." The senses, memory, and language perception depend on "input systems" that represent the world to make it accessible to thought. These systems deal with restricted kinds of input; their operation is involuntary; we do not normally have any conscious awareness of their processes, only of their output; they work extremely fast; and they are "informationally encapsulated," i.e., largely unaffected by any other information the subject possesses. They are associated with fixed neural architecture in the brain, and they exhibit characteristic patterns of development and breakdown. Fodor describes them as mental modules, and he claims that this functionally specified class constitutes a natural kind for psychology.

But none of this applies to Fodor's "central system." This seems to be just a label for a person's ability to take into account all the evidence he is aware of that is relevant to a given proposition, and to arrive at a reasoned judgment. This "central" mental functioning is applicable to any topic, it is subject to voluntary control, open to conscious awareness, and comparatively slow, and it is *not* informationally encapsulated; indeed it displays the kind of evidential holism that is characteristic of empirical science. The presumption is that these domain-free inferential capacities are a late evolutionary development, superimposed on aboriginal "input analyzers." In a later book Fodor (2000) frankly admits that this highest level of our mentality defies explanation by the computational models of cognitive science. The central system could well be called "the conscious mind," "the self," or even "the soul." One suspects that the philosophical problems have not been solved; they have just been bundled into the central bit of the mental black box.

Lehrer simplifies Fodor's story by talking of an input system *in the singular:*

The mind contains an input system that receives information from the outside world and provides us with a representation of that information as an output. That output is the input for a higher-order system, a central system, that evaluates the lower-level information represented by the input system. The evaluation may result in acceptance of the lower-level information or in rejection of that information. The output of such evaluation—acceptance, for example—is a functional state that plays a special role in memory, inference, and action. It is the sort of state that ordinarily results from reflectively judging the information to be correct, but the same sort of functional state also arises unreflectively from the processing of information. We arrive at the same sort of functional state by more than one historical route.

(Lehrer 1990a: 2)

A few pages later, Lehrer offers an explicitly metamental account of acceptance, as opposed to belief:

Acceptance is a metamental operation. Belief, for the most part, is a lower-level operation. In the usual case, belief is carried over into acceptance. Indeed, the default mode of the central system is to accept what is believed, especially in the case of perceptual belief....But the default mode...will be overridden when background information indicates that perception is untrustworthy. One function of the central system is to sort lower-level representations, accepting some as evidence, others as hypotheses, and refusing to accept others at all.

(Lehrer 1990a: 11)[14]

Cohen also verges toward this metamental conception of acceptance, when he writes: "The fact is that in deciding what to accept we often need to presume that our subconscious belief-forming mechanisms—and especially those of perception and memory—have operated veridically" (Cohen 1992: 17). But neither Lehrer nor Cohen seems to have realized that this notion of acceptance as a metamental operation is quite different from a context-relative policy, decided on quite voluntarily for certain purposes only.[15] For all that we know about the central system, what it accepts (whether by default, or after critical review of the evidence) may be retained quite independently of changes of context, plans, and purposes.

The metamental conception of acceptance seems more like what Price distinguished as reasonable assent as opposed to primitive credulity. However, there is an important ambiguity in Lehrer's use of the notion of the metamental. He introduced it (in the first quotation) as meaning mental states or operations that have as their intentional contents other mental states or operations. But then (in the second quotation) he makes the distinction between input and central systems, with the associated distinction between functional states (e.g., of acceptance) that arise from unreflective or reflective mental processes. That allows that acceptance sometimes arises in the unreflective way, when the central system operates "in default mode."

Later (in the third quotation) he tells us that acceptance is a metamental operation, and what that means here seems to be that it is a function of the central system rather than the lower-order input system(s).

But it is not obvious that what is accepted by the central system (whether by default or by reflection) is necessarily metamental in the sense that Lehrer first attached to the term, i.e., as having mental states or operations as contents. Surely much perception is of the inanimate world, so many of the propositions that are accepted will be about purely material, nonmental, states of affairs (even if some such acceptances are arrived at by reflection or critical review conducted by the central system). Conversely, some at least of our beliefs and/or acceptances are about the mental states of others; and it is surely evident that many of them are arrived at immediately and unreflectively, when we see people's behavior, body language, and facial expressions and hear what they say and the tone of voice in which they say it. Lehrer's notion of the metamental thus seems ambiguous between two distinctions:

Having only material states as content/having mental states as content
Arrived at by unreflective processes/arrived at by reflection

Lehrer himself seems to realize this when he says that the functional or computational character (what I have called the reflective nature) of states of the central system is what enables us to attribute higher-order states (thoughts about thoughts—even about one's own thoughts) to people, "without supposing that those states are the objects of conscious reflection" (Lehrer 1990a: 4).

V. THE DISTINCTION BETWEEN INFORMATIONAL STATES AND BELIEFS

In *The Varieties of Reference* Gareth Evans wrote of "the informational system, which constitutes the substratum of our cognitive lives" (1982: 122). In perception, we gather information about the world; we retain it in memory, and transmit it by communicating with others. These are platitudes, but Evans goes beyond them in proposing to use the notion of an informational state as a primitive technical term, distinct from belief. This distinction between information and belief is surely related to Fodor's distinction between "what the input systems compute and what the organism (consciously or subdoxastically) *believes*."

It is as well to reserve "belief" for the notion of a far more sophisticated cognitive state: one that is connected with (and, in my opinion, defined in terms of) the notion of *judgment,* and so, also, connected with the notion of *reasons.* The operations of the informational system are more primitive. Two of them after all, we share with animals [obviously, Evans means perception and memory here]; and I do not think we can properly understand the mechanism whereby we gain information from others unless we realize that it is already operative at a stage of human intellectual development that pre-dates the applicability of the more sophisticated notion.

(Evans 1982: 24)

Evans refers to Wittgenstein's point in *On Certainty* that we receive information by accepting the testimony of other people as soon as we begin to understand and use language in childhood, well before we can make reasoned judgments:

The child learns by believing the adult. Doubt comes *after* belief.

...I believe what people transmit to me in a certain manner. In this way, I believe geographical, chemical, historical facts etc. That is how I *learn* the sciences. Of course learning is based on believing.

...Perhaps someone says "There must be some basic principle on which we accord credence," but what can such a principle accomplish? Is it more than a natural law of "taking for true"?

(Wittgenstein 1969: *160, 170, 172)

Like de Sousa, Evans proposes to reserve the term "belief" for the higher of two kinds of mental functioning. But *which* distinction does he have in mind? He says more about this later:

So far I have been considering the non-conceptual content of perceptual informational states. Such states are not *ipso facto* perceptual *experiences*—that is, states of a conscious subject....it seems abundantly clear that evolution could throw up an organism in which such advantageous links were established, long before it had provided us with a conscious subject of experience.

...[W]e arrive at conscious perceptual experience when sensory input is not only connected to behavioral dispositions in the way I have been describing—perhaps in some phylogenetically more ancient part of the brain—but also serves as the input to a *thinking, concept-applying, and reasoning system*; so that the subject's thoughts, plans, and deliberations are also systematically dependent on the informational properties of the input. When there is such a further link, we can say that the person, rather than just some part of his brain, receives and processes the information.

(Evans 1982: 57–58)

The term "belief" does not occur in this passage, but in view of Evans's previous connection of it with judgment and reasons, it is clear that for him beliefs are functions of "the thinking, concept-applying, and reasoning system." He makes an explicit link with experience and consciousness, and an implicit one with language, for it seems that for him concepts must be expressible in words.[16] Yet in the earlier passage he wanted to locate the child's unreflective acceptance of what he is told at the lower mental level, apparently not deserving the title "belief." I suggest we need to distinguish three kinds of mental functioning:

1. Nonlinguistic informational states in animal perception and memory
2. The child's unreflective use of language, in response to perception, and in the uncritical (primitive) reception of testimony
3. The adult human's reasoned judgments

Evans's talk of the reasoning system now appears somewhat ambiguous. Concepts (of an elementary sort) occur at (2)—or even perhaps at (1), depending on how we legislate for the use of that slippery word—but reasoning is confined to (3). The notions of "thought" or "consciousness" are notoriously vague, for they can be applied at (3) alone, or at (2) plus (3), or even perhaps at all three. Also ambiguous are the notions of "act" or "action," "voluntary," and "will." Many of our witnesses allude to the *active*, voluntary, willed or free nature of the "higher" side of their distinctions.[17]

VI. RECONCEPTUALIZING BELIEF: LOCATING THE JOINTS AT WHICH TO CARVE

We have heard from quite a cloud of witnesses, and now it is time to try to construct a coherent overall story. But we had better ask ourselves what sort of inquiry we are conducting. Can the elucidation of mental concepts be done a priori, independent of all empirical inquiry into what kinds of mental states and processing there are? The facts about animal and human mentality tend to be more various and complex than are dreamt of in the words of ordinary language or the armchair reflections of the greatest philosophers (even Kant!). Animals differ greatly over the evolutionary scale: baboons, dolphins, and parrots have more sophisticated levels of mentality than lizards, spiders, or worms, and we may be surprised to discover just what is involved in each case. Human children obviously go through various stages of mental development, but theories about the underlying nature of these changes are controversial; and in adults there often seem to be different kinds or levels of mentality at work at the same time. So we had better frankly allow that empirical research may throw light on our questions, and that inquiry into the mind needs to be interdisciplinary.

Everyone has to agree that there is an animal kind of perceptual awareness that does not involve language (those who are fastidious about talking of "belief" here can call it a more primitive belief-like state). In contrast, Price's "primitive credulity," Evans's conception of the informational role of testimony, and Lehrer's and Cohen's concept of human belief as opposed to acceptance all involve the understanding of *sentences*. So, as we saw in the preceding section, three kinds of mental functioning can be distinguished:

1. Nonlinguistic information processing
2. Linguistic but primitive, not involving reasoning or critical judgment
3. Linguistic and involving the exercise of reflection or reasoning

Price and Evans talk of *conscious* mental states, and so presumably does Cohen when he talks of "feeling that p." But it may be wise not to appeal to the obsessively discussed notion of consciousness, which I suspect may be as ambiguous or many-faceted as that of belief. Rather, I will proceed in the hope that some independent elucidation of belief and related mental states may be feasible.

I propose to superimpose on the above three levels of cognition Lehrer's distinction between mental and *meta*mental states, where the latter have as their content other mental states.[18] This first-order/higher-order distinction is different from the primitive/reasoned distinction. A child—and an adult—may make unreflective, noninferential judgments about the mental states of others, in response to perceived behavior, speech, facial expressions, or tones of voice (e.g., "Dad is angry," "Fido wants to play"). Conversely, there can be reasoned judgments about nonmental, material states of affairs. So I am now using the following three distinctions to carve up the field of cognitive mental states:

A. Arrived at by some sort of reasoning or critical assessment (reasoned)/ primitive (unreasoned)
B. Higher-order (having mental states as content, mind-directed)/first-order (having only material states as content, object-directed)
C. Linguistic (expressible in language by the subject)/nonlinguistic

Distinctions B and C are to do with the sort of *content* a token mental state has. C concerns whether or not the content is expressible by the subject in a system of symbols with propositional meanings established by convention. This involves the first kind of Kantian spontaneity that I distinguished at the end of essay 7, which characterizes those levels of mentality that involve *language-based conceptualization*.

Distinction B concerns whether the content is material or mental states of affairs (in the latter case, it may be either other-mind-directed, or about the subject's own mental states). Price, Lehrer, and Cohen are clear that the right-hand side of their distinction is mind-directed, involving thoughts about thoughts. De Sousa and Dennett do not apply this criterion—their distinction can be made within object-directed beliefs.[19]

Distinction A is a matter of the causal history of a token mental state in a particular subject at a particular time—has it been arrived at by some process of conscious judgment on the basis of evidence or reasons? Epistemologists routinely distinguish basic (noninferred) beliefs from inferred ones, but what I have in mind here is rather Price's distinction between primitive credulity and reasonable assent. The latter involves the second kind of Kantian spontaneity, namely, the *reflective control* of judgment by the conscious evaluation of reasons, as opposed to the unreflective, quasi-automatic, primitive kind of belief formation.

To illustrate the application of A, consider someone's belief that the bird she sees in the bush is a Lesser-spotted Godtwit: this would be a case of primitive credulity if she has unquestioningly accepted it on the authority of the leader of the bird-watching group, but it would be reasoned assent if she arrives at it by peering at the bird, consulting her bird book, and making her own judgment. Her belief would also count as reasoned if she accepts it from the tour leader *not unquestioningly*, but only after reflecting that someone in his position is supposed to know about the local fauna. This example concerns the acceptance of testimony, but the point can be extended to linguistically expressible beliefs formed on the basis of perception or memory (remember the talk about how the central system normally accepts what "the input systems" put in, but can sometimes override them). In any situation where someone raises the question "Is it really the case that p, of does it only seem that way?" or "I seem to remember that p, but did it really happen?" and then arrives at a judgment about p, the resulting belief counts as reasoned in the sense I intend. If she simply trusts her perception or memory without any such reflection, her belief is "primitively formed."

When two distinctions are crossed, four possibilities are generated, but sometimes one of them gets immediately eliminated on conceptual grounds. (Kant ruled out the analytic a posteriori, while claiming to discover the synthetic a priori.) When three distinctions are involved, there are eight prima facie possibilities. So do A, B, and C reveal as many as eight different kinds of mental states? Crossing B and C first, we have the following:

nonlinguistic object-directed
nonlinguistic mind-directed

linguistic object-directed
linguistic mind-directed

The second of these may look dubious, for it might be wondered how there could be a creature without language yet with higher-order mental states. It would be foolhardy to rule this out a priori, however. Consider the psychological studies of primates interpreting them as "mind-reading" within their social groups.[20] To explain their behavior it is proposed to credit them with thoughts about each other's thoughts, e.g., "If I mate with his female behind this rock, he won't be able to see us at it from over there." This is to put the thought in language, of course, but cartoons can express it in pictures, using thought bubbles that contain not words but pictorial representations of thoughts about how the other creature sees the state of affairs. Further subtleties in behavior might justify crediting a languageless creature with self-directed thoughts. Deceptive behavior can apparently be interpreted this way, e.g., "If I pretend not to have noticed that banana, then when this fellow goes away I will have it all to myself." Of course, it can be debated whether this is the *right* way to interpret the relevant behavior, but the issues involved here are empirical: Are the observed behaviors capable of any simpler explanation? My point is that we cannot rule out the possibility of mental states that are mind-directed yet nonlinguistic; and indeed that there is prima facie evidence for their existence.

If we now cross distinction A with the above four possibilities, we would have reasoned and unreasoned versions of each. However, A does not apply to animals or infants, for we do not ascribe the relevant sort of doubting, reasoning, or reflective judgment to them. My application of the term "reasoned" includes raising and answering doubts, whether out loud or internally in one's own mind—and it is hard to see how the latter could be possible for a creature who cannot formulate questions in words. We thus get a list of six rather than eight kinds of mental functioning:[21]

1. Nonlinguistic, object-directed
2. Nonlinguistic, mind-directed
3. Linguistic, object-directed, and primitively formed
4. Linguistic, mind-directed, and primitively formed
5. Linguistic, object-directed, and reasoned
6. Linguistic, mind-directed, and reasoned

I suggest that all these are instantiated in human beings, and sometimes even simultaneously. This fits with the Aristotelian view that we are rational animals, possessing the basic forms of animal mentality but with extra mental functions built on top; and it also fits with the theory of evolution.[22]

VII. SIX KINDS OF BELIEFS?

I will now summarize my distinctions between six kinds or levels of beliefs or belief-like states:

1. *Nonlinguistic object-directed beliefs*—this is the lowest or most basic mental level, which includes the perceptual "beliefs" (or belief-like mental states) of animals and prelinguistic infants about their material environment. There are surely also perceptual states in adult humans whose content we cannot formulate in words, e.g., those involved in the perception of music, or in any rapid spatial navigation or skill, like avoiding bumping into people in a crowded street. There seem to be similar states involved in certain types of visual or aural memory.[23]

2. *Nonlinguistic mind-directed beliefs*—those belief-like mental states of higher animals and prelinguistic children that can reasonably be interpreted as being about the mental states of other creatures, usually conspecifics (for example the primates studied by Byrne and Whiten 1987). There are surely some such nonlinguistic informational states in our adult perceptions of each other, e.g., in our awareness of body language—the emotive or erotic expressiveness of others' facial expressions, tones of voice, bodily movements, and gestures. For the self-directed case, see Bermudez (1998) on the nonconceptual informational states involved in our psychological self-awareness.

3. *Linguistic object-directed primitively formed beliefs*—our first example of this was linguistically expressible beliefs resulting from primitive credulity in humans, namely, our tendency to believe whatever we are told. Young children cannot do otherwise, and probably all of us believe things in this way much of the time.[24] (Con men rely on this uncritical kind of belief formation in their victims: when one realizes one has been conned, one thinks, "How could I have been so credulous?") There is something similar in the way in which our linguistically expressible perceptual and memory beliefs are normally produced. Usually, we just find ourselves with such beliefs, primitively and passively formed in our minds; to raise or settle doubts about them is comparatively rare and involves a higher, more active, reason-involving kind of mental functioning.

4. *Linguistic mind-directed primitively formed beliefs*—linguistically expressible but primitively formed beliefs about the mental states of others (or perhaps oneself), such as those beliefs that a child expresses when she says "Mummy can see me," "Dad doesn't want me to do that"; and in the self-directed case "I can see the rabbit," "I just saw the ball go in the hole."

If asked how she knows these things, or whether she has any doubts, the child may have nothing further to say.

5. *Linguistic object-directed reasoned beliefs*—those of our beliefs about the material world that are arrived at by reasoned judgment, that is, the weighing of evidence or justification, where the deliverances of one's senses, one's memory, or testimony are put into question, or where the evidence is ambiguous or conflicting. In such cases we ask, and often have to answer, questions of the form:

It looks to me (from here) as if p, but is p really the case?

I seem to remember that p, but did p really happen?

So-and-so told me that p, but should I believe him?

We have some evidence that p, but we also have evidence against p—so what should we believe?

We thought we had evidence that p, but now we have been given reason to question the validity of that "evidence"—so what should we believe?

Anything that is accepted *after* the raising of such a question (explicitly, or in the mind) counts as reasoned in my sense, even if one concludes that there is, after all, no sufficient reason to distrust one's informant, one's memory or one's senses, or the previous evidence.

6. *Linguistic mind-directed reasoned beliefs*—the highest or most sophisticated kind, which includes all the cases in which the kinds of doubt-resolving judgment or reasoning involved in 5 are applied to arrive at beliefs about mental states of others (e.g., Is he rudely ignoring us, or did he not hear my request? Does she really feel friendly toward me, or is her smile commercially motivated?). The same sort of reasoned judgment can also apply to one's *own* mental states (e.g., Was I really so angry with that student, or was it because of that previous confrontation with X? Am I in love with Y, or is it just a passing fancy?). The notion of acceptance that Cohen and Lehrer distinguished from belief in terms of its voluntariness and context-relativity surely involves this highest kind of mental functioning. As an act or policy, it is under the control of the will; and it is for a purpose, so there is a reason for acceptance (in the relevant context) that the subject can surely formulate in words.[25]

You can say, if you like, that these are six kinds of beliefs—or if you prefer, belief-like mental states—to replace the "messy," ambiguous folk concept of belief from which we started. Am I thus eliminating folk psychology, or proposing an improvement within it? Some may say that belief is not a genus with six species, but a disparate bundle tied loosely together by family resemblances. Others may claim that "belief" is not the right word to apply to levels 1 and 2, even on a family resemblance basis. But having done all this work elucidating similarities and differences, I confess to not being terribly interested in these questions, unless they can be shown to involve substantial issues rather than mere verbal choices.[26]

In one sense it is possible for the same belief to occur at more than one level (remember the bird-spotting example above), but what is meant here is that the same *proposition* is believed by different people in different circumstances, or by the same person at different times. However, a particular mental state of someone's *believing* in the proposition can only be at one level. What the scheme fundamentally classifies is *token mental states* of a person A's believing that p at time t. Types of belief identified by very general kinds of content or origin, e.g., perceptual beliefs, memory beliefs, or testimony-based beliefs, can be instantiated at more than one level.[27]

The distinctions in the scheme are not *primarily* between kinds of mind (or stages of mental development), but between different kinds of token mental states, many or all of which may be present together in adult humans. However, a derivative set of questions can be asked, namely, whether there can be kinds of creatures—or stages of human mental development—that instantiate only some of the levels. (Is talk of lower and higher "levels" really justified here, or should we just say they are different *kinds* of mentality?) Prima facie, there are plenty of animals that instantiate only level 1, but if the primate psychologists are right, some of the intensely social higher animals display 2, without using anything that can count as linguistic symbols (at least in the wild). Whether certain humanly taught primates count as using language, at least in the primitive way involved in 3 or 4, is still under debate.

It may not be clear to casual observation whether children go through a stage when they are aware of things *before* they are aware of the mental states of other people—thus instantiating 1 but not 2, or 3 but not 4—but there has been a proposal to interpret autistic children in this way.[28] It seems fairly obvious, however, that children go through a stage when they instantiate 3 and 4 without 5 or 6, i.e., they use language only in the primitively unreflective way. Possibly autistic adults instantiate 5 without 6—but that is a matter of delicate interpretation of the facts. So there is at least the empirical possibility of a hierarchy of the six levels.

The third kind of Kantian spontaneity that I identified at the end of essay 7, the kind that characterizes *reason* in Kant's technical sense, where *ideal concepts* are employed—whether in the scientific explanation of observed phenomena (the pure theoretical use of reason), or in deciding what one is morally required to do or strive toward (the pure practical use of reason)— surely belongs at levels 5 and 6.

VIII. DISTINGUISHING THE SIX LEVELS IN DESIRES
AND EMOTIONS

Let me test this rather ambitious scheme by sketching how it might extend to other kinds of mental states talked of in folk psychology. If a similar six layers can be discerned among desires and emotions, this would tend to confirm the validity of this new "anatomy of the soul."

1. *Nonlinguistic object-directed desires and emotions*—most of the desires of higher animals and prelinguistic infants belong here, along with related kinds of emotion, e.g., fear of large objects approaching, frustration or anger at not being able to do something. (For anyone who thinks "emotion" is an inappropriate term to apply at this level, we can call them "states of arousal"). Of course, *we* have to use words to identity such desires or emotions, but we do not thereby attribute any linguistic understanding to their subjects.

2. *Nonlinguistic mind-directed desires and emotions*—the desires of social animals and human infants that are (in a nonlinguistic sense) about the mental states of other people, e.g., wanting Mummy's attention, wanting a conspecific to see (or *not* see!) one doing something, wanting all the available food for oneself. There are also other-directed emotions at this level, e.g., anger with another creature (for an attack, a stealing of food, or a challenge in the pecking order), fear that they may attack, a baby's delight at a parent's attention and playfulness.

3. *Verbally expressible, object-directed primitive desires and emotions*—the linguistically expressible desires and emotions of young children who have not learned to reflect on them or inhibit them, e.g., as expressed in the words "More ice cream!," "Let me stroke the cat," "I'd love to go to the movies" (said as soon as the idea is mooted), "I'm so excited," "I'm sad we can't go." Children at this stage have learned some vocabulary, however limited, with which to express their conative and emotional states.

4. *Verbally expressible, mind-directed primitive desires and emotions*—linguistically expressible but unreflective desires and emotions concerning the mental states of others, e.g., as expressed by the words "Daddy, watch me do this," or "Mum's angry with Joe," or "I'm afraid she'll be angry with me too." (Levels 3 and 4 will involve the same range of examples as in 1 and 2, but here we *are* attributing understanding of relevant words: the subjects can *say* what they want, and to some extent how they feel.) The unreflective desires and emotions of adults, perhaps indeed the majority of human states of desire and emotion, will be at the unreflective levels 3 and 4.

5. *Verbally expressible, object-directed reasoned desires and emotions*—this level will include those of our desires that are inferred by some kind of practical reasoning, i.e., cases in which we want something not for its own sake but only because we see it as a means, e.g., wanting a key to open a box. Some emotions are inferential or reasoned in an analogous way, e.g., panic at seeing a white powder on the floor because one thinks it may be anthrax; delight at seeing the geese flying north because one knows it's a sign of spring.

6. *Verbally expressible mind-directed reasoned desires and emotions*—e.g., a desire that Jeremy will do his homework tonight, because he'll be in trouble at school if he doesn't (and he needs to develop good working habits). As examples of emotions at this level, consider the anger one may feel when one's daughter's room is untidy, not so much because one cares that much about the state of the room, but because she *promised* she would clear it up *today*; consider also the gratitude one may come to feel to someone when one realizes just how much she has done for one over the years. All the most distinctively *human* mental states, the topics of ethics and literature, belong at this level.

Perhaps you will conclude that rule-following, rationality, free will, responsibility, self-consciousness, personhood, ethics, self-development, and spirituality all involve level 6. But steady on!—we must beware of the temptation to bundle everything high and mysterious into one mental black box. (Remember Fodor's central system, alias the mind or soul in scientific disguise.) Further distinctions may well be needed for deeper understanding.[29]

ESSAY 9

A Kantian Defense of Free Will

It will take me quite a while to get around to discussing what to make of Kant's very controversial thoughts on free will. I will be attempting to construct a defensible philosophical position using some of the materials he bequeathed to us rather than engaging in systematic exegesis of his texts. But first I want to lay a secure foundation by a more careful elucidation of the concepts of determinism and causality than seems common in this perennial area of philosophical pondering.

I. THE STATUS OF DETERMINISM

Determinism is standardly understood as the thesis that at every moment of time the laws of nature, together with the state of the universe at that time, imply that only one state of things can come about in the next instant of time—and indeed that there must be a similarly unique outcome at each future time.[1] That is a metaphysical claim, an assertion about the most general structure of the world. Laplace famously expressed it in more epistemological form: if a superintelligence ("Laplace's demon") knew the total state of the universe at any given time, and also knew all the laws of nature, then the demon (replaced these days by a supercomputer) could do the requisite calculations and predict every subsequent state of the universe with mathematical certainty. Laplace assumed that every fact about the world can be expressed by a measurable quantity (or at least that all other truths are determined by the values of such variables), and that the laws of nature can be expressed in mathematical formulas. His metaphysical picture was a generalization from the dramatically influential success of Newton's laws of mechanics applied to the solar system to an imagined application to everything in the universe.

But before we get to physics, let alone philosophy, there is a purely mathematical difficulty in the way of a Laplacean demon or computer. Nonmathematicians tend to assume that the calculations can be straightforwardly (even automatically) performed, that all one has to do is formulate the equations that express the laws of nature, feed in the observed values of the variables, then turn the handle (metaphorically speaking)—i.e., make the appropriate inferences, or set the computer program working—and the results will fall out. But that is to betray ignorance of the complexity of the mathematics involved. Consider the paradigm case of Newtonian gravitation: the laws tell us the force acting on a given body in a given direction, and hence (given its mass) its acceleration—the double derivative of distance with respect to time. To know its velocity at any time we have to integrate the differential equation, and to predict its position we have to integrate again. If we imagine two bodies in space, with no other forces acting on them than their mutual gravitational attraction, then the prediction comes out easily that they will accelerate toward each other, and indeed that the acceleration will itself increase with the decreasing distance. But if we imagine *three* masses similarly isolated from all other forces, the derivation of predictions about their relative motion poses the classic "three-body problem" that is still, I gather, unsolved in principle,[2] though there are methods of making approximate predictions, so that we were able to send men to the moon and back. Given the masses of the bodies and their positions at any one time, their instantaneous accelerations can be readily derived, but the problem is to predict, with complete precision, their *subsequent* positions, motions, and accelerations—the central difficulty being that the forces change as the distances between the bodies change. The moral of the story is that even in this very simple and artificially isolated case, although we believe that the future states are completely determined by the laws and the initial state, neither our best mathematicians nor our most powerful computers can derive predictions with complete mathematical precision. The elegance of mathematically expressed laws is often remarked upon, but their application is a different matter. Even before we apply them to the real physical world, the mathematics of some simple imaginary cases can get messy.

That is the first difficulty in the Laplacean picture. Next I want to point out how much idealization is involved in the epistemological version of it. There is absolutely no prospect of anyone ever *knowing* the *total* state of the universe at a time, including the size and shape of every leaf, the movement of every molecule of air, the exact mixing of genes in every act of reproduction, the firing of every neuron in animal and human brains—let alone whatever happens on other planets and in other galaxies. There may seem to be a rather better prospect of human beings (or, at least, the scientists among us) getting to know all the laws of nature—if we could assume that the laws are finitely expressible and relatively small in number. But could we ever be sure of that? How could we know that we had got absolutely all the laws of nature down in our textbooks or computers? I shall let that pass, however, for the impossibility of our ever knowing a total state of the universe is itself enough to relieve us from the nightmare (if that is what is) of a Laplacean demon predicting every event unto the end of time. (Of course, there is a temptation to replace the presumably finite demon with an infinitely well-endowed God. But the very idea of an infinite mind raises problems of its own, and you may be relieved to know that I do not propose to enter into theology here.)

Some philosophers are not impressed by mere epistemological impossibility and want to maintain that it does not show the *metaphysical* thesis of determinism to be false, or meaningless. For all that we have seen so far, it seems perfectly coherent to suppose that there *exists* both a total state-description of the universe at any given moment and a complete set of laws of nature, and that these together entail what must happen at every subsequent time. Moreover, it has seemed to many that it is not merely intellectually respectable but *compulsory* to believe this, in the light of the progress of science in the last few centuries and our commitment to scientific method. To be sure, the advent of quantum mechanics has shaken belief in universal determinism embracing all levels of nature (though famously it did not shake Einstein's faith that God does not play dice with the universe), but the theory of quantum indeterminism at the microlevel has hardly undermined the widespread assumption of determinism at the level of perceptible objects, including human behavior. Yet the possibility cannot be ignored that undetermined microevents may result in some degree of indeterminism at the macrolevel, as illustrated by the notorious thought experiment of Schrodinger's cat, and also, I understand, by recent developments in quantum computing and cryptography.[3] But if there is any such indeterminism in the human brain, it is not at all clear how it could provide for free will, which surely involves some intelligible connections between a person's decision and her previous thoughts and feelings, beliefs and attitudes. Thus philosophers have continued to worry about the implications for free will *if* determinism were true, and to exercise their conceptual ingenuity on a variety of compatibilist and incompatibilist positions. There remains a widespread assumption that determinism is a coherently statable, very general, yet ultimately empirical claim about the overall character of the universe, and that physical science has provided strong evidence for it at any level above the atomic.

However, I am going to argue that determinism is not an empirical proposition at all, not even one of great generality, but rather an *idea* in Kant's sense. That is, it is a concept or conception that is not meaningless—for it is one we quite easily form and understand—but we arrive at it by a process of intellectual idealization from the empirical realities that we deal with, and it can never be directly applicable to them, though it may perhaps serve as an ideal to be approached but never exactly instantiated. As we have seen, the definition of determinism requires the conception of a total state-description of the universe at any one time. That contains two idealizations—to the ideal of describing *all* the states, and of describing *each particular state exactly as it is*.

Let me first address the ideal of exact description. This surely implies measurement, for although there are many everyday descriptions that do not involve numbers (e.g., "purple," "noisy," "fragrant," "annoying," "celebrity," "old-fashioned," "sexy"), most serious physical science involves numerical values of empirical variables. But how precise can measurement be? The advance of technology has improved our techniques, but even the most skilled operator of the most up-to-date kit has to admit, if pressed, that her observations are accurate only within a certain margin of error.[4] The metaphysically minded philosopher may say in his lofty way that this is only a matter of human sense-organs and gadgets, and that there remains a clear distinction between physical reality—which he maintains must be determinate in every detail—and our human descriptions and approximate measurements of it. The claim would be that there is a completely precise right answer for every question of measurement. The numbers will typically go into decimal points—but how far into that infinite range? There is no *theoretical* limit, so the imaginable set of answers stretches into the rational numbers, and perhaps into the reals.

The existence of precise numerical values for all physical variables is crucial for the thesis of determinism, which needs an *exact* state-description of the world at any time, to be fed into the laws of nature stated in mathematical equations, and thence to predict all future states. *No doubt we humans cannot* perform the relevant computations, but the thought is that an idealized computer could do so. However, some recent developments in the mathematics of so-called chaotic systems show that for some kinds of equations the predictions that can be computed from initial states can vary dramatically, depending on very small differences in the initial states (e.g., the famous "butterfly-wing" effect on the weather).[5] "Chaotic" is perhaps not the best label for these systems, for the outputs remain mathematically determined by the inputs; it is just that tiny differences in the input variables can make huge differences to the outputs. This means that in practice, given that all of our actual measurements have limits of accuracy, some of our predictions are liable to large errors for complex types of system such as the weather—and perhaps the human brain. The point is also instantiated in simpler systems that we use to generate "random" outcomes such as toss-ing a coin, or dropping a ball to bounce down through an array of pins, or the more elaborate devices used in lotteries; in these cases, a human action starts a physical process whose result cannot be predicted. It is not just that we presently lack the technology to make sufficiently precise measurements of the relevant variables; the systems are designed to have so much multipli-cation of tiny differences that no human measurement could ever make realistic predictions of outcomes. As Elizabeth Anscombe noted, we here get indeterminateness arising from the limits of measurement, even where Newtonian mechanics is assumed to apply.[6]

Realist-minded philosophers may still want to say that these practical limits on our knowledge of the present and predictions of the future do not affect the underlying facts about how reality is "in itself." On the other hand, Michael Dummett (who coined the expression "anti-realism") says that the assump-tion that every measurable quantity must have a precise value given by a real number is "a realist fantasy which, though deeply embedded in our thinking, must be rejected."[7] It is a nice irony that realism, which surely intends to acknowledge reality, may be fantastic, i.e., out of touch with reality. But there are at least two kinds of dissociation between thought and reality: we may *under*estimate what there is, or we may *over*estimate it. The thesis that a certain "transcendental" kind of realism involves deep philosophical error is central to Kant's thought, but we have yet to see if this has any relevance to our present topic. Dummett is bold enough to say that reality itself may be in certain respects indeterminate; and he does not mean causally undetermined events, but questions to which there is no true or false answer.

I do not know any conclusive way of resolving this standoff between realist and antirealist over exact measurement. The realist claim can hardly be classed as meaningless, for it seems readily enough intelligible (and philosophers' attempts to draw sharp limits around the meaningful do not have a promising track record). The antirealist will naturally point out that the realist's claim can never be confirmed or disconfirmed by experience, but the realist will not be fazed by that, for it was part of his view from the start that the truth on some matters may forever outrun empirical test. The best I think the antireal-ist can do is to show that the ideal of *completely* precise measurement plays no essential role in our dealing with the world, not even in the most theoretical parts of science. To be sure, science expresses laws in the form of mathematical formulas, and computations can be performed in the abstract as it were (in classroom examples and school homework), by feeding integral or rational numbers into the equations. But when it comes to testing those laws or using them to predict anything, we have to use *actually measured* values, which are accurate only within a margin of error and cannot be strictly identified with numbers abstractly conceived as rationals, let alone reals.

It may be tempting to suggest that the idea of exact measurement functions as a Kantian ideal, to be approximated to but never actually reached. But even that is open to question, for although it sounds like good advice to say that our measurements should be as accurate as we can make them, our standards of precision will quite reasonably vary depending on what we are measuring, and for what purpose: there will be no point in trying to measure the width of a road or the height of a growing child to hundredths of a centimeter. And even when it is important to micromeasure up to the limits of available technology, in cosmology or atomic theory, for example, there is a sense in which although new technology can increase the accuracy of our measurements, we never get any nearer to coming up with an *infinite* row of decimals, for the distinguishing feature of an infinite set is of course that however many members of it you count, there always remain infinitely many more. Thus the ideal of complete precision is not really *approached*, for it constantly recedes over the horizon.

Let me now address the first of those two idealizations I identified in the idea of determinism, namely, the idea of a *total* state-description of the world at a time. I find it remarkable how casually philosophers tend to help themselves to this notion in discussing determinism. Of course, it will be readily admitted that nobody could ever *know* such a total description, so the claim would have to be that nevertheless there *is* such a description, which would have to be a monstrously large (yet presumably still finite) proposition, consisting of a conjunction of all the true propositions about the world at a time. Some may want to insist on a distinction between true propositions and the facts or states of affairs that make them true, propositions being thought of as abstract entities, and facts as concrete entities that are "in the world." But my skepticism applies equally to both, for there is surely a one-to-one correlation between them, i.e., to every proposition there corresponds a unique fact, and vice versa. This entails that facts or states of affairs are conceptually structured, like propositions (as we saw in essay 1). Yet facts and propositions can be thought of as outrunning the conceptual resources of any particular language as it has developed up to a certain time. There were electrons and protons in the universe, and rocks and reptiles on the earth, long before we developed concepts of them, indeed for aeons before there were any languages at all (on this planet, anyway). And we have to allow that the sciences will almost certainly develop new concepts in the future, to identify aspects of reality that presently lie beyond our ken but are all around us now.

Conceptual innovation is not confined to the sciences, either: consider, for example, the concepts of bassoon, A-minor scale, symphony, cobalt blue, golden section, pointillism, tragedy, sonnet, novel, general election, prime minister, fascism, insurance contract, subprime mortgage, pedophilia, and soap opera. Each of these concepts has been developed at some stage of human history, and some of them may be applied retrospectively to instances that existed before the relevant concept was added to our language. The notion of a stupendously large proposition conjoining *all* the truths about *everything* in the world, involving *all* the concepts that are not just actual but *possible* (for any species of rational being, anywhere in the universe?) must now be seen as a very great idealization indeed, and one that it is hard to see as having any possible use in our thinking. However, those sympathetic to determinism may want to cut down the set of *all* facts to a more manageable size by saying that the state-descriptions in any realistic thesis of determinism will have to prescind from any such riot of aesthetic, political, and sociological concepts, and should be expressed austerely in terms of basic physical concepts that apply universally to the matter or energy of which everything is composed.

This raises a cluster of issues centering around reductionism and emergence, which could take whole books to discuss. There is first a question of whether we can ever be sure that we have identified the most basic level of physical reality, for the history of science shows a series of steps down the levels, and there is no guarantee that our present subatomic physics is the end of the story. Next there are subtle questions about how the basic level relates to the other levels of reality, from the chemical and the biological up to the psychological, social, historical, political, aesthetic, and whatever else goes into the mix. If we accept the weakest possible form of materialism and say that everything is *composed* of whatever entities are recognized by the basic level of physics, that will exclude dualism of mind and matter but leave almost everything else open. If we accept the weakest form of supervenience, namely, that if there is a difference between two bodies, states, events, or processes there must be some difference between them at the basic level, we have to acknowledge how very little this amounts to. All it implies, for example, is that if orchestra A gives an exciting performance of Beethoven's Fifth Symphony whereas orchestra B is underwhelming with it, there must be some difference at the acoustic level between those two sound events—which is hardly news. And if C takes the risk of accepting D's offer of a drink, there must be some difference (though conceivably only at the subatomic level) between C's state and the state she would have been in had she declined. But there is absolutely no prospect of our being able to detect *all* the microphysical similarities and differences within such highly complex systems as human bodies, so the supervenience thesis would seem to be unfalsifiable and devoid of empirical content.

We could try approaching the issue from the top, as it were, with the strongest possible reduction thesis, namely, that all the concepts at level n can be defined in terms of the concepts of level n − 1, so that all the truths (or facts) expressible at level n can be defined in terms of true propositions at level n – 1. Repeated applications of such a principle would reduce all concepts and truths to those at level 1. But there is no prospect of such an extremely strong reduction being carried out. Each level has its own distinctive concepts, and the idea of defining all the vocabulary of music, politics, history, psychology, biology, ecology, and meteorology in terms of physics is laughable, if only because familiar words such as "car," "prime minister," and "insect," though designating physical objects, allow of *multiple realization*, i.e., there are many different physical types of each, and new types can turn up, so not even a disjunctive physical definition will do.

It thus appears that the would-be reductionist cannot cut down the set of all the facts to those expressible in the microphysical vocabulary. Whether we like it or not, the world is an irreducibly complex place, as we noted in essay 5. The notion of "all the facts," or a total state-description of the world at any one instant, is an idealization vastly inflated from anything we can ever hope to know. So, therefore, is the notion of determinism—for this and the other two reasons discussed above, namely, the complexity of the mathematics and the inexactness of all measurement.

II. CONCEPTIONS OF CAUSATION

So far I have not invoked the concept of cause, causality, or causation. But determinism has often been expressed as the claim that every event has a cause, by which is often understood a preceding state of affairs upon which the event follows in accordance with a law or rule, hence with a certain kind of necessity such that if the relevant preceding state (the cause) occurs, then the event (the effect) *must* follow. So let us scrutinize this well-worn claim that every event has a cause. It has sometimes been taken in a very strong sense, to mean that for any event there is a preceding *total* state of the world that, given the laws of nature, implies that that event must happen—i.e., determinism as we elucidated it above. But there is a much weaker way of interpreting it. Take the example of an apple (that paradigm fruit of Newtonian Paradise!) and consider how it could be detached from its tree by at least three different kinds of cause—a gust of wind, the decay of the last strand of its stalk, or the tweak of a human hand. It is one thing to say that any particular event of apple detachment must have some cause or other in the immediately preceding vicinity, where by "cause" we just mean an event of a kind that *normally* results in an effect of the relevant type. But it is quite another thing to assert that for every event of apple detachment there must have been some preceding *total* state of the universe that made it *inevitable*. That is a highly speculative thesis that goes way beyond the homely generalizations of apple-picking folk and other ordinary talk of causes.

It is thus apparent that the apparently simple generalization "Every event has a cause" is *deceptively* simple, for it suffers from ambiguities in the notion of cause, and the associated notions of law, rule, and necessity. There is an everyday usage of the word "cause" that amounts to: *what made a certain event happen in the circumstances*, or perhaps: the most distinctive thing in that set of circumstances that made or allowed the event to happen (where what counts as "most distinctive" often depends on human interests in apportioning praise or blame, e.g., was the crash caused by pilot error, extreme weather, a design fault in the aircraft, or a combination of two or more of these?). But this informal notion of what *made* something happen by no means implies that it absolutely *had* to happen, that nothing whatsoever could have stopped it. The possible causes of apple detachment mentioned above could each be prevented from having their usual effect: the pressure of the wind could be stopped by a wind shield, the decay of the stalk might be arrested by a chemical spray, and the apple picker's grasp might be interrupted by something diverting her attention (the voice of Adam, perhaps). In the aircraft case, the absence of any one of the above-mentioned factors might be enough to avoid a crash; it is harder to see how it could be prevented if all three factors were to combine, but it is not inconceivable—perhaps another freak in the weather might allow the pilot to stabilize the falling plane.

I am thus backing up Anscombe's claim that our ordinary notion of causality does not imply determination or necessitation. It would seem to involve only *what usually leads to the effect, if no interfering factor prevents it*— and the vagueness of the word "usually" matches the vagueness of our notion of "cause." Perhaps even "usually" is too strong, in the light of Anscombe's examples of people sometimes, but not always, catching diseases when exposed to infection. If A develops the symptoms of flu after being in a room full of sneezes, we may say with great confidence that that was the cause of A's catching flu, even if we know that B was also there but did not get it. Even if a majority of those sneezed upon escape the flu, we may still believe, not unreasonably, that for those who do catch it their exposure was the cause. Similarly, we may be quite certain that it was last night's storm that brought down our beloved beech tree, though previous storms of equal or greater ferocity did not. And we may ascribe Joanna's appreciation of the difference between Kantian and utilitarian ethics to her taking course 101 in Moral Philosophy, even if most of her inattentive classmates fail to come away with any such understanding. So if "usually" is taken to imply "in a majority of cases," we will have to downgrade still further to the bathetic "quite often." No wonder that the young and boisterous Bertrand Russell described the law of causality as "a relic of a bygone age, surviving, like the monarchy, only because it is erroneously supposed to do no harm."[8]

Even if not disposed to be quite so iconoclastic about the concept of cause, readers will be itching to protest that the lamentable imprecision of most of its applications is due to our ignorance. If we get to know more about the operations of viruses and the human immune system, the strength of tree roots and their dependence on the weather, the intelligence and industry of particular students (and perhaps some detail of their brains?), then surely we will be able to come up with more precise analyses of the causal factors that are relevant in each case, and thus make more confident explanations and predictions. Now I do not deny for a moment that we can make progress in identifying more causal factors, and in understanding how they can make a difference to outcomes; indeed, much of science consists of such inquiries. But I insist that many of the generalizations that result will still need to hedge their bets, and take the form: if A, B, and C occur then D will usually, or normally, or nearly always, happen, or: if A, B, and C occur then D will happen unless something intervenes to prevent it. For anything as complex as immune systems, human psychology, and perhaps even the growth of trees, there seems to be no prospect of achieving a complete and perfect understanding of *all* the factors involved in their behavior. So any summary of the state of the science about them needs to acknowledge a fringe of ignorance and make allowance for interfering factors that remain unknown or imperfectly understood. Scientific research increases our knowledge, but it does not reduce our ignorance to zero. Science is not omniscience.

But though this point may be admitted for complex systems where complete understanding and predictability are humanly impossible, anyone who has learned a bit of science will want to say that at the microlevel of chemistry and physics we have discovered fundamental laws that are genuinely exceptionless, and need no hedging about with reference to possible interfering factors. Our paradigms tend to remain Newton's laws of motion, and Maxwell's equations for electromagnetism, and perhaps the formulas for chemical reactions (though the need for catalysts may muddy those waters). However, there is an important distinction between textbook examples involving such laws and their application to real-life situations. The examples in the books invite us to consider simple situations *in isolation*, as if nothing else existed in the world—or nothing else that is relevant, anyway. Newton's first law says that a body *not acted upon by any forces* will continue in its state of rest or of motion in a straight line—but of course there is no such totally isolated body anywhere in the universe. Newtonian mechanics achieved striking success in explaining and predicting the motions of the solar system and has thereby exerted a stranglehold over our imaginations, leading many people to suppose that science has proved the truth of determinism (as Anscombe also noted). But that success rests on the contingent facts that the sun is enormously massive compared with the planets and moons, that they in turn are very massive relative to the asteroids and comets, and that all the stuff in the rest of the universe is so distant that its gravitational effects can be ignored. The impressively accurate predictions of eclipses, etc., are based on *approximations* which work to the scale of accuracy that concerns us. But for the smaller bodies like the asteroids their motions can still not be computed with any similar long-term accuracy, so that future asteroid impacts on the earth can be neither predicted nor ruled out. The solar system is quite complex after all, and not every detail is predictable. There is plenty of room for our rough-and-ready concept of cause, without commitment to determinism.

III. KANT AND CAUSALITY

Now at last it is time to relate our discussion to Kant. There is a widespread impression that, being strongly influenced by the Newtonian paradigm like everyone else in the eighteenth century, Kant believed in determinism, and moreover argued for its synthetic a priori status in his Second Analogy of Experience, in the Analytic of the *Critique of Pure Reason*. And it is usually assumed that he carried forward this supposed result to his discussion of determinism and free will in the third antinomy, in the Dialectic. However, Graham Bird has questioned these assumptions (Bird 2006: 19.2, 20.1, 27.1), and my discussion will be much indebted to his.

Admittedly, the headline of the Second Analogy tends to encourage us to read Kant as a determinist. In A the claim is: "Everything that happens (begins to be) presupposes something which it follows in accordance with a rule" (A189). In B Kant reworded this as: "All alterations occur in accordance with the law of the connection of cause and effect" (B232). It is very natural to take these sentences as asserting that every event has a cause,[9] but Bird finds some wiggle room in the fact that the first talks of "presupposition," and the second of "in accordance with"; and he proposes that the "General Causal Principle" that Kant argues for is only that every event must be "contained within a general causal network." Bird offers various formulations of this weaker principle (Bird 2006: 482, 485, 692):

Ai.   Every phenomenal event presupposes some causal connection.
Aii. The concept of an event in general is synthetically dependent on that of a cause.
Aiii. The concept of an event in general requires reference to, presupposes, that of a cause.

as opposed to the increasingly stronger principles:

B. Every event has a cause.
C. Every phenomenal event is the outcome of a necessary causal law.
D. All phenomenal, natural events are subject to causal laws related by necessity, and form a complete determinate series.[10]

If Bird is right, what Kant's subtle but obscure discussion in the Second Analogy shows is that our recognition of events in the world as objectively ordered in time, distinct from our successive perceptions of them, requires that we locate all events within a general causal framework, i.e., a web of relations that includes a great deal of causal connection. Not every alteration in our perceptual experience represents an alteration in the object perceived. A house does not normally change as one surveys it, so one can presume that its features remain in simultaneous existence as one moves through it. Kant's inquiry in the Second Analogy is into the necessary conditions of our being able to distinguish between changes in our perceptions and changes in the things we perceive. I am not entering into detailed exegesis of that difficult text here, but the main line of argument is that to make this type of distinction we need to rely on regularities in the persistence and changes of familiar sorts of thing, and on the causal dependence of our perceptions on our proximity to objects and the normal workings of our sense organs. We could not apply the concept of objective event unless we also find plenty of application for causal conceptions, as Ai–iii assert.

But if Kant makes a plausible case for A, that need not imply B, let alone C or D. Once a general causal framework is in place, could there not be conceptual room for some "uncaused" events? After all, we are told that quantum mechanics has shown that random, undetermined events continually occur at the subatomic level, and that there can be no "hidden variables" to explain them. At one stage in twentieth-century cosmology, before the advent of the big bang theory, it was suggested (by Fred Hoyle) that the expansion of the universe might be explained by postulating the spontaneous creation ex nihilo of hydrogen atoms in interstellar space; that is not now believed, but the idea was rejected on empirical rather than a priori grounds. Come to think of it, even the old folktale of babies being found under gooseberry bushes may have a similar epistemological status. Of course, it is not being *found* under a bush that poses a puzzle, for the overwhelming presumption would be that any such foundling had been left there by someone who wanted rid of it; what would be truly startling is the idea that babies come into existence ex nihilo (and could be observed and videotaped doing so). In medieval times people believed that lower forms of life were spontaneously generated in dust and slime, and though we now know they were wrong, they surely had enough of a general causal framework in place to be able to distinguish their perceptions from objects perceived; they would seem to have satisfied the (weakly interpreted) requirements of Kant's Second Analogy while nevertheless believing that some events lacked causes. Of course any such spontaneous generation would play havoc with our biology, chemistry, and physics and their conservation laws, which rule out the coming into existence of living beings without the normal processes of reproduction and growth. But that just shows that such deeply entrenched scientific beliefs ultimately rest on empirically observed regularities in the world, rather than a priori grounds. At present we lack a thorough understanding of what causes cancer in individual people, and its occasional unexpected remission which is sometimes greeted as miraculous. We all hope medical science will make further progress on this, but suppose evidence were to emerge that the starting and stopping of cancerous growths sometimes depends on undetermined, inherently unpredictable events at the quantum level. Would the lack of causation in such cases prevent us distinguishing our perceptions from objects we perceive?—surely not.

Much depends here on what we mean by this weaselly little word "cause," whose ambiguity I have already noted. If we see any of the above possibilities of uncaused events as not ruled out a priori, it is surely because in those scenarios the relevant events are envisaged as *frequently*, though unpredictably, occurring *in certain specifiable conditions*. Any allegation about a *one-off* uncaused event would quite reasonably be disputed on grounds like those Hume adduced against believing any testimony about miracles (*Enquiry*, section X): it would be said that the observer must have been mistaken, that the recording apparatus was not working properly, and so on. But if in a certain type of condition C, events of type A are quite often observed to happen, but in ways that we cannot explain by any intervening factor B, it seems we have a choice. We could insist that there must *exist* some such explanatory factors, however many times we have failed to find them, and thus maintain that every event has a cause as a matter of unfalsifiable faith. Or else—so my argument suggests—we could say that these A-events have no causes in the sense of something that necessitates them to happen. However, they could still be said to have a cause in what is perhaps the weakest possible meaning of that conceptually overstretched word— namely, a type of condition C in which As are known to sometimes occur (perhaps with a quantifiable measure of probability). That usage would weaken any connotation of C *making* As happen, but it could retain Anscombe's notion of C being the *source* of As, that from which As derive, or in which As tend to come into being.

We would still believe that every event has an *effect*—or at least that it *could have* an effect on suitably placed observers or instruments—but we would give up the belief that every single event has a cause in that sense of something involving a necessary connection between cause and effect. Kant obviously had that stronger sense in mind when he wrote:

> For this concept [of cause] always requires that something A be of such a kind that something else B follows from it *necessarily* and *in accordance with an absolutely universal rule.*
>
> (A91/B124)

> There must therefore lie in that which in general precedes an occurrence the condition for a rule, in accordance with which this occurrence *always* and *necessarily* follows.
>
> (A193/B238-9, with my emphasis)

Just after that first quotation, Kant wrote that the concept of cause has a "dignity" and necessity that an empiricist approach like Hume's fails to accord it. (Perhaps he would accuse me, too, of casting aspersions on its dignity!) To be sure, Hume famously found "necessary connexion" to be part of our idea of cause—and he performed some extraordinary mental acrobatics in trying to find an empirical origin for it (*Treatise* I.iii, sections ii, vi, xiv)—but the sort of "necessity" that he offered was far too subjective and contingent for Kant's taste. And although Hume talked of *constant* conjunction as the foundation of our causal beliefs, in later sections he allowed that *probable* reasoning can be founded on chances and on causes where past evidence contains "contrary instances" in which similar states of affairs have produced different results (*Treatise* I.III.xi–xii). He thus recognized a probabilistic conception of cause. Both philosophers talk of *regularity,* and of things happening *in accordance with a rule,* but both could avail themselves of the ordinary language reflection that neither phrase need imply the total absence of exceptions, e.g., "Snoggins attends our parish church regularly"—though not when he is ill, or on holiday; "As a rule, heavy smoking leads to lung cancer"—but for reasons that we do not understand, it does not always do so. Kant had a notably rigorist cast of mind, and he was obviously concerned to analyze and emphasize the a priori elements in causation and the necessity of causal connections as he understood them, but he knew perfectly well that there is such a thing as probable empirical reasoning (A728–9/B756–57; A775/B803; A820–22/B848–50), so I suggest that he too could have accepted the idea of probabilistic causation, though I do not know of any text where he explicitly does so.

The outcome of this section is that although the wording of the Second Analogy strongly suggests that Kant thought he had proved C, i.e., the need for scientific-style exceptionless laws as a prerequisite for experience of an objective world, it may be that all that he succeeded in supporting was A (in any of its formulations) and B in the weakest possible sense of probabilistic cause or originating condition. An edifying moral of the story is that there are various different conceptions of causation, some of them having more "dignity" or necessity than others.

IV. KANT AND DETERMINISM

Let me now examine Kant's attitude to the strongest of Bird's formulations:

D. All phenomenal, natural events are subject to causal laws related by necessity, and form a complete determinate series.

I take it that "complete determinate" implies "completely determined," so that this is as Bird says (2006: 693) a version of universal causal determinism. Now that we are about to address what Kant wrote about his third antinomy, we must be careful to remember that although in setting out the Antinomy he presents arguments for opposing theses plus some relevant observations, he is not thereby *endorsing* those arguments or observations. Kant describes the whole Dialectic section of the *Critique* as a "logic of illusion"; and in the four antinomies he presents what he takes to be inherent but mistaken tendencies in human reasoning. He only begins to speak for himself again when he offers his elaborate diagnosis of what goes wrong in these arguments that seem to support contradictory conclusions.

The nerve of the two opposing arguments presented in the third antinomy can be summarized as follows:

> *Thesis:* If causality in accordance with laws of nature is the only kind of causality, then every cause must itself have a cause, and on to infinity; so there would never be a first beginning, and there would be "no completeness of the series on the side of the causes," but this would contradict "the law of nature" which "consists just in this, that nothing happens without a cause sufficiently determined a priori."
>
> (from A446/B474)

> *Antithesis:* If there were "freedom in the transcendental sense," i.e. "a faculty of absolutely beginning a state," then nothing would precede it "through which this occurring action is determined in accordance with constant laws," but this would be "contrary to the causal law," so that no "unity of experience" would be possible.
>
> (from A447/B475)

Now suppose we do not yet take into account the great deal that Kant finds to say in the rest of the Antinomy chapter, and just consider these arguments on their face value, in the light of the considerations broached in this essay so far. As Kant's observations on it say, the thesis argument (if it shows anything) only shows the need for a First Cause in the whole history of the universe (whether big bang or divine creation remains to be seen), and such a First Cause would itself have to be uncaused (or self-causing—if that makes sense). But if *one* such "absolutely spontaneous" cause can be admitted, there would seem to be no *logical* bar to postulating a host of others all down history, including a decision by Kant to rise from his chair (the only case I know where he uses himself as an example!). The whole force of the thesis argument rests on the so-called law of nature, that "nothing happens without a cause sufficiently determined a priori"—but it is very unclear what that means, and whether we have any reason to accept it. We have allowed that in the Second Analogy Kant makes at least a plausible case for A (in any of the formulations Ai–iii) and for B (that every event has a cause) though only in the very weak sense of a condition in which events of the relevant type are known to occur quite often. But the crucial premise of the thesis argument seems to be either C (a much stronger sense of cause) or D (a formulation of total determinism). Armed with our own reflections on causality and determinism, and with what we have found acceptable from Kant's Second Analogy, we seem easily able to resist the blandishments of the thesis argument.

The same applies to the antithesis argument. What exactly is "the causal law," to which uncaused events would be contrary? The claim that no "unity of experience" would be possible without it is a clear reference back to the supposed result of the Second Analogy, but our discussion in section III cast doubt on any claim that C or D (or B in a more than probabilistic sense) is a necessary presupposition of experience. Suppose, as many of us believe already, that some natural events, at least human actions, are free and uncaused in the strongest sense you can conceive: that may make life complicated and unpredictable in many ways, but is the Kantian unity of experience thereby undermined? Does it prevent us locating everything that happens, including human actions and their manifold consequences for good and ill, in a single objective world in which we all move and have our being? Surely not!

Is that the end of our inquiry, then? Given that we have seen in section I that determinism is a mere ideal, not an empirical claim that can be confirmed, and if, given our distinctions between various concepts of causation in sections II and III, there is no reason to be persuaded by either side of Kant's third antinomy as stated, can we happily conclude that causality and determinism pose no genuine threat to free will? No doubt some will welcome the chance to go home early, especially if it means not having to read any more Kant. If so, I am sorry to disappoint them, but I think there is more that needs considering, some of it indeed from the deep but difficult sage of Konigsberg.

I have cited a variety of cases in which we believe that there is causality at work without our knowing any exceptionless laws in terms of which the effects can be reliably predicted—the weather, the spread of infections, the uprooting of trees, the incidence and remission of cancers, the fall of apples—and I might have added: the shapes of trees, the antics of cats, and the decisions of people about insurance, marriage, and charitable giving. But it will be replied that in many (perhaps all?) of these cases, we can find out more about the causes involved by scientific research, delving into the relevant microstructures such as viruses, cells, hormones, and brains. And if there *is* more to be found, then don't we have to believe that there are real, intrinsic structures out there, in which proper scientific laws operate, i.e., laws of nature that are not just vague and probabilistic but exact and universal, without exceptions? And when we apply this thought to our bodies and brains, many people feel that a threat to free will remains.

Now the argument for the thesis of Kant's third antinomy (paraphrased above) seems strangely remote from this common thought that seems to lead toward a threatening kind of determinism. He talks there of a *first* cause, and thus seems to align his third antinomy more closely with the first antinomy (concerning the age and size of the universe) and the fourth (concerning a necessary being). Yet it is obvious from the *solution* Kant offers to the third antinomy, and above all from his later writings on moral philosophy and religion, that he was deeply concerned to defend human free will in a very strong sense. As the observation on it says, the thesis argument is *indirectly* connected with the conception of free will in that it defends the "transcendental freedom" that Kant takes to be a necessary presupposition of free will, namely, that there can be events that have *no* natural causes. I am therefore going to be so cheeky as to reformulate Kant's third antinomy for him, to make it touch more explicitly on free will and determinism.

Revised Constitutive Antinomy

Amended thesis: If causality in accordance with laws of nature is the only kind of causality, then everything that happens can be causally explained in that way, including human decisions and actions. But that seems to leave no room for explanation in terms of the reasons of the agent. In many of the situations we face, we have a real choice about what to do: although we may have relevant beliefs and desires, they do not determine what we do, and we have to make our own decision, which we are painfully aware could go either way. Thus we believe in "transcendental freedom," i.e., that nothing that precedes such decisions "determines them in accordance with constant laws."

Amended antithesis: If there were "freedom in this transcendental sense," "a faculty of absolutely beginning a state," then nothing would precede our free actions "through

which they are determined in accordance with constant laws." But that would be contrary to the presumption of all science, that if only we know enough about the preceding
state of the world and the laws of nature, every event, including human choices and
actions, can be predicted with certainty. And that presupposes that the laws and complete
state-description of the universe at any given time imply its next state, i.e., determinism.

Here is a modernized version of the antinomy, which I hope expresses the
philosophical problem in a form that we now find readily intelligible, and
with arguments that are plausible on first sight. But now our work on the
concept of determinism in section I will pay dividends, for we can already see
the outlines of a solution. The definition of determinism requires the concept of a complete description of the state of the universe at any given time;
remember that we found that such a notion (if it makes sense at all) is an idealization way beyond anything we can ever hope to achieve, whatever progress
we may make in science and technology. It is *this* kind of completeness—the
idea of a total state-description of the world at a time—that is more centrally
involved in the amended antinomy, rather than the completeness of a series
of causes stretching back in time. To say of any given event that it is predetermined is to say that it is necessitated by the laws of nature plus the preceding
total state-description of the world; to say of any given event that it is *not*
predetermined, but uncaused, is to say that the laws of nature plus the preceding total state-description of the world do *not* necessitate it. So both
determinism and indeterminism ("transcendental freedom") presuppose
that there *is* such a thing as a total description of the world at any given
time—but we have seen that to be highly questionable. We can therefore see
a solution to our revised third antinomy that takes the form Kant proposed
for his first and second antinomies, namely, that both sides are wrong because
they rest on a common presupposition that has to be rejected.

   Moreover, what is claimed to go wrong in all these cases is a certain kind
of attempted "completion" to a series, in which our thought tends to jump
ahead of all possible scientific inquiry, and postulate a first moment in the
history of the universe, a smallest constituent of matter, and a total state-
description of the world at any time. In each case, we can endorse Kant's
recommendation of a "regulative ideal" that encourages science to go on
(forever) seeking more knowledge of the universe great and small, and of its
constituents and operations at any one time. But (unlike Laplace) we have
no need of the notion of an end point to each of these series; that is not
something for which we will ever find empirical application. At best, it may
serve as an ideal to be pursued, but it will forever recede over the epistemological horizon and elude our scientific grasp (see also essay 5).

   And now at last we can see a connection with Kant's distinction between
appearances and things in themselves, and perhaps we can even discern

some rationale for it. Appearances can be identified with our empirically justified, but inevitably finite, partial, incomplete descriptions of reality; things in themselves (despite the plural) can, I suggest, be identified with the notion of reality, i.e., reality as it is "in itself" (see essays 1, 4 and 5). Our descriptions are of course meant to be descriptions *of reality* (and some of them turn out to be false), but they are all inadequate and partial. There can be no such thing as a complete description of reality. (But I am well aware that is not the only interpretation of this, perhaps the most hotly disputed of all Kant's doctrines.)

The conclusion of this section is that both determinism and indeterminism are precisely what Kant called "transcendental ideas":

> By the idea of a necessary concept of reason, I understand one to which no congruent object can be given by the senses. Thus the pure concepts of reason we have just examined are *transcendental ideas*. They are concepts of pure reason; for they consider all experiential cognition as determined through an absolute totality of conditions. They are not arbitrarily invented, but given as problems by the nature of reason itself, and hence they relate necessarily to the entire use of the understanding. Finally, they are transcendental concepts, and exceed the bounds of all experience, in which no object adequate to the transcendental idea can occur.
>
> (A327/B383–84)

At the end of his solution to the third antinomy, Kant says he has not been trying to establish the reality of freedom (i.e., transcendental freedom, indeterminism), and not even its possibility; he rests his case on treating freedom as a *transcendental idea* that does not conflict with natural causality (A558/B586). I fear he is not quite so clear about the status of determinism; he seems prone to overestimate what he has proved in the Second Analogy, and in one place he suggests it is a conception of the understanding, whereas it would be more consistent with the main lines of his thought to say that *causality* is a category of the understanding, but *determinism* is an idea of reason.

V. KANT AND FREE WILL

Kantians will have been jumping up and down to remind me that his official solution to his third and fourth antinomies is not that both sides are false but that each side, when suitably interpreted, can be *true*. He repeatedly makes the bold claim that natural causality and determinism can reign supreme at the level of phenomena, or things as they appear, but that "transcendental freedom" can apply at the level of noumena, or things as they are in themselves. He is, if anything, even bolder in the "Critical Elucidation" section of the *Critique of Practical Reason* (4:89–106).

But this seems to push our judgments and decisions into the unknowable and atemporal realm of noumena, and Kant's readers have always found it hard to understand how this can help, for it implies that we can have no knowledge whatsoever of these supposedly "transcendentally free" operations of human minds. It would indeed be a Pickwickian defense of free will to hide what we are most interested in behind an irremovable veil of ignorance. The problem is illustrated when Kant writes that "the real morality of actions (their merit and guilt), even that of our own conduct, therefore remains entirely hidden from us" (A551/B579, note), yet goes on to say about the example of a malicious lie that even when we believe it to be determined by its psychological and sociological causes, we may still blame the agent and regard his reason as "fully free" (A555/B583).

To be sure, the logical relationships between premises and conclusions in logic and mathematics, between evidence and hypotheses in theoretical reasoning and science, and between reasons and decisions in practical reasoning are all atemporal. Such rational relations are the subject matter of "reason" in a wide sense of the term. But our mental *acts* of realizing, reasoning, weighing-up and judging or deciding are of course events occurring in time, though their *contents* are atemporal. Even the most determined Platonist about mathematics has to recognize that mathematicians undergo birth and death, and have their moments of discovery and perhaps of fame somewhere in between. According to Kant's controversial doctrine, whatever is noumenal is atemporal, but he would be among the first to acknowledge that not everything that is atemporal is noumenal—for example, mathematics.

Nevertheless I think Kant in his erratic wisdom has left behind the means for us to see how *both* diagnoses of the revised third antinomy can be correctthat in one sense, determinism and indeterminism should be rejected, but in another sense they can both be endorsed.[11] My suggestion is based on the distinction between *constitutive* claims and *regulative* principles that Kant makes so much of throughout the Dialectic. Here is a typical statement of it:

> Thus the principle of reason is only a *rule*, prescribing a regress in the series of conditions for given appearances, in which regress it is never allowed to stop with an absolutely unconditioned. Thus it is not a principle of the possibility of experience and of the empirical cognition of objects of sense...nor is it a *constitutive principle* of reason for extending the world of sense beyond all possible experience; rather it is a principle of the greatest possible continuation and extension of experience...thus it is a principle of

reason which, as a *rule*, postulates what should be effected by us in the regress, but *does not anticipate* what is given in itself *in the object* prior to any regress. Hence I call it a *regulative* principle of reason.

(A508–9/B536–37)

Determinism and its negation (indeterminism) cannot, for the reasons I have been exploring throughout this essay, be regarded as "constitutive," i.e., as empirical assertions about the actual nature of the world.[12] But there are associated maxims or policies or regulative principles that we can and should follow. On the side of determinism, the obvious policy is to keep on looking for causes, to continually refine and deepen our understanding of how the world works and how one set of conditions leads to another. That, of course, is the mission statement of science, broadly conceived to include the social as well as the physical sciences. But we have seen in this essay and in essay 5 that we should not expect any end point to the story of science.

On the side of free will, as it were, it is perhaps less clear what the regulative ideal or practical policy should be. After all, what would it amount to, in practice, *not* to believe in free will? In one's own case, however firmly one might believe that all one's thoughts, judgments, choices, and actions are completely determined by preceding states of the universe, including the states of one's own brain and of the brains of one's significant others, one cannot thereby be relieved of the burden of deciding what to think and how to act. As we saw in essay 7, Kant made this point in *Groundwork* 4:448, with respect to judgments as well as actions.[13] Quite often one may "go with the flow" (or the Tao?) and simply accept and do whatever it occurs to one to accept or do, but there are bound to be occasions on which one will need reflectively to weigh the evidence for and against believing A, or the reasons for and against doing B, thus operating at the higher mental levels distinguished in essay 8. As for our attitude to *other* people, let us remember the elementary fact that we do talk to each other, and that this often involves offering reasons for and against doing something, or reasons for or against believing something. Frequently there is a collective "we"—a couple, a family, a committee, a board of directors—who are committed to doing things together and have to engage in discussion and in something resembling reasoning about what to do next. In such situations, the participants have to treat each other as capable in some degree of understanding, communicating, and weighing of reasons. If one is cynical enough to believe that the outcome of a particular discussion is already determined by the beliefs and attitudes of the other participants, then one may decide to save one's breath and remain silent, or if pressed to comment one might just "go through the motions" without any hope that it will affect the result. But then the point of communication is lost, and the unnaturalness of that situation shows up by contrast our normal assumption that other people (well, most of them, for some of the time at least) are amenable to reason.[14]

To be sure, this assumption sometimes breaks down. It is possible to see the speech and behavior of certain people as caused, perhaps even determined, by their physiological state and their psychological and sociological history. The clearest examples are brain damage or advanced dementia, where it may seem one has to give up hope of any real communication. But with anything beyond those extreme cases, the situation is less clear. What about addicts, those with "compulsive" disorders, the sexually abused, the severely traumatized, the autistic, those who have been ideologically conditioned from an early age, Kant's malicious liar—the list goes on. Should one treat them as determined by their past, and hence as beyond all serious communication and reasoning, and so as subjects for "management," manipulation, and the use of drugs or force when necessary? (It is very tempting for those who have the difficult task of dealing with such people to simplify and shortcut in such ways, to label people as falling under certain types, and thereby to give up hope that they can transcend the types into which one has cast them.) There is an enormous range of human types and conditions, and obviously it is way beyond the scope of this essay to go into the empirical details. But I think there is one important lesson that emerges from our discussion, namely, that we can never know for certain that someone is beyond all communication, or that their behavior is totally determined by the type under which they admittedly fall. Even with brain damage and dementia, unexplained recoveries and lucid moments sometimes occur: there is, and presumably always will be, much we do not understand about brain function, especially in abnormal cases. With less extreme conditions, the attempt to communicate (in a way that respects the person) may well help to induce recovery and mental or moral growth. Hope or faith in the actual or potential personhood of the other can be self-fulfilling. Here perhaps is the most appropriate object for the Kantian attitude of moral faith (*Glaube*) that I investigated at some length in essay 6.

What, then, of Kant's malicious liar, the seemingly hardened criminal, the long-term abuser, or *l'homme moyens sensual*—the averagely self-centered self-indulger (i.e., most of us most of the time?) It is vital to recognize that we never know just how hardened, how impervious to moral considerations, someone has become. We may be told much about their past, but we will never know it all; we may be able to study increasingly sophisticated brain scans, but we can never know the detail of every neuron, let alone every thought. Kant's saying that the real morality of actions, even of our own conduct, remains hidden from us is surely wise. In the *Religion* (6:37–48) he argues passionately that despite the "radical evil" in our

human nature, namely, our constant temptation to prefer our own inclinations to the demands of morality, each of our actions remains fundamentally free, and a radical revolution in our disposition is always possible. And
there are examples of murderers becoming writers, of terrorists turning into
democratic politicians, and of former enemies achieving reconciliation and
forgiveness. It remains open, and I would suggest obligatory, to respect the
humanity, the personhood, of even the most apparently hardened wrong-
doer and to hope that our respect may elicit respect in return, along with
acknowledgment of responsibility for their own actions. I conclude that
both sides of the following antinomy can be endorsed with consistency,
and with enthusiasm:

Regulative Antinomy

> *Thesis:* We should treat people as amenable to reason as far as possible, and be amenable
> to reason ourselves.
>
> *Antithesis:* We should pursue scientific research into causes as far as possible (including
> brain science and evolutionary psychology).

Perhaps, dear reader, you are still wondering how all this relates to the
timeworn philosophical debate between compatibilism and incompati-
bilism? Well, I put it to you that determinism (as a constitutive claim) is a
paper tiger: there is nothing there that you need to worry about being compatible or incompatible with. But do you wonder if all this really counts as a
defense of free will after all? Do you still hanker in your heart after the idea
of undetermined acts of will, possessing that "transcendental freedom" that
Kant alleged to be essential to practical freedom? Well, as Laplace said to
Napoleon about God, I have no need of that hypothesis. To recapitulate:
first, Kant himself ended up saying that this is a "transcendental idea," of
which we cannot understand even the possibility; second, I have backed
this up by arguing that both determinism and indeterminism are figments
of our philosophical imaginations; and third, in the conception of treating
each other as amenable to reason (in the very broad sense outlined here),
we have all the free will worth wanting.

NOTES

ESSAY 1

A slightly earlier version of this essay appears in the March 2011 issue of *Diametros*, an online journal of philosophy published by the Institute of Philosophy in the Jagiellonian University of Cracow in Poland: (http://www.diametros.iphils.uj.edu.pl/?l=2&p=anr100&m=101M)

1. A phrase, if ever there was one, that betrays what Wittgenstein called the philosophical "craving for generality"!

2. *Vorstellung* and *Gegenstand* in the letter to Herz. In the first *Critique* Kant sometimes uses *Objekt* instead of *Gegenstand*, but English has only the one word "object." See note 17 below.

3. In a complete treatment we would also need to give an account of our representations of properties and relations—the kinds of "thing" or "object" (in a still more general sense) that are meant or expressed (or "referred to," according to Frege's theory) by predicates and relational expressions.

4. Allison defines an "epistemic condition" as "a necessary condition for the representation of objects" (2004: 11), and presumably he still means this to cover both objects and states of affairs, as he said in the first edition. But his label "*epistemic* condition" is potentially misleading, suggesting as it does a condition for knowledge: a better term might be "*representational* condition." He himself suggests the neologism "*objectivating* condition" but does not use it.

5. Descartes ([1641] 1986: 28). His use of the phrase "objective reality" means precisely the opposite of what more recent philosophers (including Kant) would understand by it: Descartes means representational content, independent of whether it actually relates to anything outside the mind of the subject.

6. Somebody might try to ask an even more fundamental question, not about *how* but *whether* we can represent particular items, which would pose a yet more radical form of skepticism about the very existence of representation even in the internal sense. But I do not think that Kant was raising *that* question, and nor am I; indeed it seems incoherent, for it tries to use the notion of representation while allowing the supposition that we do not have any specific representations.

7. Frege called them "thoughts" (*Gedanken*). In his technical use of this everyday term there can be many thinkings (by different people, or by one thinker at different times) of one and the same thought, or proposition.

8. As Wittgenstein put it, "naming is not so far a move in the language game" (1953: *49).

9. Where there is no distinction between *seems* and *is*, there can be no such thing as *is*—as Wittgenstein famously argued (1953: *258).

10. Searle has written a whole book about intentionality while denying that there are any such things as intentional objects (1983: 16–18).

11. Evans (1982); McDowell (1998).

12. See the articles "Externalism/Internalism," "Content (1)," and "Content (2)" in *A Companion to the Philosophy of Mind*, ed. Samuel Guttenplan (1994).

13. This suggests that our notion of *proposition* may need to be split up into broad (world-involving) and narrow (purely mental) versions, but I will not go down that road here.

14. "…a person goes by a sign-post only in so far as there exists a regular use of sign-posts, a custom"; "…'obeying a rule' is a practice" (Wittgenstein 1953: *198, *202). So there cannot be such a thing as a logically private language, one that it is logically impossible for more than one person to understand.

15. "Empirical realism" is a misleading label, for Kant manifestly does not think of it as an empirical, a posteriori claim.

16. Waxman (1991) offers some more blatant interpretations of Kant's transcendental idealism, which I do not think represent his meaning, and which I cannot believe, anyway: "The subject must create the entirety of the physical cosmos within itself" (p. 19); "one of the cardinal tenets of Kant's philosophy: the thesis that objects themselves, in their own right, are representations and not things in themselves. This claim is justifiable—indeed, has sense—only if objects conform a priori to the constitution of a mind, that is, *are its products no less than the representations of them are*" (p. 275, with my emphasis).

17. In the German, Kant wrote of the object (*Gegenstand*) as object (*Objekt*) of the senses, which suggests that he might have been using these two words to make our modern distinction between actual and intentional objects. But this temptingly neat idea does not seem to be borne out by further tracking of his usage.

18. Kant's systematic classification of representations at A320/B376 divides cognitions or "objective perceptions" (by which he seems to mean all mental states with representational content of some sort) into intuitions (i.e., states with nonconceptual content) and concepts.

19. Heidegger's *Zuhandensein* ("ready-to-handedness").

20. Quite often in philosophy we need to ask "Who exactly are *we*?"

21. Gardner acknowledges that "it is impossible to even determine whether reference to them [things in themselves] should be singular or plural" (1999: 281), yet later in that same chapter (on the meaning of transcendental idealism) he continues to write, without qualification, of things in themselves in the plural (1999: 295–97).

22. A sense that Kant explicitly recognizes when he says that "appearances can certainly be given in intuition without functions of the understanding" (A90).

23. Of which I was an early supporter in my own small way (Stevenson 1972).

24. Rescher's "Summary Overview" (1973: 195–97) is useful, especially in emphasizing that his "conceptual idealism" is not a doctrine about the nature of reality itself, but about the nature of our *thought* about reality.

ESSAY 2

This is a revised version of my paper in *Philosophy and Phenomenological Research* 60(2), 2000, pp. 281–305, used with permission from Wiley-Blackwell.

1. I have been influenced by, among recent writers, Patricia Kitcher (1990), Andrew Brook (1994), and John McDowell (1994). Brook claims that Kant noticed some fundamental aspects of mental functioning that contemporary cognitive science has hardly yet got to grips with.

2. Despite Strawson's scorn for the "imaginary subject of transcendental psychology" (1966: 32), there is more to Kant's psychological talk than Strawson was prepared to allow when he wrote *The Bounds of Sense*, and perhaps more than McDowell (1994) realized.

3. This seems to be an afterthought added in the A preface. Kant does not systematically apply any such distinction in the main text, though it may explain the lesser prominence of synthesis or "combination" in the B Transcendental Deduction. Walsh (1966) argued that despite Kant's emphasis on the a priori, his philosophy ultimately rests on empirical foundations. Kitcher (1990: Ch.1) gives a fuller treatment of these issues, interpreting Kant's theory of mind as proto–cognitive science.

4. It may be that our concepts of experience, perception, and consciousness have been developed to apply to the normal and normative kinds of cases, and have only questionable or analogical extensions to nonstandard cases. See Nagel (1971).

5. McDowell (1994) uses the vivid metaphor "saddled with" to express this passive element in perceptual experience: the fact that however much we may actively move ourselves around and focus our attention, what we perceive at any given place and time is in the end up to the world, not up to us.

6. In the Schematism chapter Kant makes a similar remark about the "schematism of our understanding" being "a hidden art in the depths of the human soul, whose true operations we can divine from nature and lay unveiled before our eyes only with difficulty" (A141/ B180–81). Hume theorized about the subconscious workings of "the imagination" in remarkably similar terms ([1739] 2007: I.iv.ii), as Strawson (1971) noted and as I have elaborated on (2003b).

7. Alas, this passage comes rather late in the *Critique* as an explanation of Kant's terminology. He was adapting older philosophical terminology to express his radical new insights, but he had trouble keeping his usage under consistent control.

8. See also Kant's account of sensations (at B207) as "merely subjective representations, by which one can only be conscious that the subject is affected." It thus emerges that Kant's "objective perceptions" with representational content are precisely those mental states that Descartes described as having "objective reality" (see note 5 to essay 1). Aquila (1983) has written a whole book about representation in Kant and his predecessors.

9. Sellars (1968, Ch.1.3–18); but as he notes, there are other ways of interpreting Kant's talk of intuition (see essay 3).

10. Sellars (1968, Ch.2.3).

11. Graham Bird (2006) has done a great deal more to reduce the pressure toward an idealist interpretation of Kant.

12. The example is of course Kant's at A192/B237. He introduces it in the course of his famous argument about causality, whereas I am using it for a more phenomenological, but not unrelated, point.

13. Frank Jackson (1976) uses this point to argue for the existence of mental objects; but that raises questions about what we mean by "existence." All I assert here is that "A seems to see something red, and seems to see something square" does not imply "A seems to see something red and square."

14. Merleau-Ponty ([1945] 1962) makes a similar point about looking at a landscape upside down.

15. If Merleau-Ponty is right, the experience of the congenitally blind is not just like ours with all visual elements removed, nor can the experience of someone who is suddenly given his sight be understood as simply adding the visual to what he already had. See Merleau-Ponty ([1945] 1962), Part 1, Ch.3, "The Spatiality of One's Own Body and Motility," pp. 115–20, and Part 2, Ch.1, "Sense Experience," esp. pp. 222ff.

16. See Merleau-Ponty ([1945] 1962), Part 2, Ch.3, "The Thing in the Natural World."

17. This is the B version of the headline thesis of Kant's Third Analogy.

18. Strawson (1971), where he makes amends for his brusque dismissal (1966) of Kant's theory of synthesis and "the imaginary subject of transcendental psychology."

19. Could that be what Brook (1994) meant by "a global representation"? I hope not!

20. See Nagel (1971) and Marcel (1994).
21. See Sacks (1985: Ch.2).
22. I intend no empirical implications about the laying down of physical traces in the brain, the size of memory capacity, or the efficiency of retrieval mechanisms.
23. Sellars adopted the practice of numbering each paragraph he wrote, and I am using asterisks to indicate his paragraph numbers.
24. Thus Kantian/Sellarsian sense impressions are quite different beasts from the conceptualized "sense data" beloved of Moore, Russell, and Ayer.
25. See my principle entitled "Scene" above, and essay 3.
26. Ignoring the curvature of the retina itself, which presumably is not functionally relevant.
27. Though given certain conventions of visual representation using blurred images, or a sequence of "frames" in comic strips, some pictures can be *interpreted* as representations of movement.
28. One is tempted to say that the subject has to see the footsteps *as* a trail—but one must be careful not to assume that we can adequately model temporal relations on spatial ones.

ESSAY 3

1. Much later on, in the Antinomy chapter in the Dialectic, Kant refers back to the Aesthetic as having "sufficiently proved" transcendental idealism (A490–91/B518–19) but claims that his resolution of the antinomies also provides an indirect proof of it (see essays 4 and 5).
2. Could the sheer number of books that Rescher has published since 1973 have distracted philosophers' attention from the considerable merits of this one?
3. See Bird (2006: 132).
4. Rescher (1973: Ch.1, and Summary Overview).
5. Graham Bird emphasizes this strain in Kant (2006: Ch.3.1, 9.3).
6. Unless we can count the passage in the Antinomy chapter where he refers to "the real things of past time" (A495/B523).
7. Rescher (1973: 125).
8. Patricia Kitcher (1990) wrote a whole book about this.
9. Falkenstein (1995) treats us to 400 pages of patient and thorough interpretation and critique of Kant's mere 40 pages in the Transcendental Aesthetic.
10. Waxman (1991).
11. See also A97–106, where Kant elaborates on the threefold synthesis, and A115ff. where he summarizes the story as told in A.
12. For more on Kant on the imagination see Gibbons (1994), and on the imagination more generally see Stevenson (2003).
13. Waxman also asserts briefly (1991: 52) that his version of transcendental ideality, in which "spontaneity is wrested free from temporality," is essential for Kant's defense of "transcendental freedom"—a topic I touch on in essays 8 and 9, though not to defend Waxman's view.
14. No doubt the scholars will have taken this discussion further in the fifteen years since Falkenstein's book.
15. Sellars put it well: "Kant is fighting his way towards a clarity of structure which he never achieves, and which is in his thinking only as the oak is in the acorn" (1968: Ch.1*5). (Don't we all know the feeling?)
16. In the B Transcendental Deduction Kant introduces some bewildering new technical terms: "figurative synthesis (*synthesis speciosa*)" as distinct from "intellectual synthesis (*synthesis intellectualis*)" at B151; a distinction between "productive" and "reproductive" imagination at B152; and between "form of intuition" and "formal intuition" in the footnote at B160–61.

17. Including his notes for the popular lecture course "Anthropology from a Pragmatic Point of View" that he delivered over many years, and finally published in 1798.
18. As Quine rather unappealingly put it.
19. Just in case anyone is eagle-eyed enough to inquire what relation this essay bears to the three kinds of transcendental idealism I distinguished thirty years ago (1981b), the answer is not very much, except that the third kind there is pretty much the first here.

ESSAY 4

1. Reported (with extraordinary repetitiveness!) in Rescher (2000).
2. Confusingly, Graham Bird labels them the other way around (2006: 602).
3. Wittgenstein also insisted on a sharp demarcation between science and philosophy, in both his early and his later philosophy.
4. I investigated testimony as a source of knowledge in Stevenson (1993).
5. "The transcendental object [is unknowable] because it is, as the concept of an object prior to any constitution, not an entity at all" (Gardner 1999: 155).
6. See also *Reflexion* 5554, in which the transcendental object "is no real object or given thing, but a concept, in relation to which appearances have unity."

ESSAY 5

An earlier version of this essay is to be published by Palgrave Macmillan in a collection entitled *Kantian Metaphysics Today*, edited by Roxana Baiasu, Adrian Moore, and Graham Bird.

1. Kant said in a letter that it might have been better to start with the Dialectic.
2. This is an appeal to Leibniz's Principle of Sufficient Reason, applied to Newton's concept of absolute time.
3. This is Leibniz's rejection of Newton's concept of absolute space in favor of the view that space consists only in the spatial relations between material objects; see also A431–33/ B459–61.
4. This opposition between "conceptual" and "a posteriori" should not be identified with the standard empiricist distinction between "analytic" and "synthetic." There is a special Kantian conception of the "conceptual" that includes the synthetic a priori conditions for experience.
5. Kant himself made an early contribution to the scientific study of the remote past, with his nebular hypothesis about the formation of the solar system.
6. Charles Darwin presupposed Charles Lyell.
7. And he may have been inhibited from voicing doubts about the existence of a first human pair by awareness of the theological opprobrium that would have come down upon his head.
8. Kant argued for it transcendentally in his first Analogy.
9. Thus deserving Kant's title of "the unconditioned"? (see essay 4).
10. Some metaphysically or theologically inclined physicists do this too, e.g., Paul Davies.
11. These points also arise in essay 9.
12. Guyer 1987: Part V and Afterword.
13. Labeled P2 in essay 4, following Michele Grier.
14. Yes, it is there in the German.
15. Well, *almost* universally accepted – it has been questioned by some radically postmodernist philosophers.

ESSAY 6

This is an abbreviated and revised version of my paper in the *Kantian Review* 7 (2003): 72–101, used with the permission of the editors. The original has some academic bells and whistles that are not essential to the main argument; they remain there in the journal for those with a taste for that sort of thing.

1. I touch on the second question at the end of essay 9.

2. Presumably it had been handed down from medieval philosophy, for Aquinas makes a similar threefold distinction in his *Summa Theologica*, II.II, Q.1, art.2 and Q.2, art.1. St. Thomas said that faith is midway between science and opinion: *fides* is a propositional attitude that differs both from *scientia* (rational knowledge derived from first principles) and from *opinio* (uncertain or probabilistic belief about matters of fact). For him faith is the acceptance of propositions that can only be revealed; the assent of faith is voluntary; yet faith involves firm commitment, unlike opinion. Apparently Aquinas's treatment of the epistemological trio derives from Hugh of St. Victor, who worked in Paris in the preceding 12th century, and wrote, "Faith is a form of mental certitude about distant realities that is greater than opinion and less than science"—see the footnote on p. 11 and appendix 4 by T. C. O'Brien in *St. Thomas Aquinas, Summa Theologiae*, Vol. 31 (London: Eyre and Spottiswoode 1974).

3. Kant habitually used the trio of *meinen, glauben*, and *wissen* as a framework in which to organize his thoughts on epistemology. See the *Blomberg Logic* (24:148ff., 24:228ff.), the *Vienna Logic* (24:850ff.), the *Dohna-Wundlacken Logic* (24:732ff.), and the *Jäsche Logic* (9:66ff.)—in Kant's *Lectures on Logic*, translated by J. Michael Young (Cambridge, UK: Cambridge University Press, 1992). These lecture notes by various hands can hardly be accorded the same authority as Kant's published works, but they provide useful supplementary evidence of the development of his thinking, especially on topics not represented in his publications. The *Jäsche Logic* was prepared for publication by Jäsche with the approval of the aging Kant, so it can be taken with a bit more confidence as representing his late views on these topics. "Logic" in eighteenth-century usage covered much more than (Aristotelian) formal logic; it included topics in what we now call epistemology, theory of meaning, and philosophy of mind. See Patricia Kitcher (1990, Ch.1).

4. Rendered by the neologism "opining" by Kemp Smith in his translation of the *Critique of Pure Reason* (London: Macmillan, 1929), and by J. M. Young in translating the logic lecture notes.

5. In everyday usage, people tend to think of knowledge and belief as mutually exclusive, for example when Jung said "I don't *believe* that God exists, I *know* it." But such cases can be treated in terms of Gricean "conversational implication": in most contexts, when someone says "I believe p," he conversationally implies he does *not* know p, though that is not logically entailed. For to say one believes p in a situation in which one knows p (or thinks one does) is to mislead one's hearers into assuming that one thinks one has insufficient grounds for p.

6. Guyer and Wood translation (1992: 687n).

7. Kant's *Critique of Judgment* ([1790] 1987: 360, n.75).

8. Kant was not very careful about the distinction between a disposition and its actualizations. "Here the talk is not of truth but of holding-to-be-true.... This is judgment in relation to the *subject*" (the *Dohna-Wundlacken Logic* 24:731–32); "the judgment through which something is *represented* as true...is, *subjectively, holding-to-be-true*" (the *Jäsche Logic* 9:65–66).

9. This is the first appearance of Kant's "moral theology" in the critical philosophy; it is developed at length in the Dialectic of the *Critique of Practical Reason*, in sections 86–91 of the *Critique of Judgment,* and in *Religion within the Boundaries of Mere Reason.*

10. I examined differences between first- and third-person judgments more systematically in Stevenson (1999).

11. See the *Blomberg Logic* 24:148ff.; the *Vienna Logic* 24:850ff.; the *Dohna-Wundlacken Logic* 24:732ff.; and the *Jäsche Logic* 9:66ff.

12. Many subtle varieties of justification have been distinguished in recent epistemology, and in the light of the internal/external distinction it has been questioned whether there is any single conception of justification; but we need not bring in these modern distinctions here unless they turn out to be necessary to make sense of Kant. It is clear that by "objective sufficiency" he means more than just having some minimal amount of evidence (enough, perhaps, to make it not blameworthy to believe the proposition); and for *wissen* he requires *certainty*—but it remains to be seen what such certainty can amount to.

13. In his Commentary on the second *Critique* L. W. Beck remarks that "subjective" in Kant does not mean arbitrary and contingent; it just means "dependent upon the nature of the subject" (1960: 256). (He goes on to say, obscurely, that this can be interpreted either a priori or posteriori: perhaps alluding to the distinction between species-dependence and individual-dependence.)

14. Wood (1970: 14–16).

15. From the translation by Allen Wood in Kant's *Religion and Rational Theology.*

16. From the translation by J. M. Young, in Kant's *Lectures on Logic.*

17. The section heading is "On What Kind of Assent Results from a Practical Faith."

18. Kant had touched on the topic of testimony in earlier logic lectures, implying that it can, in favorable cases, be a source of well-justified beliefs that amount to empirical knowledge. See the *Blomberg Logic* 24:30–31 and 245, and the *Dohna-Wundlacken Logic* 24:749–50. I treated testimony on my own account in Stevenson (1993).

19. Kant is closer to Locke than Plato in time and in doctrine, but he is prepared to say that we can have knowledge of the material world by induction and testimony, whereas Locke would say we can only have a lesser grade of probability called belief, assent, or opinion (*Essay concerning Human Understanding* IV.xv.3). And Kant has a distinctively practical account of religious faith, whereas Locke still treats it as a special kind of theoretical belief, based on revelation - the alleged testimony of God Himself (*Essay* IV.xvi.14; IV.xviii.2).

20. From the translation by J. M. Young, in Kant's *Lectures on Logic.*

21. See the *Blomberg Logic* 9:228, where the middle degree of holding to be true is characterized as "to believe, or to hold something to be true to such a degree that it is sufficient for action and for deciding to act"; and 9:241–42, where it is said "one can opine something without believing.... Here I hold something to be true without its having an influence on our actions."

22. But there may be no uncontroversial way to assign numerical values to degrees of belief in general, aside from the easy cases of finite numbers of equiprobable outcomes, as in the fall of a fair dice. (Not everyone will be prepared to bet about anything!)

23. The degree of someone's belief may also depend on his aversion to risk, e.g., someone may be unwilling to bet his last ducat, even on very favorable odds. Not all values can be measurable in monetary terms.

24. Wood compares Kant with Kierkegaard and Pascal on the personal nature of faith (1970: 16 and 25).

25. For further comment on the use of *meinen, glauben, wissen,* and other words in the eighteenth- and nineteenth-century German epistemic vocabulary, especially for the association of *Glaube* with religious faith, see the entries on "Belief, Faith and Opinion" and "Knowledge, Cognition and Certainty" in Michael Inwood, *A Hegel Dictionary* (Oxford: Blackwell, 1992).

26. I address these issues in Stevenson (2001) and (2006).

ESSAY 7

This is a revised version of my paper in the *British Journal for the History of Philosophy* 12, no. 2 (2004): 223–46, used with the permission of the editors.

1. Not Descartes's term, but it expresses the analogy between his treatment of cognitive error and the theological problem of evil - see Cottingham (1988).
2. Descartes, *Meditations on First Philosophy*, in 2008: 56 and 59–60; page numbers of the French edition by Adam and Tannery [AT VII]).
3. Hence the notorious problem of "the Cartesian circle": how can the premises and inferences in those arguments for God's existence be exempt from the sort of doubt that Descartes maintains can only be assuaged by knowledge of their conclusion?
4. Fourth Meditation, AT VII 57, with my interpolation.
5. *Ethics*, Appendix to Part 1, and II.48; *Treatise* 2.3.2.
6. Sidgwick (1901), Appendix on "The Kantian Conception of Free Will."
7. Descartes's allusion to the mysterious possibility of divine grace is something for which Sidgwick's studiously agnostic approach finds no place.
8. Descartes, *Principles of Philosophy*, in 2008: Part 1, *39, AT VIIIA 19.
9. Descartes, *Discourse on the Method*, in 2008: Part 3.
10. *Principles of Philosophy,*, in 2008: III 45 (AT VIII 100).
11. This question arises for Kant too. I will touch on it in essay 9.
12. On Spinoza's view, if one has "confused" or "mutilated" ideas one's judgments may be false, but if all one's ideas are "adequate" one's judgments will be true (*Ethics* II.34, Scholium to I.49).
13. *Treatise* 1.3.12, with my interpolations.
14. Such statements surely express the youthful boldness and enthusiasm with which Hume, while still in his twenties, wrote his miraculous masterwork.
15. *Enquiry concerning the Human Understanding*, edited by L. A. Selby-Bigge (Oxford University Press, 2nd edition 1902), section 9.
16. The locus classicus is Descartes's *Discourse on the Method*, in 2008: Part 5.
17. "The principles [in the imagination] which are permanent, irresistible (*sic*) and universal"; "the general and more establish'd properties of the imagination" (*Treatise* 1.4.4, 1.4.7).
18. "The principles [in the imagination] which are changeable, weak, and irregular"; "the trivial suggestions of the fancy" (*Treatise* 1.4.4, 1.4.7).
19. *Treatise*, 1.3.9: "education is an artificial and not a natural cause" [of beliefs].
20. See Hume's *Natural History of Religion*, section 8.
21. I take a further look at animal/human differences in essay 8.
22. In the wide eighteenth-century sense of "logic," which includes topics in epistemology, philosophy of mind, and language, as well as (Aristotelian) formal logic.
23. Published in English in Kant (1992).
24. The *Blomberg Logic* 24:156, with my interpolations.
25. See also the *Jäsche Logic* section 9 (9:73–75), which derives from lectures in the 1790s and was published by Jäsche with Kant's approval in 1800.
26. *Groundwork of the metaphysics of morals* 4:448. See also Reflexion 5413: "In order to judge objectively, universally, that is, apodictically, reason must be free of subjectively determining grounds; for if they did determine reason, the judgment would be as it is only contingently, because of subjective causes" (18:176).
27. Or "from outside," as H. J. Paton translated it.
28. See A738/B766ff. and Kant's essay "What Is Enlightenment?"
29. "Brutely" enough—if that means outside our control—though what we see and touch depends partly on where we look and feel, as noted in essay 2. We have also come to recognize that our moods of elation or depression may be caused by drugs, hormones, or biochemical changes in our brains.
30. Though confusingly, he labels our faculty for conceptual thought in several different ways: as "the understanding," "the faculty of representation," "judgment," or "reason."
31. *Prolegomena to Any Future Metaphysics* 4:290.

32. I offered an abbreviated, compact overview of this and other Kantian ambiguities in Stevenson (1998a).
33. Kant contemptuously dismissed Hume's notion of spontaneity as "a wretched subterfuge" in the *Critique of Practical Reason* at 5:95–96.
34. Here it is significant that Kant's German idealist successors saw a transcendentally realist Spinozism as the main rival to Kantianism, which they felt Kant had not done enough to exclude. See the symposium "From Kant to Post-Kantian Idealism" by Sebastian Gardner and Paul Franks, in *Proceedings of the Aristotelian Society,* Supplementary Volume 76 (2002). Today the main rival is obviously a thoroughgoing scientific naturalism.
35. *Critique of Practical Reason* 5:96.
36. There is also Kant's distinctive notion of moral belief or faith (*Glaube*) that involves the will in its own distinctive way, as we saw in essay 6.

ESSAY 8

This is a revised version of my paper in *Philosophical Explorations* 5, no. 2 (2002): 105–24, used with the permission of the editors. (http://www.informaworld.com)
1. More recently, Brandom has endorsed Davidson's form of argument for the conceptual priority of the linguistic sense of "belief," while allowing that there is a derivative sense in which animals can be said to have beliefs (Brandom 1994: 150–55). This is a position with which I will not, in the end, disagree.
2. I offered some reflections on the method of reflective equilibrium in Stevenson (1999, section 5).
3. Richard Jeffrey judiciously applied his theory of deliberate action to his cat (1965: 59).
4. As a bridge between his two concepts of belief, de Sousa (1971) offers "assent," a mental act that is like "a bet on truth alone, solely determined by epistemic desirabilities." He claims that this notion can be abstracted from sincere assertions and can be understood as an *act* since it is caused "in a certain way" by wants and beliefs, though not in the ordinary sense voluntary. He defines "belief (proper)" as a disposition to assent.
5. See Davidson et al. (1957); these studies were described by Carl Hempel, paradoxically, as evidencing "a type of conscious decision which is non-consciously rational with quantitative precision" (1965: 483).
6. Dennett doesn't get de Sousa quite right—no doubt because of his dangerous expository method of "claiming that he says things he doesn't quite say" (1978: 301n)—for de Sousa *does* call the longer-lasting states that result from assentings or judgings "beliefs (proper)."
7. Price credits Alexander Bain with the invention of the term, and the Victorian thinker Walter Bagehot with the most forceful expression of the conception. Bagehot ([1871] 1986) argued that what we commonly call "belief" includes an emotional element that has been neglected by philosophers. The power of an idea to cause such intense commitment depends, he claimed, on several factors: its clearness, its intensity (due to the exciting nature of the circumstances), its constancy (how frequently one meets with it from other people), and its interestingness (its power to gratify some wish).
8. The innate human tendency to believe what others say had already been noted by Hume (with disapproval) and Reid (with approval). For more on Hume's and Reid's treatment of testimony see Stevenson (1993).
9. Yet another version of the distinction is expressed in vividly metaphorical terms in Boyer's evolutionary psychological/anthropological account of religious belief. We tend to think that "what happens in the mind seems to require two different functions or organs. One of them is the Representations' Attorney and the other one is the Belief-Judge. The Attorney produces various representations.... This is for the benefit of the Mental-Judge, who considers them and hands over his verdict." But Boyer suggests that "among the hundreds of

special systems that compose a normal brain, many seem to be their own Attorney and Judge at the same time. That is, mental systems do not present their evidence in front of a mental-judge or jury. They *decide* the case even before it is presented to any other system....So we have two quite different pictures of how a mind reaches a verdict. On the one hand, we sometimes weigh evidence and decide on its merit. On the other hand, there seems to be a great deal of underground belief-making work going on that is simply not reported" (Boyer 2001: 348–49).

10. Lehrer offers a much more contentious example when he suggests it could be reasonable for someone to accept a logically inconsistent religious proposition "for the purposes of faith"—whatever they are supposed to be! In accepting such a doctrine, the person may not thereby believe it (for that is not within her immediate power), but Lehrer (following Pascal) says she can *strive* to believe it, she can do whatever tends to induce the state or habit in which believing it would consist.

11. He first made the distinction in Cohen (1989); he explains it in more detail and applies it in wider contexts in Cohen (1992).

12. See Evans (1982: 225): "in making a self-ascription of belief, one's eyes are, so to speak, or occasionally literally, directed outward—upon the world." Cohen surely overstates his view, anyway—for surely one cannot literally introspect the presence of the disposition; rather one might introspect the feelings that actualize it. His appeal to "credal feelings" seemstoo stuck with a neo-Humean introspective approach. De Sousa's definition of belief as a disposition to assent (which is a publicly manifestable action) seems the right corrective.

13. Cohen offers another quite different criterion of distinction: that acceptance is *closed under deduction*, whereas belief is not (1992: 29). That would imply that one doesn't *know* the full content of what one accepts until one has performed the relevant logical deductions.

14. The qualification in the claim that "belief, *for the most part*, is a lower-level operation" suggests there is further complexity involved. Lehrer throws in another theoretical consideration when he writes: "The higher-order system also adds representations and, contrary to some theorists, is genuinely constructive in producing *new* representations that are not mere combinations of some previous conceptions" (1990a: 12).

15. Bas van Fraasen (1980) also distinguishes belief from acceptance, but only with respect to scientific theories. To accept a theory is to believe it is "empirically adequate," i.e., that what it implies about all *observable* states of affairs is true. Van Fraasen understands such acceptance as involving an associated research program, trying to explain observations in its terms, and a commitment of resources. His conception of belief is thus weaker than acceptance in one way, and stronger in another. But this sort of acceptance is definitely a more *sophisticated* notion than belief, for it involves the relatively subtle distinction between theoretical and observable statements.

16. For Evans this is the same question as whether the content is conceptual rather than non-conceptual—but not for Kenny or Peacocke, who allow that nonlinguistic creatures may be said to possess concepts (Kenny 1975: 51 and Peacocke 1992: 31). On Evans's side is Bermudez (1998), who defends a "priority principle" to the effect that conceptual abilities are constitutively linked with linguistic abilities in such a way that conceptual capacities *cannot* be possessed by nonlinguistic creatures (1998: 42–43).

17. Some so-called acts or "actions" are involuntary, e.g., reflex actions in animals or humans. Many philosophers will insist that these are not actions in the proper sense of the word; but others are prepared to apply the term "action" here, and to follow ordinary language in talking even of the "action" of chemical substances—e.g., Kenny (1975: 46). Kenny is prepared to say that animals perform voluntary actions wherever they have an obvious choice

between alternatives, although he maintains that they cannot properly be said to possess a will (1975: 52).

18. Obviously I am assuming some workable distinction between the mental and the non-mental here, and questions can of course be asked about that. How can we tell when a mental state has as its content the *mental* state of another creature, rather than just the state (or behavior) of their body? I don't think I have anything original to say on this—I am presupposing a functional conception of the mental as those states of a creature that may be caused (in part) by perception, that can interact with each other, and that can combine to cause action.

19. De Sousa claims that nothing he has said about reasoning at the level of *first-order* beliefs involves *second-order* belief in any way (1971: 77).

20. See Richard Byrne and Andrew Whiten (1987), and in more detail their edited collection (1988).

21. Another route to the same result is to apply the reasoned/primitive distinction to the three levels already identified in sections 3 and 5.

22. Perhaps this architectural metaphor can be literally applied to the structure of the brain (reptilian, mammalian, hominoid layers?), but that is a thoroughly empirical question.

23. See Evans (1982) and Fodor (1983, 2000) on nonconceptual informational states in perception and memory. The unconscious subjective probabilities and utilities invoked to explain the results of certain experiments on human subjects, such as those reported by Davidson et al. (1957), may also belong at this level—but the role of such postulated unconscious states would deserve more extended scrutiny.

24. Simon (1990) suggests an evolutionary explanation for primitive credulity in humans.

25. More work on acceptance has been done by Engel (2000).

26. Brandom accepts that the issue is partly factual and partly verbal (1994: 155). It is interesting to compare results with John McDowell's *Mind and World* (1994). He distinguishes very sharply between human and animal mentality. Adult humans are responsive to reasons and norms; we can judge and act in conscious awareness of our reasons for doing so, and thus we exercise our freedom. McDowell talks of spontaneity, consciousness, and concepts where I have talked of mental states being reasoned, mind-directed, and linguistic. But he seems to assume that these three criteria coincide, so for him there is just one huge difference between animal and human mentality. My recognition of intermediate levels does not obliterate the distinction, but it makes it less of a yawning chasm with no intervening steps.

27. Linda Zagzebski says it is a mistake to treat perceptual beliefs as paradigms of rationality and justifiability (1996: 69). But if I am right, no one level of the mind contains *all* perceptual beliefs (or all those based on personal memory, or testimony). Beliefs at levels 1 to 4 hardly conform to our ideal of rationality, but those at levels 5 or 6 may do so.

28. Simon Baron-Cohen (1995).

29. Harry Frankfurt (1988), by making so much of second-order desires, i.e., desires about our own desires, has in effect endorsed Lehrer's thesis that the human mind is a metamind. Keith Frankish (2004) has written a whole book advancing the thesis that belief is not a unitary psychological kind, and arguing that we need (at least) two levels in our theory of mind.

ESSAY 9

1. Peter van Inwagen explains determinism rather more precisely, in terms of *propositions* that express the total state of the world at a given instant; presumably they would have to be enormously large, yet still finite, conjunctions. He can then define determinism, with elegant brevity, as the thesis that any such world-encompassing proposition about one time, taken in conjunction with the laws of nature, entails all such propositions about any subsequent time (van Inwagen 1983: Ch.3, reprinted in Watson ed. 2003). I have not

expressed determinism in terms of propositions, but the adjustment is easily made, if desired.

2. "Solutions of the three-body problem may be of an arbitrary complexity and are very far from being completely understood" according to a website curated by Dr. Alain Chenciner: http://www.scholarpedia.org/article/Three body problem

3. Website: en.wikopeida.org/wiki/Schrodinger%27s_cat

4. I am reminded of the Irish story about a student of engineering who got talking to the men digging up the road in Belfast; when he remarked that in *his* work he had to be accurate to within the thousandth part of an inch, the sturdy fellow at the bottom of the hole replied: "Boys, youse is lucky! In our work we've gotta be *dead on!*"

5. Website: dept.physics.upenn.edu/courses/gladney/mathphys/subsection3_2_5.html

6. Anscombe (1971). The point is also made by the distinguished mathematician Roger Penrose (1989: 224–25, 559).

7. Dummett (2006: Ch.7, p. 87). ("Thought and Reality" is indeed a capacious title for a slim volume!)

8. Russell (1913). (His subversive remark about the British monarchy must have had far more shock-value in pre-1st-world-war England than it has now.)

9. For a recent defense of this traditional interpretation see Longuenesse (2005: Ch.6).

10. Bird is primarily concerned to distinguish between Ai-iii on the one hand and B, C and D on the other. I am not sure whether he intends any substantive difference between B, C and D, but it seems to me that distinctions can be drawn.

11. This could be described as a metasolution to this meta-antinomy.

12. Physicists may say that in quantum mechanics we now have an *empirically justified* indeterminist theory; but I cannot enter here into the extremely difficult issues in the philosophy of quantum mechanics, even if I were qualified to do so. I can only offer the thought that a future scientific breakthrough to an even deeper and perhaps more deterministic level cannot be conclusively ruled out.

13. The point has been argued at length by Bok (1998).

14. This is a version of P.F.Strawson's point about the impossibility of our abandoning our reactive attitudes in his classic paper "Freedom and Resentment" (1963).

BIBLIOGRAPHY

Allison, Henry E. 2004. *Kant's Transcendental Idealism: An Interpretation and Defense*. Revised and enlarged edition. New Haven, CA: Yale University Press.

Anscombe, G. E. M. 1971. *Causality and Determination*. Cambridge: Cambridge University Press. Reprinted in Sosa, ed., 1975.

Aquila, Richard E. 1983. *Representational Mind: A Study of Kant's Theory of Knowledge*. Bloomington: Indiana University Press.

Bagehot, Walter. [1871] 1986. The Emotion of Conviction. In *The Contemporary Review* 17: 32–40. Reprinted in *The Collected Works of Walter Bagehot*, ed. Norman St. John-Stevas. Vol. 14: 46–57. London: The Economist.

Baron-Cohen, Simon. 1995. *Mindblindness*. Cambridge, MA: MIT Press.

Beck, L. W. 1960. *Commentary on Kant's Critique of Practical Reason*. Chicago: University of Chicago Press.

Bermudez, J. L. 1998. *The Paradox of Self-Consciousness*. Cambridge, MA: MIT Press.

Bird, Graham. 2006. *The Revolutionary Kant: A Commentary on the Critique of Pure Reason*. Chicago: Open Court.

Bok, Hilary. 1998. *Freedom and Responsibility*. Princeton, NJ: Princeton University Press. [The chapter "Freedom and Practical Reason" is reprinted in Watson, ed., 2003].

Boyer, Pascal. 2001. *Religion Explained*. London: William Heinemann.

Brandon, Robert B. 1994. *Making It Explicit*. Cambridge, MA: Harvard University Press.

Brook, Andrew. 1994. *Kant and the Mind*. Cambridge: Cambridge University Press.

Byrne, Richard, and Andrew Whiten. 1987. The Thinking Primate's Guide to Deception. *New Scientist* 116: 54–6.

———, eds. 1988. *Machiavellian Intelligence*. Oxford: Oxford University Press.

Churchland, P. M. 1981. Eliminative Materialism and the Propositional Attitudes. *Journal of Philosophy* 78:67–90.

Cohen, L. J. 1989. Belief and Acceptance. *Mind* 98:367–69.

———. 1992. *An Essay on Belief and Acceptance*. Oxford: Oxford University Press.

Cottingham, John, 1988. The Intellect, the Will, and the Passions: Spinoza's Critique of Descartes. *Journal for the History of Philosophy* 26:239–57.

Davidson, Donald, P. Suppes, and S. Siegel. 1957. *Decision Making: An Experimental Approach*. Stanford, CA: Stanford University Press.

Davidson, Donald. 1975. Thought and Talk. In *Mind and Language*, ed. Samuel Guttenplan, 7–23. Oxford: Oxford University Press. Reprinted in *Inquiries into Truth and Interpretation*, 155–70. Oxford: Oxford University Press 1984.

De Sousa, Ronald B. 1971. How to Give a Piece of Your Mind, or The Logic of Belief and Assent. *Review of Metaphysics* 35:52–79.

Dennett, Daniel C. 1978. How to Change Your Mind. In *Brainstorms*, 300–309. Hassocks: Harvester Press.

Descartes, Rene. 2008. *Selected Philosophical Writings*. Ed. John Cottingham, Robert Stoothoff, Dugald Murdoch and Anthony Kenny. Cambridge: Cambridge University Press.

Dummett, Michael. 2006. *Thought and Reality*. Oxford: Oxford University Press.

Engel, Pascal, ed. 2000 *Believing and Accepting*. Dordrecht: Kluwer.

Evans, Gareth. 1982. *The Varieties of Reference*. Oxford: Oxford University Press.

Falkenstein, Lorne. 1995. *Kant's Intuitionism: A Commentary on the Transcendental Aesthetic*. Toronto: Toronto University Press.

Fodor, Jerry A. 1983. *The Modularity of Mind*. Cambridge, MA: MIT Press.

———. 2000. *The Mind Doesn't Work That Way*. Cambridge, MA: MIT Press.

Frankfurt, Harry G. 1988. *The Importance of What We Care About*. Cambridge: Cambridge University Press.

Frankish, Keith. 2004. *Mind and Supermind*. Cambridge: Cambridge University Press.

Gardner, Sebastian. 1999. *Kant and the Critique of Pure Reason*. London: Routledge.

Gibbons, Sarah. 1994. *Kant's Theory of Imagination: Bridging Gaps in Judgement and Experience*. Oxford: Oxford University Press.

Grier, Michelle. 2001. *Kant's Doctrine of Transcendental Illusion*.

Guttenplan, Samuel, ed. 1994. *A Companion to the Philosophy of Mind*. Oxford: Blackwell.

Guyer, Paul. 1987. *Kant and the Claims of Knowledge*. Cambridge: Cambridge University Press.

Hawking, Stephen. 1998. *A Brief History of Time*. Updated edition. London: Bantam Press.

Hempel, Carl G. 1965. *Aspects of Scientific Explanation*. New York: Free Press.

Hume, David. [1739–40] 2007. *A Treatise of Human Nature*. Ed. David Fate Norton and Mary J. Norton. Oxford: Oxford University Press.

———. [1748] 2000. *An Enquiry concerning Human Understanding*. Ed. Tom L. Beuchamp. Oxford: Oxford University Press.

———. [1779 and 1757] 2008. *Dialogues concerning Natural Religion*, and *The Natural History of Religion*. Ed. J.C.A. Gaskin. Oxford: Oxford University Press.

Hurley, Susan. 1994. Unity and Objectivity. In *Objectivity, Simulation and the Unity of Consciousness*, ed. C. Peacocke, 49–77. Oxford: British Academy.

Jackson, Frank 1976. The Existence of Mental Objects. *American Philosophical Quarterly* 13:23–40.

James, William. [1890] 1950. *Principles of Psychology*. 2 vols. New York: Dover.

Jeffrey, Richard C. 1965. *The Logic of Decision*. New York: McGraw-Hill.

Kant, Immanuel. [1781] 1998. *Critique of Pure Reason*. Trans. and ed. Paul Guyer and Allen W. Wood. Cambridge: Cambridge University Press.

———. [1790] 1987. *Critique of Judgment*. Trans. Werner Pluhar. Indianapolis: Hackett.

———. [1798] 2006. *Anthropology from a Pragmatic Point of View*. Trans. and ed. Robert B. Louden. Cambridge: Cambridge University Press.

———. 1992. *Lectures on Logic*. Trans. and ed. J. Michael Young. Cambridge: Cambridge University Press.

———. 1996a. *Practical Philosophy*. Trans. and ed. Mary J. Gregor. Cambridge: Cambridge University Press. [This contains the *Groundwork of the Metaphysics of Morals* of 1785 and the *Critique of Practical Reason* of 1788.]

———. 1996b. *Religion and Rational Theology*. Trans. and ed. Allen W. Wood and George Di Giovanni. Cambridge: Cambridge University Press. [This contains the *Religion within the Boundaries of Mere Reason* of 1793.]

Kenny, Anthony. 1975. *Will, Freedom and Power*. Oxford: Blackwell.

Kitcher, Patricia. 1990. *Kant's Transcendental Psychology*. Oxford: Oxford University Press.

Kolakowski, Leszek. 1968. *Towards a Marxist Humanism*. New York: Grove Press.

Lehrer, Keith. 1990a. *Metamind*. Oxford: Oxford University Press.

———. 1990b. *Theory of Knowledge*. London: Routledge.

Longuenesse, Beatrice. 2005. *Kant and the Human Standpoint*. Cambridge: Cambridge University Press.

Marcel, Anthony. 1994. What Is Relevant to the Unity of Consciousness? In *Objectivity, Simulation and the Unity of Consciousness*, ed. Christopher Peacocke, 79–88. Oxford: British Academy.

McDowell, John. 1994. *Mind and World*. Cambridge, MA: Harvard University Press.

———. 1998. Woodbridge Lectures. *Journal of Philosophy* 95, no. 9: 431–91.

Merleau-Ponty, Maurice. [1945] 1962. *Phenomenology of Perception*. Trans. Colin Smith. London: Routledge.

Millar, Alan. 1991. *Reasons and Experience*. Oxford: Oxford University Press.

Nagel, Thomas. 1971. Brain Bisection and the Unity of Consciousness. *Synthese* 22:396–413. Reprinted in J. Glover, ed., *The Philosophy of Mind, 111–25*. Oxford: Oxford University Press, 1976.

Neiman, Susan. 1994. *The Unity of Reason: Rereading Kant*. New York: Oxford University Press.

Peacocke, Christopher. 1992. *A Study of Concepts*. Cambridge, MA: MIT Press.

Penrose, Roger. 1989. *The Emperor's New Mind*. Oxford: Oxford University Press.

Price, Henry H. 1969. *Belief*. London: George Allen and Unwin.

Rescher, Nicholas. 1973. *Conceptual Idealism*. Oxford: Blackwell.

———. 2000. *Kant and the Reach of Reason: Studies in Kant's Theory of Rational Systemization*. Cambridge: Cambridge University Press.

Russell, Bertrand. 1913. On the Notion of Cause. *Proceedings of the Aristotelian Society, 1912–13*. Reprinted in *Mysticism and Logic*. London: George Allen and Unwin, 1917.

Sacks, Oliver. 1985. *The Man Who Mistook His Wife for a Hat*. London: Duckworth.

Searle, John. 1983. *Intentionality*. Cambridge: Cambridge University Press.

Segal, Gabriel. 1994. Belief (2), Epistemology of. In *A Companion to the Philosophy of Mind*, ed. Samuel Guttenplan, 146–52. Oxford: Blackwell.

Sellars, Wilfrid. 1968. *Science and Metaphysics: Variations on Kantian Themes*. London: Routledge.

Sidgwick, Henry. [1888] 1901. The Kantian Conception of Free Will. *Mind* 13 no.51. Reprinted as an appendix to *The Methods of Ethics*. 6th ed. 509–14. London: Macmillan.

Simon, H. A. 1990. A Mechanism for Social Selection and Successful Altruism. *Science* 250:165–68.

Sosa, Ernest, ed. 1975. *Causality and Conditionals*. Oxford: Oxford University Press.

Spinoza, Baruch. [1677] 2000. *Ethics*. Ed. and trans. G. H. R. Parkinson. Oxford: Oxford University Press.

Stevenson, Leslie. 1972. Relative Identity and Leibniz's Law. *Philosophical Quarterly* 22, no. 87: 155–59.

———. 1979. Recent Work on the Critique of Pure Reason. *Philosophical Quarterly* 29, no. 117: 345–54.

———. 1981a. Things in Themselves and Scientific Explanation. *Indian Philosophical Quarterly* 8, no. 2: 208–15.

———. 1981b. Three Kinds of Transcendental Idealism. In *Akten des 5.Internationalen Kant-Kongresses*, ed. G. Funke, I.2, 1050–59. Bonn: Bouvier.

———. 1982a. *The Metaphysics of Experience*. Oxford: Oxford University Press.

———. 1982b. Wittgenstein's Transcendental Deduction and Kant's Private Language Argument. *Kant-Studien* 73, no. 3: 321–17.

———. 1983. Empirical Realism and Transcendental Anti-Realism. *The Aristotelian Society*, supplementary volume 57:131–53.

———. 1988. Meaning, Assertion and Time. *Australasian Journal of Philosophy* 66, no. 1: 13–25.

———. 1993. Why Believe What People Say? *Synthese* 94:429–51.

———. 1995. Experiences in the Cave, the Closet, and the Vat—and in Bed. *Philosophy* 70, no. 272: 167–89.

———. 1998a. Kant's Many Concepts of Appearance. *Cogito* 123:181–86.

———. 1998b. Things in Themselves: A Dialogue between Kant, Michael Dummett and Liesel. *Comparative Criticism* 20:87–103.

———. 1999. First-Person Epistemology. *Philosophy* 74290):475–97.

———. 2001. Is There Any Hope for Kant's Account of Religion? In *Kant und die Berliner Aufklarung: Akten des IX. Internationalen Kant-Kongresses*, ed. Volker Gerhardt, Rolf-Peter Horstmann, and Ralph Schumacher, Band 3, 713–20. Berlin: de Gruyter.

———. 2003. Twelve Conceptions of Imagination. *British Journal of Aesthetics* 43, no. 3: 238–59.

———. 2006. Kant's Approach to Religion Compared with Quakerism. In *Kant and the New Philosophy of Religion*, ed. Chris L. Firestone and Stephen R. Palmquist, 210–29. Bloomington: Indiana University Press.

Stich, Stephen. 1983. *From Folk Psychology to Cognitive Science: The Case against Belief.* Cambridge, MA: MIT Press.

Strawson, Peter F. 1963. Freedom and Resentment. *Proceedings of the British Academy*: 48:1–25. Reprinted in Watson, ed., 2003.

———.1966. *The Bounds of Sense.* London: Methuen.

———. 1971. Imagination and Perception. In *Experience and Theory*, ed. L. Foster and J.W. Swanson. Amherst: University of Massachusetts Press. Reprinted in Ralph C. S. Walker, ed., *Kant on Pure Reason.* Oxford: Oxford University Press 1982.

Van Fraasen, Bas. 1980. *The Scientific Image.* Oxford: Oxford University Press.

Van Inwagen, Peter. 1983. *An Essay on Free Will.* Oxford: Oxford University Press. Ch.3 is reprinted in Watson ed. 2003.

Walsh, W. H. (1966). Philosophy and Psychology in Kant's Critique. *Kant-Studien* 56:186–98.

Watson, Gary, ed. 2003. *Free Will.* 2nd ed. Oxford: Oxford University Press.

Waxman, Wayne. 1991. *Kant's Model of the Mind: A New Interpretation of Transcendental Idealism.* New York: Oxford University Press.

Wiggins, David. 2001. *Sameness and Substance Renewed.* Cambridge: Cambridge University Press.

Wilson, Edward O. 1998. *Consilience: The Unity of Knowledge.* London: Little, Brown.

Wittgenstein, Ludwig. 1953. *Philosophical Investigations.* Trans. Elizabeth Anscombe. Oxford: Blackwell.

———. 1969. *On Certainty*, Trans. Denis Paul and Elizabeth Anscombe. Oxford: Blackwell.

Wood, Allen. 1970. *Kant's Moral Religion.* Ithaca, NY: Cornell University Press.

Zagzebski, Linda. 1996. *Virtues of the Mind.* Cambridge: Cambridge University Press.

INDEX